WOMEN OF POWER

WOMEN OF POWER

FORMIDABLE FEMALES OF THE MEDIEVAL WORLD

TERESA COLE

AMBERLEY

First published 2023

Amberley Publishing
The Hill, Stroud
Gloucestershire, GL5 4EP

www.amberley-books.com

British Library Cataloguing in Publication Data.
A catalogue record for this book is available from the British Library.

ISBN 978 1 4456 9874 8 (hardback)
ISBN 978 1 4456 9875 5 (ebook)

1 2 3 4 5 6 7 8 9 10

Typesetting by SJmagic DESIGN SERVICES, India.
Printed in the UK.

Contents

Introduction

The stereotypical medieval woman is a pious, helpless creature of little intelligence, and still less drive and ambition. Completely at the mercy of the men in her life, she was married young, had copious offspring and died, often in childbirth, to make way for another, younger model. At best, she may have inspired music (made by men), art (made by men), or poetry (made by men), but clearly, she was incapable of doing anything for herself.

While this may have been true of many, it was certainly not true of all. At the lowest social level, in this as in all ages, peasant women were not at all helpless, taking a full share in working the land. They may not have undertaken the heaviest labouring jobs, but were certainly involved in planting, weeding, caring for livestock and poultry and in all matters relating to the harvest. Higher up the scale, particularly in towns, women are known to have engaged in trade, often alongside their husbands but sometimes on their own account. In particular, a widow might continue a business after her husband's death, especially if the marriage was childless or if the children were very young. In no circumstances, however, were positions of power, even on a local stage, open to such women.

Restricted in many ways in a misogynist age, they would, at least, have had some small measure of control over their lives. They may even have had some say in the choice of marriage partner, though this was often decided as a matter of family or business connection, by the father or brother who was regarded as head of the household. By contrast, their more 'privileged' sisters at the higher levels of society frequently had their lives mapped out for them almost from birth. Daughters of earls and counts were regularly bartered for family advantage, while princesses could seal a peace treaty. Betrothals of babies in their cradles were common, and if one 'husband' failed to make it past childhood, a substitute could be quickly found. An heiress, even in a small way, was a saleable object, her inheritance belonging to her husband from the date of the marriage. She would usually be well guarded by father, brother, or other guardian, but abductions and, indeed, forced marriages occurred in more lawless times.

Such high-born women may well have achieved considerable influence, depending on the personalities involved, but actual power – the ability to make their own decisions and enforce their choices – was rarer. It might be achieved by turning one's back on marriage and entering a convent, a course frequently chosen by noblewomen of the time. There, an abbess or prioress could taste real power, albeit on a limited scale and subject to the supervision of the local bishop. Occasionally one, such as Hildegard of Bingen, transcended even that limitation. Hildegard (later St Hildegard) was rightly famous in her own time for her visionary writings, music, preaching and works on herbs and medicines.

The women featured in this book – Emma of Normandy, Matilda of Tuscany, Empress Matilda, Matilda of Boulogne, the crusader women of Outremer and Eleanor of Aquitaine – would all have begun their lives as stereotypical puppets to be manoeuvred by men. Their personalities, though, took them far beyond that traditional mould. While some were placed in positions of power by events outside their control, others actively pursued it and once achieved, did all they could to hold on to it. If they were subtle, they might be praised as wise and capable. If they were forceful, they were described as 'manly', a word that might be the highest compliment or the gravest insult, depending on the circumstances.

Some are famous names, others almost unknown outside their own region. Some had their histories written in their lifetimes, while others let future generations give their own verdict. In every case, however, the choices they made and the lives they lived had a profound impact on their own times, while, for some, their influence lasted well beyond their own era. Unlike many of their meek and subservient fellows, these women were truly Women of Power.

Maps and Family Connections

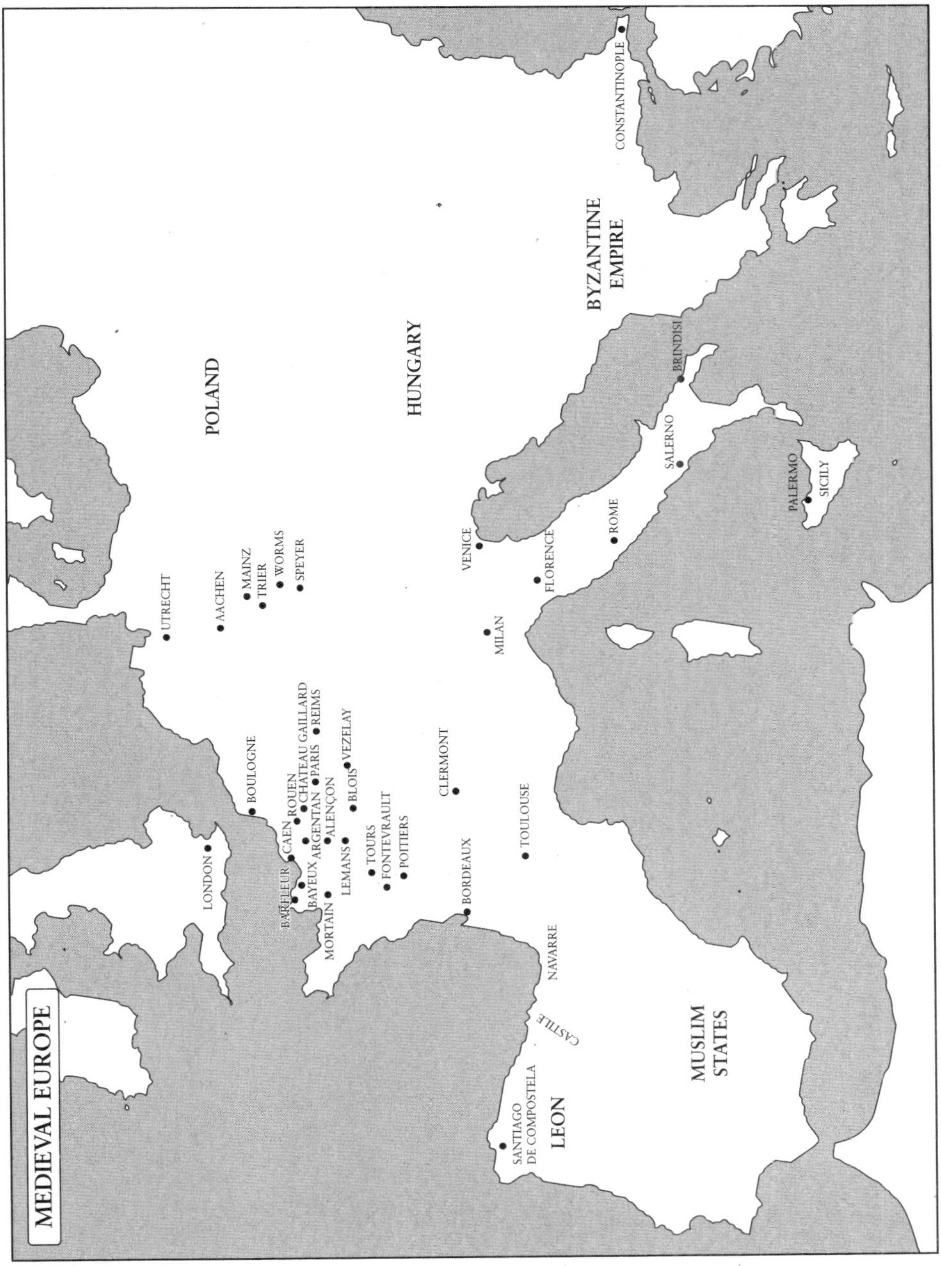
MEDIEVAL EUROPE
POLAND
HUNGARY
BYZANTINE EMPIRE
CONSTANTINOPLE
BRINDISI
SALERNO
PALERMO
SICILY
ROME
VENICE
FLORENCE
MILAN
UTRECHT
AACHEN
MAINZ
TRIER
WORMS
SPEYER
BOULOGNE
ROUEN
CHATEAU GAILLARD
REIMS
PARIS
VEZELAY
CAEN
ARGENTAN
ALENÇON
BLOIS
LONDON
BARFLEUR
BAYEUX
MORTAIN
LEMANS
TOURS
FONTEVRAULT
POITIERS
CLERMONT
BORDEAUX
TOULOUSE
NAVARRE
CASTILE
LEON
SANTIAGO DE COMPOSTELA
MUSLIM STATES

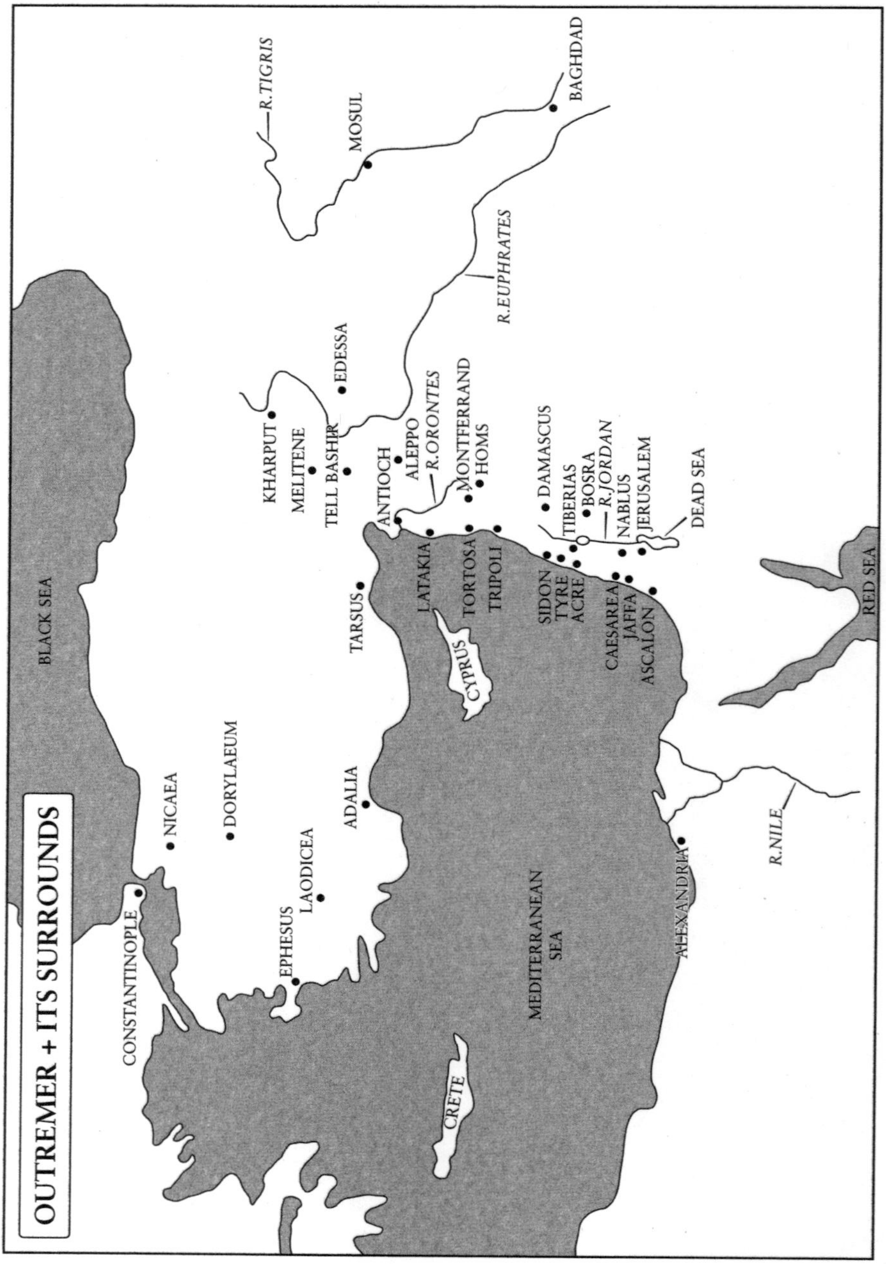
OUTREMER + ITS SURROUNDS
BLACK SEA
CONSTANTINOPLE
NICAEA
DORYLAEUM
EPHESUS
LAODICEA
ADALIA
TARSUS
KHARPUT
MELITENE
EDESSA
TELL BASHIR
ANTIOCH
ALEPPO
R.ORONTES
MONTFERRAND
HOMS
LATAKIA
TORTOSA
TRIPOLI
DAMASCUS
SIDON
TYRE
ACRE
TIBERIAS
BOSRA
R.JORDAN
NABLUS
JERUSALEM
CAESAREA
JAFFA
ASCALON
DEAD SEA
RED SEA
CYPRUS
CRETE
MEDITERRANEAN SEA
ALEXANDRIA
R.NILE
R.TIGRIS
MOSUL
BAGHDAD
R.EUPHRATES

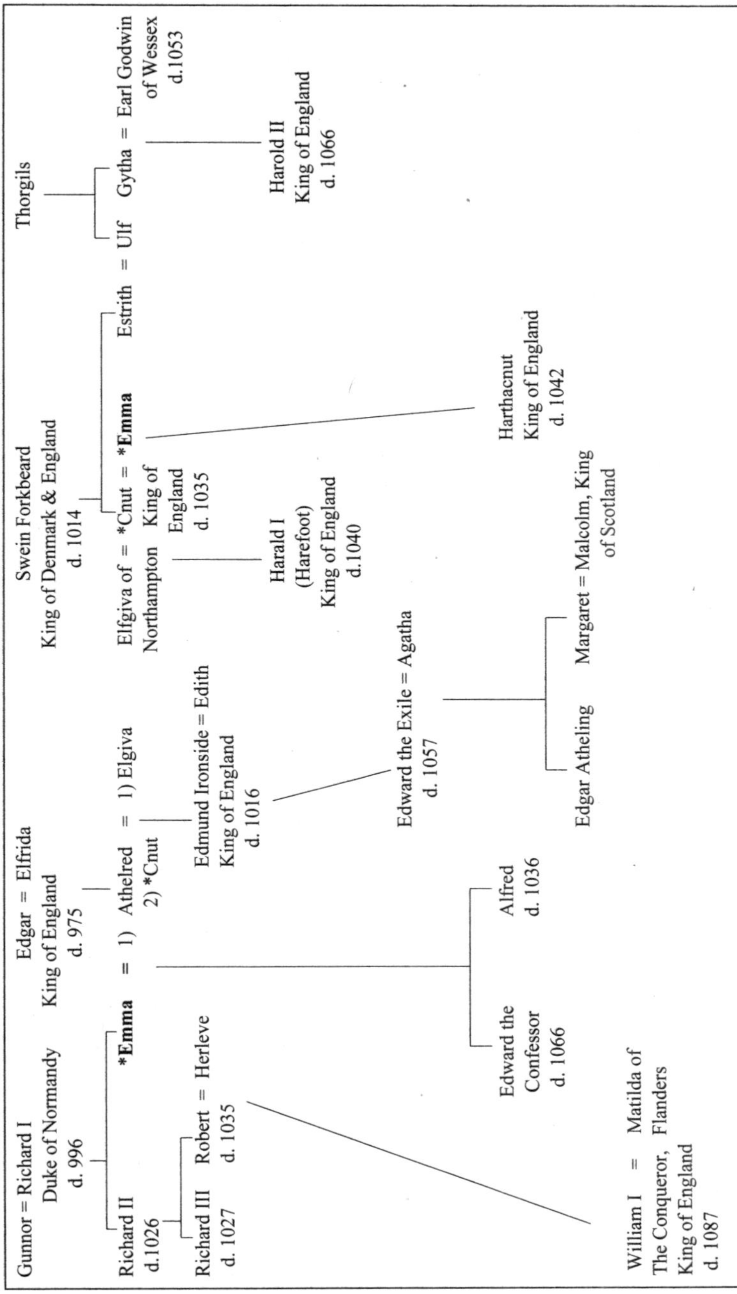

Fig.1 Selected Family Connections of Emma of Normandy

N.B. Where the same person appears in different parts of a diagram, this is indicated with an *

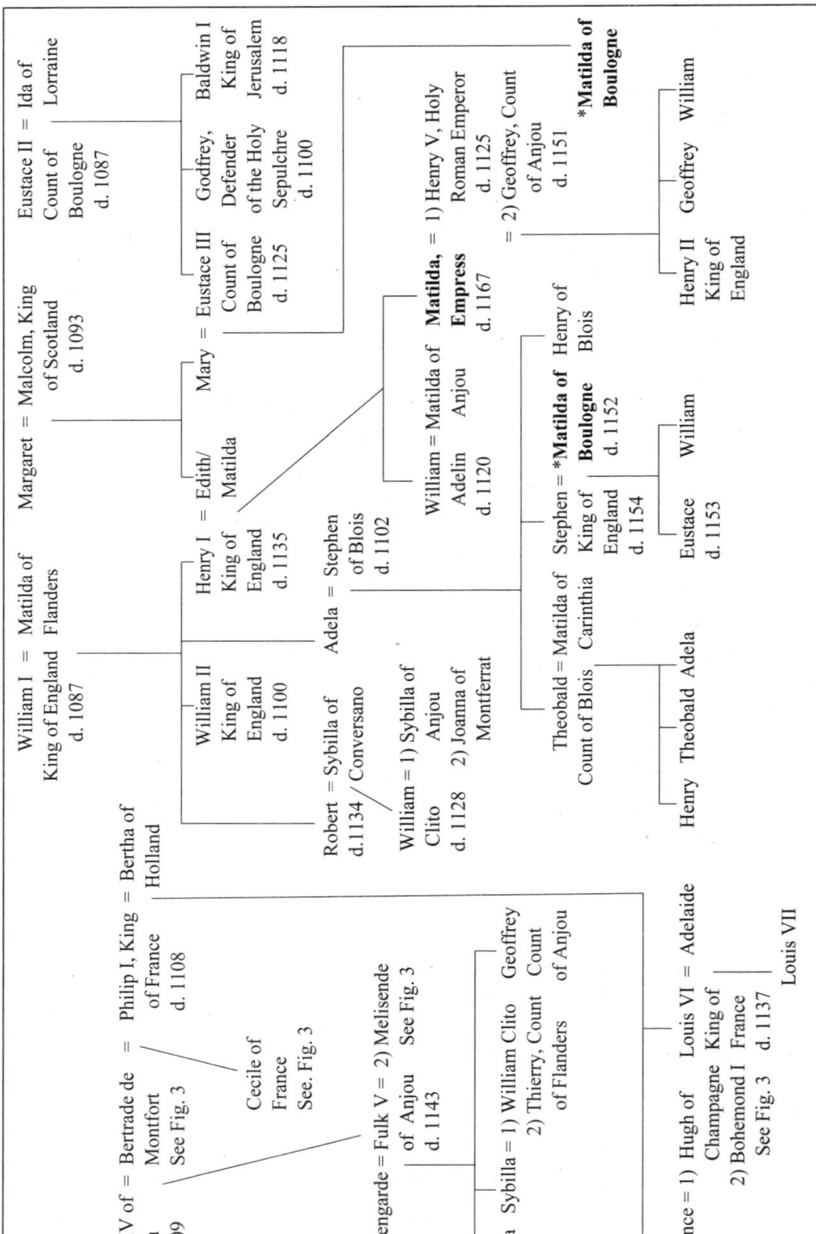

Fig. 2 Selected Family Connections of Matilda the Queen & Matilda the Empress

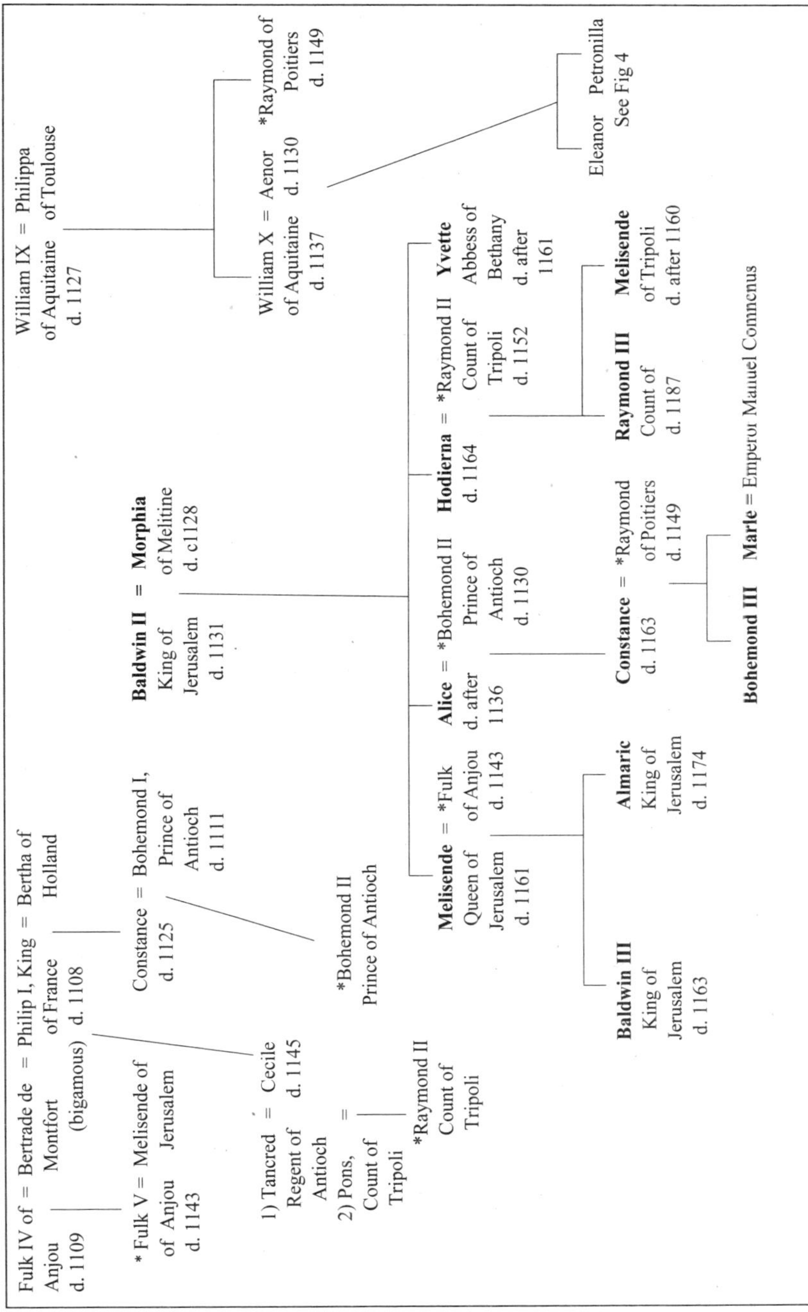

Fig. 3. Selected Family Connections of Melisende of Jerusalem

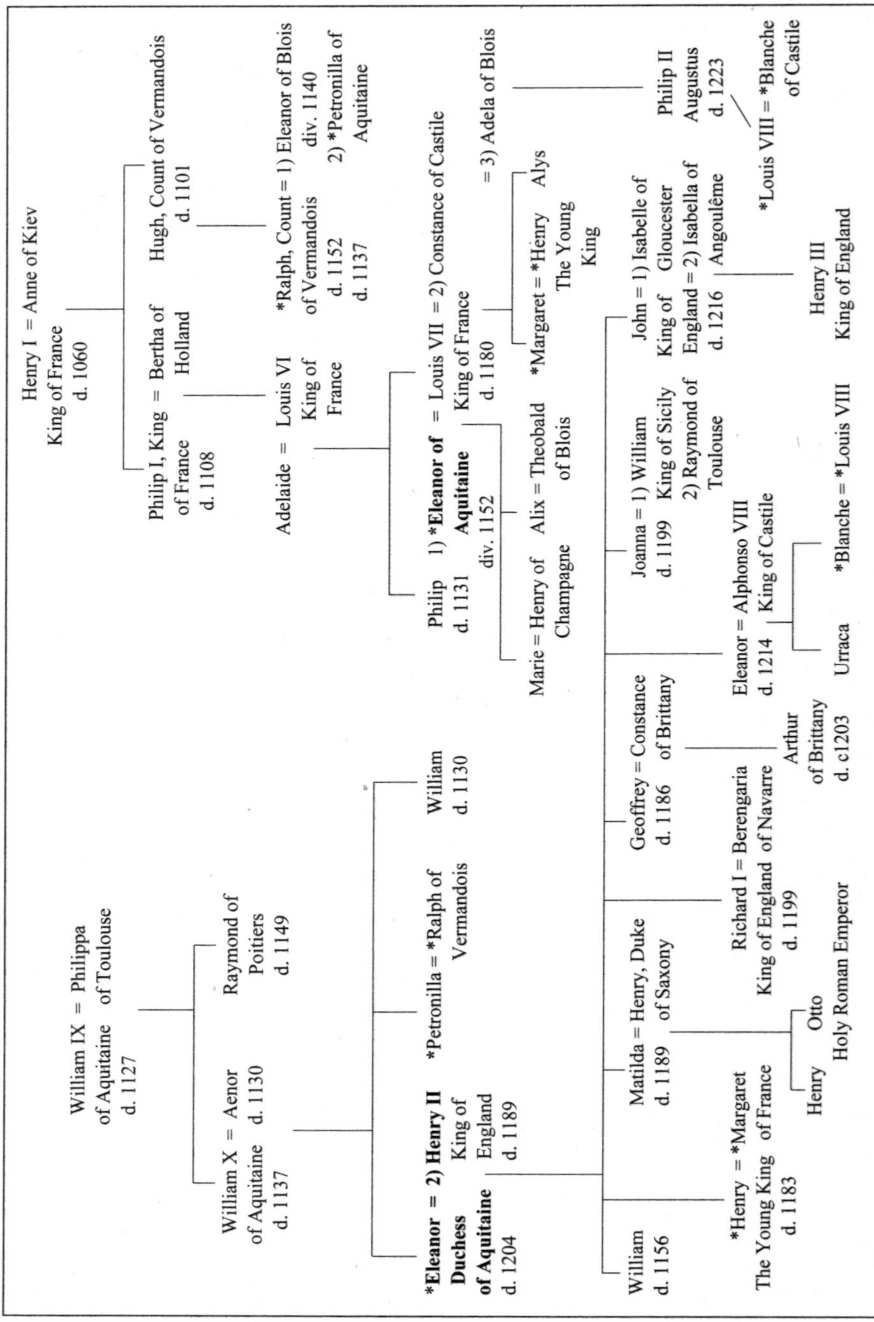

Fig. 4 Selected Family Connections of Eleanor of Aquitaine

1

Emma of Normandy: The Great Survivor

To marry one English king might be seen as an achievement: to marry two is the unique accomplishment of Emma of Normandy. Nor is there much similarity between the two. The first, Athelred the Unraed, has gone down in popular history as 'the Unready', a chronically incompetent failure. The second has been referred to as Cnut the Great, and Emperor of the North, having conquered not only England but Norway, too, to add to his homeland, Denmark. How much choice the lady had in either of her marriages is unclear, but the fact that she out-lived both husbands, and largely maintained her position through the turbulent times of six different kings, suggests that Emma had survival skills of the highest order.

We know a great deal about her – or at least about how she wanted to appear to history – as, towards the end of her life, and at the height of her power, she commissioned an anonymous Flemish cleric to write an account of her rise to glory. His approach to this work, known as the Encomium Emmae Reginae – Queen Emma's Encomium – is clearly shown by the Prologue, in which he declares that no-one would be capable of doing justice to her excellence, and he seriously doubts being equal to the task laid on him. We need to bear this in mind when reading the detailed account that follows, though even the half-truths and evasions that are apparent are revealing of the characters involved, their interactions and motives. It may well be that the author himself was aware of the limitations imposed on him, and that he intended as a subtle warning the comment that the reader who has scanned the work with a penetrating eye should understand it was devoted entirely to praising Queen Emma.

The background to both of her marriages, and, indeed, to the whole of her life, was the relationship between the established rulers of the recently united land known as England, and the Vikings of the north, whose thoughts had by now turned to conquest and settlement. Emma herself was of Viking descent on both sides. Her great-grandfather was Hrolf the Ganger, known to the French chroniclers as Rollo, whose persistent attacks on the lower Seine valley so depopulated the area that he was able to colonise it, eventually winning grudging acknowledgement of that fact when, in AD 911, Charles the Simple, king of the Franks, granted it to him on condition that he became, at least nominally, a Christian.

In the three-quarters of a century between then and the birth of Emma, these Norsemen, or 'Normans' as they had become, expanded their territory to the west to take in the Cotentin peninsula, south as far as Mont St. Michel, and east as far as the River Bresle. In those years, too, particularly from around 965, they took on much of the culture of their adopted land, becoming more solidly Christian, speaking Norman French and adapting their institutions to the Frankish model. Emma's father, Richard I, was generally known as Count of Normandy, but her brother Richard II would securely hold the title of 'duke'.

It was Richard I who commissioned Dudo of St Quentin to write the Historia Normannorum – the History of the Normans – which he began immediately after Richard's death with the encouragement of his son Richard II. He worked mainly from oral tradition rather than from the scanty documents available, so the history is presented as the family wished it to be seen. Thus, when Dudo says of Emma's mother, Gunnor, that she was 'a maiden of shining majesty, descended from an exceedingly famed family of noble Danes', we must remember that she may well have been 'of shining majesty' when he was writing in the early eleventh century, but she may also have been looking over his shoulder at the time. Others have suggested a humbler background, as a child of a Danish family recently settled in the Cotentin area. This chimes better with the story of how she met Count Richard, as recounted by the much later chronicler, Robert of Torigni. According to him, Gunnor's sister was married to a forester in the Pay de Caux region, at whose house the count called on a hunting expedition. Despite having a noble wife, and probably a number of 'concubines', Richard became smitten with the forester's wife, but to preserve her virtue, she sent her sister, Gunnor, to his bed instead. Gunnor thereafter became a mistress with far higher status than the others, and eventually the second wife of the count.

There is a great deal of confusion about dates here. Dudo is careful to tell us that the count's first noble wife was dead before he married Gunnor, and she is believed to have died around 968. It is very likely that Richard and Gunnor had children before that time, but quite impossible that the son who became Richard II could have been born in 963, as frequently stated, if he was still five years short of his majority on his father's death in 996. An alternative date of 978 is more plausible, but that would mean that his younger brother Robert was at most ten years old when he was appointed Archbishop of Rouen in 989, which again seems unlikely.

There is another story that it was only to legitimise Robert, and thus enable that appointment, that Count Richard and Gunnor married. Dudo, smoothing the family history, makes no such suggestion, instead claiming it was at the urging of the Norman nobility that Richard agreed to turn his 'alliance of forbidden union' into a Christian marriage, 'lest, lacking an advocate and heir after the mournful loss of your death-day, foreign nations tread us under foot.' Since he has already told us of at least two other sons, it is clear that only the offspring of Richard and Gunnor are going to be regarded as heirs to Normandy, whenever they were born, and again it is possible to detect the presence of Gunnor herself hovering over the author, as, for a second time, he lists all her virtues. She is recommended by the nobles as 'the woman you (Count Richard) now cherish ... beautiful and elegant in her appearance, circumspect and prudent in her deliberations, of devout mind, disciplined heart, discreet speech, gentle comportment, diligent and wise in every matter.' Following their advice, therefore, at some point Richard married Gunnor 'according to matrimonial law in the presence of a gathering of bishops', thus apparently rendering their children past and present acceptably legitimate in the eyes of the church.

Whether born before or after this event, we can be a little more precise as to the birth date of the daughter of this paragon, Emma of Normandy. It is unlikely she would have been much younger than fourteen at the time of her first marriage in 1002. Nor would she be much over thirty-five years old when her last child was born in 1020. This gives us a range from roughly 985 to 988 as the year of her birth. By that time her first husband, Athelred, had been king of England for nearly ten years, and had already experienced the first of the Viking raids that were to be a constant blight on his life.

William of Malmesbury wrote his *Gesta Regum Anglorum* – the Deeds of the Kings of England – well over a century after this time, and, though striving to copy the Venerable Bede in his diligence and commitment to reporting only facts, he confesses that, for events before his time, he had to rely on earlier accounts that might be less careful. Nonetheless, he holds nothing back in his description of Athelred as a king who, having obtained a kingdom, 'occupied rather than governed it'. 'The career of his life,' Malmesbury tells us, 'is said to have been cruel in the beginning, wretched in the middle and disgraceful in the end.' The cause of all this he attributes to the manner in which Athelred came to the throne.

Athelred's father, King Edgar, known as 'the Peaceable', had been fortunate enough to live in a time between the major waves of Viking attacks. Although there were by then considerable numbers of settlers, particularly Danish, in the north and east of his kingdom, they all acknowledged his authority, and in the words of the contemporary *Anglo-Saxon Chronicle*, 'God granted him that he dwell in peace the while that he lived.' When he died, however, in 975, he left two potential heirs, both of them well short of their majority.

By his first wife, Athelfleda, he had a son, Edward, who was then around thirteen years of age. His second (or possibly third) wife, Aelfthryth, or Elfrida, was, however, the only one to have been crowned as queen alongside her husband, and she pushed hard for her own son, Athelred, to be recognised as rightful heir, although he was only seven years old. There was no automatic rule of primogeniture at the time. The issue of succession to the throne was decided by the Witanagemot, the council made up of leading churchmen and nobility who advised the king. It was generally made on the basis of the most suitable person for the prevailing circumstances, chosen from a number of 'throne-worthy' candidates sometimes referred to as 'athelings', and it was not unknown for sons, particularly young sons, to be passed over entirely in favour of some other close relative. In this case, despite a number of nobles supporting the queen, the choice fell on Edward, who was duly consecrated and crowned, as by family tradition, at Kingston-on-Thames.

A little under three years later, however, Edward was murdered while on a visit to his stepmother Elfrida and half-brother Athelred at Corfe Castle. The story goes that he was set upon and stabbed by members of the household as he leaned from his horse to accept a cup of wine on his arrival. The act was clearly pre-meditated, and since the household was that of Elfrida, this 'wicked stepmother' was soon being given the blame, though Malmesbury's claim of 'concurrence' on the part of ten-year-old Athelred seems unmerited. One version of the tale declares that Edward's body was originally thrown into a swamp then hastily retrieved, while Malmesbury simply says he was 'ingloriously interred at Wareham', the *Anglo-Saxon Chronicle* adding that the burial was 'without any kind of kingly honours'. Within weeks Athelred had been crowned king in his place.

This murder, then, which he may or may not have actually witnessed, is the cruelty with which Athelred's reign began, and the taint of it clung to him for a considerable time. 'There has not been, amid Angles, a worse deed done than this, since first they came to Britain,' says the *Anglo-Saxon Chronicle*, and when it began to be claimed that miracles were occurring at the grave of the murdered king, the by all accounts fairly obnoxious teenager was declared a saint and a martyr. 'Men murdered him, but God glorified him,' declared the Chronicle, adding that in the same year, after the coronation of Athelred, 'a bloody cloud' was seen in the sky, 'oftentimes in the likeness of fire'.

So when, within two years, the Viking raids began again on the south coast of England, it was clear that this was a punishment for the murder of Edward the Martyr. Raid and withdrawal became the pattern for the next few years, then a gap, then more raid and withdrawal, and increasingly it became apparent that the withdrawal was not home to Denmark, but the much shorter journey across the Channel to Normandy. The Normans had not become so assimilated to France that they would refuse winter shelter to their kin from the north, and hostility between England and Normandy was threatening to turn to open warfare when, in 990, Pope John XV intervened. At the end of that year he sent his envoy, Bishop Leo of Treves, to Athelred, and obtained from him a promise of 'the firmest peace for all his sons and daughters, present and future, and all his faithful people, without deceit', if Richard I in Normandy would promise the same. Presented with this offer, Richard agreed, with the condition that injustices committed should be fairly redressed. The agreement was signed on behalf of Athelred and Richard at Rouen in March 991, but the most important point seems to have been almost a footnote. 'Moreover,' it says, 'Of the king's subjects or of his enemies, let Richard receive none, nor the king of his, without their respective seals,' that is, without their due authorisation.

This seems to represent the first diplomatic contact between the two leaders, and how effective it was is uncertain, for the Viking fleet brought to England by Olaf Trygvasson in 991 was a game changer. Olaf was a great-grandson of Harald Fairhair of Norway and had been to Britain before, but the ninety-three ships and the warriors he brought with him this time had more the appearance of an invasion force.

They didn't have matters all their own way, nor, indeed, had the earlier raiders, despite history representing the Anglo-Saxons as supine. In East Anglia they came up against the ealdorman Britnoth, whose chivalrous permission for them to fight on level terms at the battle of Maldon cost him his life. It has been suggested, however, that he wanted to be sure they fought there lest they sailed off to another landing place where no army awaited them. Certainly, while the Danes won the battle, they were so badly mauled, according to English sources at least, that they had barely enough fit men left to man their ships. It was after this, however, that Athelred began to live up to the nickname later bestowed on him. The Anglo-Saxons were notably fond of wordplay. 'Athelred' – in Old English Ǽthelraed – translates as 'noble counsel', while the word tagged on 'Unraed' means literally 'bad counsel' or 'badly advised', thus providing a rather weak pun on his given name.

In the early years of his reign his mother had been effectively regent for her young son, and though she dropped into the background when he began personal rule around 984, this forceful woman still seems to have retained considerable influence. Among other things, according to the will of Athelred's eldest son, it was she, rather than his first wife, who brought up his children. Another major advisor, as he had been for King Edgar, was Archbishop Dunstan, later St. Dunstan. His death in 988 seems to have de-stabilised the regime, and it was his successor, Archbishop Sigeric, who now advised Athelred that he should pay the Vikings to go away.

As it turned out it was a serious mistake. Malmesbury calls it an 'infamous precedent', though even King Alfred had used the tactic before, buying time to assemble forces to oppose the Danes when they returned. Athelred tried something similar. Having paid £10,000 to get rid of Olaf, he attempted to assemble a fleet and reinforced the defences of the boroughs established by Alfred. Nevertheless, a further £16,000 had to be paid by London the following year, and in 994, when Olaf returned with a new (and unlikely) ally, Swein Forkbeard of Denmark, they had to be bought off again with both money and provisions. This time Olaf, already baptised as a Christian, was confirmed in the faith with Athelred as his sponsor and promised never to return. He was as good as his word, taking himself off to become king of Norway. Swein Forkbeard, however, made no such promise.

By now it must have appeared to all Viking raiders that England's defences were ineffective, and that this wealthy nation could be milked of cash and other resources again and again, the staggering sums involved being raised by a land tax that became known as 'danegeld'. By the late 990s raids were a regular feature, and once again the raiders were wintering close at hand, in Normandy, and even on the Isle of Wight. It was against this background that a marriage was arranged between Athelred and young Emma of Normandy.

It is assumed his first wife must have died by this time, having given him at least eight and possibly more children. She is not named in the contemporary chronicles, nor is there much fanfare for the arrival of Emma. A half-sentence in the *Anglo-Saxon Chronicle* simply records that 'Richard's daughter, Emma Elfgiva' arrived during Lent in the year 1002. Henry of Huntingdon, writing in the 1120s but closely following the earlier chronicle, is a little more effusive, probably with the benefit of hindsight. He calls Emma, 'the flower of Normandy' and also ascribes a motive for the marriage. According to him, Athelred, 'in order to strengthen himself on the throne', wanted to marry Richard's daughter because he was 'a valiant prince and all powerful in the kingdom of France'. Since Richard I had died in 996, unless the negotiations were extremely protracted, Athelred must, in fact, have been dealing with Emma's brother Richard II, or, if the story of his minority is correct, more likely with her mother Gunnor, who would still have been regent at the time.

It was, of course, a purely political marriage. Emma was probably in her mid-teens and Athelred a good twenty years older. He was, however, a king, and king of a wealthy country at that, so the match was probably attractive to the Normans. It seems likely they also insisted on Emma being granted proper status. Unlike her predecessor she was crowned as queen, and must immediately have been granted estates in England since her reeve or steward was already installed in Exeter by the following year. She also features high on the witness lists of charters, sometimes even ahead of the royal princes, though lower than the position the king's mother had occupied until her death a year or two before. She appears as 'Aelfgifu', later rendered as 'Elfgiva', the name the English gave her in place of the Norman 'Emma'. Apparently both names continued in use, sometimes joined, as in the Chronicle entry for her arrival. Frequently, however, chronicles simply referred to her as 'the Lady'.

If Athelred had anticipated help from Normandy against the Danes, he was to be disappointed. There is only one suggestion in the records of him later asking for such help, and none was received. Nonetheless, Henry of Huntingdon suggests it was because the king was 'so elated with pride' after his marriage that, later that year, he made his second and most serious mistake in his dealings with the Danes.

'And in that year,' says the *Anglo-Saxon Chronicle*, 'The king ordered all the Danish men who were in England to be slain.' It must have been only months after his wedding, for the action was to be carried out on St Brice's Day, 13 November, and the Chronicle gives a reason for this order. Apparently, 'it was made known to the king that they would treacherously bereave him of his life, and afterwards all his witan ... and have his kingdom without gainsaying.' We are not told how this alleged plot was hatched, or who told the king of it, and later writers show considerable scepticism. Malmesbury declares there was 'light suspicion only', while Henry of Huntingdon says the Danes were 'living peaceably in England' and were 'treacherously massacred'.

How many Danes were killed, and where, is not at all clear. Despite Huntingdon's claim that the English rose up 'everywhere on the same day and at the same hour', it is fairly certain that the order was not carried out in that part of England known as the Danelaw. This was a region roughly to the north and east of a line from London to Chester, which had been granted semi-autonomous status by King Edgar in what the Chronicle calls his 'one misdeed'. Outside that area, however, Malmesbury says there were other Danes distributed around the towns and countryside, and some at least of these are recorded as murdered on that day, in one case burnt inside a church where they had fled for sanctuary.

By tradition, among those killed on St Brice's Day were the sister and brother-in-law of Swein Forkbeard, now not only king of Denmark but effective ruler of Norway as well, having defeated and replaced his erstwhile ally Olaf Trygvasson. The massacre provided a suitable excuse, if one were needed, for renewed attacks on England, with an eye to adding that land to his growing empire.

It shows something of the suspicion with which the English regarded their new foreign queen, that, when Exeter was attacked and largely destroyed the following year, the *Anglo-Saxon Chronicle* claims it was 'entered by storm, through the French churl Hugh, whom the Lady had appointed her steward'. Why the queen's steward should arrange the destruction of her property is not considered. In 1004 attacks were centred on East Anglia, where again the Viking force was victorious in battle, though, says Malmesbury, 'the conquerors suffered much more than the conquered.' In 1006, not only was the south-east targeted in the summer, but later in the year almost the whole of Wessex was visited and plundered. 'No man could think or discover how they could be driven out of the land,' says the Chronicle, but the method found, proposed by 'the king with his witan', was to follow the earlier precedent and pay them to go away. This time it cost £36,000.

Throughout this period we know very little of the circumstances of Queen Emma except that she was dutifully adding to the number of the king's children. A son was born, probably in 1003, and christened Edward. It has been suggested that this shows Athelred making peace with the ghost of his murdered half-brother, but since all his previous sons had been named in order after his predecessors on the throne, beginning with Athelstan and working down to Edgar, he may equally well have now begun working in the opposite direction. Athelstan's predecessor was Edward the Elder, and before him came Alfred, the name bestowed on the second son of Queen Emma. There was a daughter, too, born around 1004 and christened Godgifu.

Having bought himself some respite from Viking attacks, Athelred seemed determined to be better prepared to meet the next onslaught. Unfortunately, as with so much in his reign, his good intentions came to nought by a combination of poor judgement and sheer bad luck. Like the reverse of King Midas, everything he touched seemed to turn to tragedy or farce.

In 1007 a thegn known as Edric Streona – Edric the Grasper – was appointed ealdorman of Mercia. In theory this was a good move, providing a leader for that important Midland area around which the local forces could unite. It was in his choice of man, however, that Athelred made a serious and eventually fatal mistake. Edric 'was a man, indeed, of low origin', says the chronicler John of Worcester, writing later but based in the Midlands, 'but his smooth tongue gained him high rank.' William of Malmesbury is more damning, calling him 'the refuse of mankind … an artful dissembler, capable of feigning anything'. 'Crafty and treacherous' is the Chronicle's description, and his treachery was to cost the king dear. At this time, though, he was clearly a favoured member of Athelred's inner circle, even marrying one of the king's daughters.

If this was apparently a good beginning, the king's next step should have been even better. In 1008, says the Chronicle, 'the king commanded that ships should be speedily built throughout the English nation.' One ship was to be provided for every 310 hides of land in the country, the hide being the basic land measurement at the time. The one or more owners of the land would pay for the ships, and they were also required to provide crews and armour. It has been calculated that this would produce some 250 ships, a mighty fleet for the time, and, if properly crewed and deployed, surely enough to deter any future Viking raiders. We don't know how many ships were actually built, but certainly many more than a hundred. The Chronicle simply states, 'so many of them as never before … in any king's days'. In 1009 they were assembled at Sandwich, where 'they were to lie and defend this land against every foreign army,' and apparently the king and nobility were there as well, no doubt admiring their fleet. Then, as recounted in the Chronicle, the occasion dissolved into farce. Brihtric, the brother of

Edric Streona, accused a Sussex thegn, Wulfnoth Cild, of treachery towards the king. Wulfnoth immediately took twenty ships from the fleet and set about ravaging the south coast. Brihtric 'thought that he should acquire great fame if he could seize Wulfnoth alive or dead', and took a further eighty ships with which to pursue him. On the way, however, a great storm blew up and Brihtric's ships were smashed to pieces along the coast, whereupon Wulfnoth, who had escaped the storm, came back and burnt all that remained. When Athelred was told of this, he apparently gave the matter up as hopeless and 'went his way home', while the remaining ships were taken to London and laid up. 'They let the whole nation's toil thus lightly pass away,' says the Chronicle, 'and the hopes of the English with it.'

In that mood they were in no way prepared to meet the Viking force that arrived at Sandwich a matter of months later. This was 'Thorkell's army', much more than a raiding party, and soon after joined by two other fleets. The author of Emma's Encomium claims they were sent by Swein Forkbeard to soften up the English in preparation for his own invasion, and Thorkell had certainly fought alongside Forkbeard before. He was, however, a formidable figure in his own right, and his 'army' contained many of the famous 'Jomsvikings,' those supreme warriors trained at Jomsberg, by the mouth of the River Oder in present-day Poland.

They began in the traditional way by ravaging along the south coast and being paid by the men of Kent to go away. Nonetheless they didn't have matters all their own way. At one point the king's army had cut them off from their ships and intended to face them in a decisive battle. 'But it was then prevented,' says the Chronicle, 'through Edric the Ealdorman.' How Edric achieved this is not stated, but it was clearly not the first time Edric and his kin had thwarted the king's plans. Nor would it be the last, as evidenced by the clearly contemporary end of the sentence in the Chronicle, '... as it ever is still.'

Instead of departing to winter quarters, Thorkell made a camp at Greenwich, living off the surrounding land and repeatedly attacking London but failing to breach its walls. The following year East Anglia came under attack and, after heavy fighting, succumbed. The southern midlands were opened up, Oxford burned, and though Athelred called out all his forces, for most of the year, by accident or design, the armies seem to have played cat and mouse with each other, while the Vikings burnt and plundered most of southern England. 'When they were eastward, then were the forces kept westward,' wails the Chronicle, 'And when they were southwards, then were our forces northwards.'

By the time Athelred was brought to petition for terms in 1010, some seventeen counties were recorded as overrun by the invaders, from East Anglia in the east to Wiltshire in the west, and from Northampton in the north to Hampshire on the south coast. The price for peace this time was the huge sum of £48,000 which took months to raise. In the meantime, the plundering continued, leading in September 1011 to the sack of Canterbury and the capture of Archbishop Alphege.

At Easter the following year the money was finally paid over. Alphege, however, had refused to allow the people to be burdened with an extra ransom for himself, and thus the sixty-year-old archbishop was still in captivity, probably at Greenwich, when a rowdy, drunken Viking celebration got out of hand. They began pelting him with 'bones and the horns of oxen'. One account says Thorkell tried to intervene, but the men defied him. Finally, and possibly as an act of mercy, a man whom Alphege had baptised in the Christian faith only the day before, finished him off with a blow to the head from the blunt end of an axe.

It was immediately after this that Thorkell offered the services of himself and forty-five ship's companies to Athelred as mercenaries. Disgust at the murder may have been one reason for this startling defection, but the outright defiance of men supposedly under his command would also have acted as a motive. For whatever reason it was made, his offer was quickly accepted.

Again, it is the Encomiast who declares that this defection was the reason for Swein Forkbeard's arrival in England the following year, though he does admit Swein was already planning an invasion. After a brief foray to Sandwich, where perhaps he was deterred by Athelred and his new ally Thorkell, the Danish king made off for friendlier parts. Sailing into the mouth of the Humber and up the River Trent, he set up a base at Gainsborough in present-day Lincolnshire. Within a short time, as he had anticipated, the whole of Danish northern England had acclaimed him king, and was happily supplying him with provisions, horses and men, with which to set about the conquest of the southern part of the land.

He had brought with him his younger son, Cnut, then no more than eighteen years of age at most, with whom he must have had a better relationship than he'd had with his own father, whom he had overthrown and replaced as king of Denmark. Cnut was now to be trusted to hold the base at Gainsborough and deal with the hostages already given to Swein. Perhaps to cement his standing in the area, the young man was, at about this time, married in the Danish 'handfast' fashion to Elfgiva of Northampton. She was the daughter of Aelfhelm, an ealdorman who had held considerable lands in the Midlands. Elfgiva had no love for the English king, however, since he had apparently had her father murdered and her brothers blinded for some unspecified crimes. Some accounts link Edric Streona with these actions, as part of his rise to favour with the king.

From Gainsborough Swein set out southwards, meeting little opposition at Oxford and Winchester before turning east to attack London. London, however, was sheltering not only King Athelred, but also his younger family, Queen Emma and her children. It is likely that thought had already been given to an escape route and sanctuary for them should the position become hopeless, but for the time being, with the help of Thorkell, the city held out. According to the Chronicle, in the course of this attack Swein lost many men drowned in the Thames 'because they kept not to any bridges.' It seems hard to believe experienced sailors and river navigators would have attempted to ford such a broad tidal river, but that account is clearly contemporary as the writer declares of London, 'praise be to God that it yet stands sound.' It would not do so for much longer.

Thwarted at London, Swein drew off to the west, to Wallingford and Bath, knowing that if the rest of the country fell to him, London could not hold out alone. Everywhere he went he was acclaimed as king, and he then withdrew to Gainsborough to regroup and await the inevitable. Sure enough, before the end of the year London was ready to submit. Athelred withdrew to Greenwich where the English fleet lay, including, presumably, Thorkell's ships. From there, says the Chronicle, 'the Lady (Queen Emma) then departed over the sea to her brother Richard,' accompanied by the abbot of Peterborough. Whether her children went with her or followed soon after is not clear. The Chronicle says they were in the charge of the bishop of London, but they may have been in the same group of emigrants, perhaps in a different ship. Athelred himself went first to the Isle of Wight before joining his family in Normandy, and it may be that Emma had to intercede for him with her brother before the duke agreed to give shelter to an exiled king.

It was an ignominious homecoming for the English queen, and we have no way of knowing whether she sympathised with her husband in his capitulation to a more powerful enemy, or shared history's verdict that he was simply incompetent. A clue is perhaps given by the fact that, thus far, she herself has not appeared at all in the Encomium that she commissioned, which has been entirely devoted to the exploits of Swein Forkbeard, 'the most fortunate king of his time'. Nor is her marriage to Athelred mentioned in any part of that document, an omission which causes some difficulty to its author later, and was therefore presumably insisted on by Emma herself.

There is no record of Swein ever being formally crowned, but 25 December 1013 is frequently given as the date when he was finally accepted as king of the whole of England. His reign was to be a short one. Just over five weeks later, on 2 February, he died at Gainsborough, most probably following a fall from his horse, though different accounts muddy the story. John of Worcester declares he was killed by the ghost of St Edmund, himself a king of England murdered by Danes. This rather fanciful ending might be reconciled as an imaginative interpretation of something frightening the horse that threw him. The Encomium has him aware of his approaching death and handing over the kingdom to Cnut, with many exhortations as to how it was to be governed. Again, this may be a possibility if the injuries suffered in his fall did not immediately kill him, though the emphasis on the zealous practice of the Christian faith, supposedly given by this indifferent Christian, is more likely to have come from the Encomiast himself than from Swein Forkbeard.

However it came about, the transmission of the kingdom to the young Cnut was happily accepted by the Danes in northern England. In the south, though, it was a different matter. The three surviving sons of Athelred with his first wife – Athelstan, Edmund and Edwig – seem to have stayed in England when the younger family fled abroad, and at the least they may have influenced the Witan who now met. After some deliberation they sent to Athelred, telling him, 'no lord were dearer to them than their natural lord, if he would rule them better than he had before done.' Whether this was a reference to his incompetence or to his reputed severity is not clear, but Athelred immediately responded that he would be their loving lord and amend all they complained of, provided they would give him their full obedience without any deceit. Clearly, he had some suspicions as to their loyalty, and maybe even thought the invitation to return might be a trap. To sound out their true feelings, he sent along with the messengers his son Edward, now at most eleven years old, and possibly a pawn he was prepared to lose if treachery was in the air. In the event Edward's report was entirely favourable.

All this must have been done very quickly. Swein Forkbeard died on 2 February, and the Chronicle records Athelred 'came home to his people' during Lent, which that year began on 10 March. It must have been early in Lent, too, for by Easter, on 25 April, he had raised an army, stormed north and taken Cnut completely by surprise at Gainsborough. The young man had been in the process of gathering his own forces, but the sudden attack put them to flight, and Cnut himself immediately abandoned his new 'kingdom' and sailed away. He did not go straight home to Denmark, however, but as a last act of defiance, took with him the hostages that had been in his charge and landed them at Sandwich, having first cut off their hands, ears and noses.

The Encomiast, seeking to show Cnut in the best light, carefully explains that he was not running away at this time, but returning to Denmark to consult his brother Harald on a 'weighty matter'. He also feels the need to explain why Cnut took fewer ships and men than he had brought. Ignoring the fact that Thorkell had been fighting against Swein, he claims that that mighty warrior now chose to remain in England, along with a large part of the army, and tries to suggest that this was so he might persuade the English to surrender to Cnut, or at least to form a fifth column to betray Athelred when Cnut should return.

The 'weighty matter' taking Cnut to Denmark concerned the division of Swein's kingdoms between the brothers. Again, the Encomiast is probably wrong to claim Cnut was the older brother. That was almost certainly Harald, who, having been left in charge in Denmark, had already claimed that country as his rightful inheritance before Cnut arrived. Despite a touching description of the brothers weeping on each other's necks when they met, Harald had no intention of giving up what he had taken. Cnut's suggestion that they should share Denmark between them, go together to conquer England, and then Harald could choose which kingdom he wanted, was firmly vetoed. Hard luck if you have lost England, was the elder brother's response, and though prepared to offer ships and men to help regain it, dividing Denmark was out of the question.

In England, meanwhile, Athelred was taking his revenge on the people who had deserted him for Swein. Ravaging, burning and killing across the whole area of the Danelaw and elsewhere may have satisfied his fury at their betrayal, but did nothing to endear him to them, or secure their loyalty for the future. Cnut's desertion of them when they needed him, however, probably made him equally hated. At the time Athelred seems to have had the services of two notable Vikings, not only Thorkell the Dane, but also Olaf Haraldsson of Norway. By the end of the year, however, both had departed. Olaf returned to Norway to defeat and depose the

Danish-imposed ruler Eric Haakonsson, but Thorkell's withdrawal was the more serious.

According to Scandinavian sagas, some of Thorkell's men, possibly under the command of his brother, were treacherously killed by the English. While not mentioned in the *Anglo-Saxon Chronicle*, this would certainly give a motive for his abrupt departure with his ships and men, and the fact that he then, with a little difficulty, became reconciled with Cnut, giving him not only his service but also his detailed knowledge of the situation in England. Such knowledge would be invaluable to the young man who was still only around twenty years old, as was the return to his side of another seasoned warrior, Eric Haakonsson.

It took some little time for Cnut to organise a new invasion force, and in England meanwhile Athelred took up his reign again, though with increasing difficulties caused by disunity within the country and even his own family. We have no certain knowledge of the whereabouts of Emma and her children, but in all probability they had returned to England with, or soon after, the king. None of *them*, at that time, would have been strong enough to affect the course of affairs, but the same is not true of Athelred's older children.

In 1014 his eldest son, Athelstan, had died, though whether from illness or involvement in fighting we don't know. He certainly had time to make a will, which still exists, leaving various lands, weapons and horses to family members and others, though not to his stepmother Emma or her children. This left the next son, Edmund, later known as 'Ironside', as heir apparent. Probably in his late twenties at the time, he was clearly a man with ideas of his own, and not afraid to put them into practice.

Early the following year, Athelred called a great council to meet at Oxford. What this was intended to do we don't know, for the only deed recorded as taking place there is the murder of Siferth and Morcar, two leading thegns from the Danelaw, by Edric Streona. It is possible this was ordered by the king, perhaps as a continuing revenge on those who had deserted him for Swein. In any event, Athelred proceeded to confiscate their lands, and he shut up Siferth's widow at Malmesbury Abbey. Within a very short time, however, Edmund had 'rescued' the lady and married her, 'contrary to the king's will'. He then proceeded to take possession of the estates of both thegns in the Midlands area of Danish Mercia known as the Five Boroughs.

It is most probable that he married the lady purely to facilitate his acceptance in her former lands, although William of Malmesbury claims he was also 'enamoured'. Accepted he was, though, thereby securing for himself a power base in a region where the king and Cnut were equally hated. Into the bargain, within a very short time she bore him two sons, Edmund and Edward, who against the odds would survive to carry on the line of the kings of Wessex.

Edmund's action has been labelled a rebellion, but it seems more likely to be a simple loss of patience with his father's approach to ruling the country, and a decisive movement to secure a most important region for the English cause. Certainly, when Cnut's invasion duly commenced later in 1015, Edmund was quick to raise an army to oppose him.

So, too, did Edric Streona in the English part of Mercia, but though he was son-in-law to the king and brother-in-law to the enterprising Edmund, the treacherous ealdorman gave loyalty to no-one but himself. It seems likely Edmund was already wary, for the Chronicle declares, 'When they came together, then would the ealdorman betray the atheling, but he was not able.' Because of this they quickly parted, and instead of giving battle to Cnut, Edric soon defected to his side, taking with him forty of the king's ships.

Cnut's landing had been made, not in the Danelaw, where he was unlikely to have been welcomed, but on the Dorset coast at Poole Harbour. From there he proceeded to attack the heart of Wessex – Dorset, Wiltshire, Somerset – and then all the way up the west of England through Edric's lands to Warwickshire, where 'during the midwinter's tide (they) ravaged and burned and slew all that they could come at.'

During the autumn of 1015 King Athelred is recorded as lying sick at Corsham in Wiltshire. No details are given of his sickness, but he was approaching fifty years old, and it must have been serious to strand him at relatively unprotected Corsham when enemies were so close. By the end of the year he had recovered enough to make the journey to London, but this illness and Streona's defection does much to explain how Cnut was able to establish himself so easily in the west.

Early in the new year Edmund gathered another army, but, possibly seeing the forces marshalled against them, they refused to fight unless the king came and brought an army from London to join them. Denuding London of its fighting men was probably not a good idea, and Athelred was surely still suffering from the illness that, indeed, would take his life a few weeks later. When he eventually arrived, he stayed only a short time with the assembled forces, perhaps still suspicious of his son's actions. 'Then it was made known to the king that they would betray him,' claims the Chronicle, so Athelred returned to the safety of London.

For a short time Edmund made alliance with Uhtred, earldorman of Northumbria and another brother-in-law. Together they did all they could to ravage Streona's lands in Mercia, thereby depriving him of resources. Cnut's devastation of Northumbria, however, soon drew Uhtred away to submit 'from need', and he was promptly killed 'through the counsel of Edric.'

By this time, only London and the south-east was reliably holding out against the invaders. Around Easter time, at the beginning of April, Edmund joined his father in the city. He may have been reviewing its defences, but more likely he'd had word that the king's illness had become worse. On 23 April 1016, St George's Day, Athelred died, even as Cnut was bringing around all his ships for another attempt on the city. With, perhaps, just a touch of sympathy, the Chronicle records, 'he held his kingdom with great toil and under great difficulties the while that his life lasted,' but has no more to say about this unluckiest of kings.

It is at this point that the Encomiast runs into difficulties. Clearly under orders not to mention Athelred by name, he refers to him only as the prince in command of London, claiming that God took him away to his everlasting rest in order to avoid bloodshed. He further declares that, after burying him honourably, the people of London sent to Cnut offering to hand over the city, and that a day was fixed for his peaceful entry, only for part of the garrison to reject this plan and slip away under cover of darkness the night before, together with the son of the prince. Cnut then entered the city and 'sat on the throne of the kingdom'.

This happy little tale, casting Cnut as a wise and peaceable ruler, and Edmund – later referred to as a 'youth' – as a headstrong young rebel, is entirely at odds with the details recounted in the *Anglo-Saxon Chronicle*, written nearer the event in both time and geography. To begin with, it is Cnut that is the 'youth'. He would have been, at most, around twenty years old, while Edmund was at least five years older and probably more. Edmund was almost certainly at his father's side when he died, and immediately afterwards, says the Chronicle, 'all the peers who were in London, and the citizens, chose Edmund to be king.'

This suggests that many of the nobles had gathered for the passing of the king – and probably for their own security – within the ancient walled city. Senior churchmen would likely have been there, too, including the bishop of London, the Archbishop of Canterbury, and probably also the influential Archbishop Wulfstan of York, and it is reasonable to assume all the royal family were there as well. We have no way of knowing what relations were like between Queen Emma and her stepsons up to this point, and royal step-families in Anglo-Saxon times were notoriously tricky things. Now, however, widowed in her late twenties, with three young children to protect, she would have been wholly reliant for her safety and security on the new King Edmund, who was probably much of an age with herself.

There would have been no question of moving Emma and her family elsewhere for safety. London was by far the safest place and would be defended to the death. The Danes could not be defeated from inside London, however, and already Cnut's fleet would have been approaching. The Chronicle says he arrived at Greenwich during the Rogation days. If they were including the Major rogation, this would have been a mere two days after Athelred's death, and the Encomium may well have been right about Edmund leaving the night before. Otherwise, it would have been at the end of the first week in May, still giving a bare two weeks for him to be elected as king, make his plans and leave.

Far from inviting Cnut to take possession of the city, London closed its gates and mounted its walls against his forces, and while the new king made his way to Wessex to accept its submission and raise an army, Cnut set about establishing the siege of London. To get past the defensible barrier that was London Bridge, a ditch was dug around it on the southern bank, and some of the Viking longships were hauled around to the western side, thus preventing the city being re-provisioned by water. Another ditch was then dug around the entire city in an effort to starve them into submission, and a portion of the army left to enforce the siege. Taking London would not be a knockout blow, however, if Edmund was still loose in the country, so Cnut was forced to divide his army and set off to find and confront the English king.

Henry of Huntingdon records six major battles fought over the next few months around southern England, basing his list closely on 'ancient histories', in particular the *Anglo-Saxon Chronicle*. The first battle was at Pen Selwood – the hill of the willow wood – in Dorset, and was indecisive. This was followed soon after by another further north, at Sherston, near Malmesbury. This was 'severely contested', with Edric Streona fighting on the Danish side, but it, too, finished in a draw, when 'after great slaughter ... the armies separated themselves.'

Around midsummer Edmund came back to London, having apparently evaded his opponent. Attacking from the north through Tottenham, an unexpected direction, he scattered Cnut's forces and broke the siege, following up a few days later with a resounding victory at Brentford, causing the Danes to withdraw. Briefly, London was relieved and re-provisioned, the people no doubt overjoyed to find Cnut's Danish army was not invincible. The victory at Brentford had been costly, however, and Edmund withdrew again into Wessex to recruit a fresh army. As soon as he had gone the Danes returned and the siege was re-imposed, but the available provisions were running out for the besiegers as well.

After the failure of a mighty effort to take the city, using all the forces available to him, Cnut also withdrew, sailing away to East Anglia to plunder afresh and replenish his supplies.

Edmund was not idle while they were away, assembling a new army and preparing for a further confrontation, and when Cnut returned, he landed at the mouth of the Medway instead of at Greenwich, perhaps expecting trouble. Then, marching towards London, he was met by the English at Otford in Kent. Again, it was a decisive victory for the king. The Danes fled towards their ships with Edmund pursuing, and, says Huntingdon, 'if he had continued the pursuit the Danish war would have been ended that day.' Instead, he was met at Aylsford by Edric Streona, apparently claiming the Danes were utterly defeated and leaving for good, and begging forgiveness from the victorious king. It is, of course, with the benefit of hindsight that Huntingdon can declare that this was 'traitorous counsel', and Malmesbury that Streona 'had come over to Edmund at the instigation of Cnut, that he might betray his designs'.

If this is true, and subsequent events make it very likely, it was an effective ploy to halt the English pursuit and let the remaining Danes escape. Nor is it easy to see why Edmund would accept the apparent repentance of this slippery character. Even at the time the *Anglo-Saxon Chronicle* declares that 'no measure could be more ill-advised.' On the other hand, the king had now soundly beaten Cnut twice, and was clearly in the ascendant, and may well have believed – or wanted to believe – that his enemy was indeed drawing back, at least for a time. Moreover, Edric was still ealdorman of Mercia with a substantial force at his command, and if he was really returning to the 'winning' side, as was his wont, he could prove decisive should the Danes return.

They did indeed return in the autumn – with Streona, no doubt, claiming he had underestimated their resolve – raiding across Essex and into adjacent parts of Mercia. Once more Edmund gathered an army from across the whole of southern England, and on 18 October met Cnut in the battle variously known as 'Essandun', 'Assandune' or 'Assingdon'. Ashingdon, near Rockford, in Essex is the most likely site for this, particularly since it has later associations with Cnut.

There is little doubt Edmund was confident he could win again, and no doubt at all about why he failed to do so. With him in the battle, commanding a large section of men, was Edric Streona. As the fighting progressed, says Henry of Huntingdon, 'Edric, seeing the rout of the Danes was imminent, shouted to the English … "Flee English, flee English, Edmund is dead."' He then fled with his own men, causing others to follow, the result being a slaughter of the badly weakened English side. Much the same account is given in the Chronicle, giving a list of ealdormen and other nobles slain, and concluding, 'all the nobility of the English race was there destroyed.' The Encomium, fanciful in so many accounts, including tales of animated ravens appearing on plain white Viking banners during battle, seems to hold to the truth here. It does, though, put Edric's betrayal before the start of the battle, and adds that he fled, not out of fear, but because he had secretly promised Cnut he would do so.

Edmund himself escaped the slaughter and made his way to Gloucestershire, hotly pursued by Cnut. There are claims in both Huntingdon's and Malmesbury's accounts that single combat between Edmund and Cnut was then proposed to settle the matter. In the first case the bout took place, with Cnut pleading for compromise when losing. In the second Cnut refuses combat and suggests a compromise, as the populace is 'worn out with continual suffering'. Both these scenarios are highly unlikely, but compromise there was, negotiated, according to the Chronicle, by Edric Streona and other counsellors, when the parties came together at Deerhurst in Gloucestershire. On an island in the nearby River Severn, Edmund and Cnut swore mutual friendship, and agreed to divide the country between them, on similar lines to that accepted by King Alfred many years before. Edmund was to have Wessex, extending along the whole of the southern counties of England, while Cnut had Mercia and the Danelaw. It is not clear whether London, on the border between the two, was included in the deal, but since the Chronicle then says 'The men of London made a truce with the army, and bought themselves peace,' it suggests they had to negotiate their own settlement.

It is likely that Edmund regarded this first truce with the enemy as merely the end of the first part of the struggle, as, indeed, had Alfred before him. He would not live to begin a second round, however, dying suddenly on 30 November, St Andrew's Day, a matter of weeks after the historic meeting at Deerhurst. It is possible he died of natural causes, perhaps the effects of wounds suffered at Ashingdon, where one account at least says he was seriously injured. Most later writers, however, claim it was murder, and point the finger at Edric Streona as the organiser, if not the actual perpetrator.

It was certainly a timely death as far as Cnut was concerned. The Encomium uses the same formula as for the death of Athelred, that God took away Edmund so that the kingdom should not be torn by further conflict. There were, indeed, few left who could challenge the young Dane. John of Worcester carries a story of Cnut calling together those Englishmen who had witnessed the Deerhurst treaty, and receiving assurances from them that the intention had been that the survivor of Edmund and Cnut would inherit the whole kingdom. He also says this was a lie, but if such a gathering ever took place, it surely only formalised what was a foregone conclusion. On 6 January 1017, Cnut was duly crowned king of England at St Paul's Cathedral in London.

Throughout the roller-coaster ride of 1016, Queen Emma, now more correctly dowager Queen Emma, almost certainly remained in London. With her there would have been Edmund's wife, who not only never received a formal coronation, but is not even named in the chronicles. They would have survived two sieges, the joy of Edmund's triumphs, the despair following his defeat at Ashingdon, and possibly resignation and the hope of an interlude of peace after the signing of the treaty at Deerhurst. Now, however, they would have found themselves uniquely vulnerable and at the mercy of this new king, whose army still controlled London and all its surrounds.

Despite the appearance of consent, it was clear that Cnut had achieved his throne by conquest, and that his army was an army of occupation. The killing of a number of English nobles in the immediate aftermath was the action of a young man removing all possible threats to his position. Similarly, dividing the country into four areas, each with a military leader, confirmed his intent to stamp out any semblance of a challenge. The queens would, thus, have been well aware that along with Edmund's younger brother Edwig, their children represented the only surviving English claimants to the throne that could form a focus for rebellion.

At this point Emma had several advantages over the other widow. Her children were older and she had a ready sanctuary for them. It is even possible that Alfred and Godgifu had remained in Normandy throughout this unsettled time, and though Edward is mentioned in some accounts as fighting alongside his half-brother Edmund, the mighty deeds attributed to the fourteen-year-old in one Scandinavian saga are laughably over the top. It is clear, anyway, that by Christmas 1016 he was well on his way to join his siblings at the court of their uncle Richard of Normandy.

Edmund's wife fared less well. Her children were babies at the time. Indeed, unless they were twins it is highly likely the younger was born after his father's death. It is hard to believe Cnut was squeamish about killing these boys himself, but all accounts agree that he sent them out of the country, probably to the king of Sweden, with instructions that they should be killed by him. Instead, they were shown mercy and sent on to Hungary, beyond the reach of Cnut, where the elder died but the younger 'grew up to be a good man,' marrying Agatha, the Hungarian king's daughter. What happened to their mother is not recorded.

Edmund's brother Edwig was similarly banished, which suggests he was too young to be much of a nuisance at the time. He may, indeed, have been not many years older than Emma's elder son. He did not survive long, possibly murdered on the orders of Cnut, or dying due to extreme mental and physical suffering after returning to England, depending on which account is believed.

The name of Edric Streona is associated in several accounts with these banishments, in each case recommending the banished should be murdered. Edric was named as the military ruler of Mercia in the initial division of the country but would not have long to enjoy the fruits of his treachery. He is named as one of the nobles slain by Cnut early in 1017, with a variety of different versions of his come-uppance. In most it is his disloyalty that earns its just reward, particularly when he has been accused of involvement in the death of Edmund. In the Encomium Cnut simply recognises the essential duplicity of the man, and instructs Eric Haakonsson, 'Pay this man what we owe him,' which Eric rightly interprets as an order to behead Edric before he has an opportunity to betray Cnut as well.

We can only guess at the chronology of these various expulsions and killings, but the chances are that they all took place in the first half of 1017. The Encomium certainly suggests they were all satisfactorily settled before Cnut turned his mind to another pressing matter. Then, it says, all that was lacking for the king was a noble wife. This may have come as news to Elfgiva of Northampton, his handfast wife of some four years, who had already given him two sons, Swein and Harald. The Chronicles do not mention her whereabouts at this time, but it has been suggested that she was the 'English matron' referred to in the Encomium, who had taken the body of Swein Forkbeard back to his homeland after Cnut fled there in 1014. If she was in England, she was probably living on her family estates in the Midlands along with her young children, but nothing is heard from her while Cnut was apparently seeking a new wife.

The story Queen Emma would have us believe, as recorded in the Encomium, is no doubt how she wished events had fallen out, but it bears no resemblance to reality. Cnut sent messengers far and near, says the Encomiast, through realms and cities, searching for a suitable royal bride. Such a woman was found, by implication in Normandy, possessed of nobility and wealth, beauty and wisdom, and was, in fact, already a queen; though, with his usual restrictions, he is not allowed to say of which country. Then, he says, the woman had to be wooed by a long-drawn-out exchange of messages, royal gifts, and promises. One particular promise gets special mention. The woman has heard that Cnut already has sons 'by some other woman', the only reference at this time to his existing wife. She wants to know that she and any offspring with Cnut will rank higher, and she refuses to marry him until he swears an oath that only their sons, if they have any, will rule England after him. Only when such an oath is given and the pair find each other 'acceptable' is Emma finally named in the book she has commissioned. Cnut and Emma are then married, and everyone rejoices.

It is a good story and places Queen Emma exactly where she wanted to be placed, on the same footing as Cnut, equal bargaining with equal, leading to a happy conclusion. The same transaction is recorded a little differently in the Chronicle. 'And then,' it says, 'the king commanded the relict of King Athelred, Richard's daughter, to be fetched for his wife.'

What, if any, choice Emma might have had in her second marriage, probably comes down to where she was at the time. The Encomiast is not alone in implying she had escaped to Normandy, though even there she would have been under the control of her brother, and it would have been he, rather than Emma herself, who would have negotiated with Cnut. Later writers, Malmesbury in particular, see the wedding very much as an alliance between England and Normandy, though he strongly disapproves. Instead of helping Emma's children to their rightful throne, he says, Richard of Normandy 'married his sister Emma to the enemy and invader; and it would be difficult to say whether to the greater ignominy of him who bestowed her, or of the woman who consented to share the nuptial couch of that man who had so cruelly molested her husband and had driven her children into exile.' Malmesbury may well have been influenced by the fairy tale in the Encomium in drawing his conclusion that Emma freely consented to the marriage and was 'brought over the seas' to Cnut. He would also have known the background which the Encomiast omitted, however, including the abandonment of her children in Normandy, and it is this view, of a hard-hearted woman, presumably desperate to continue as queen of England, that was largely accepted and embroidered by later commentators.

There are a number of other writers, particularly those writing near the time, who place Emma in London at the end of 1016. William of Jumièges, for example, writing a few decades later, says Cnut took her from the city, and the implication is that she was brought from close by, and already in his power. Nor does the Encomium suggest any alliance with Normandy, all the emphasis being on reconciliation between the English and their Danish conquerors.

It is valid to ask, then, why Emma had remained in London at such a time of danger. We may discount stories that she was captured along with her children and her marriage to Cnut bought their freedom. It is known the children had already escaped to Normandy, but, if so, why had Emma not gone with them? At the least charitable end of the scale, it has been suggested that, as she was a wealthy woman in England, with many valuable estates settled on her, she could not bear to go penniless and landless to her brother's court. There, the chances were, she would be sent to a convent or married off for the advantage of Normandy. A kinder view might be that she felt some responsibility towards the people she had lived among for more than a dozen years and hoped to be able to intercede for them with their new rulers, particularly having a Scandinavian background herself. This certainly accords more with the theme of the Encomium, however doubtful the facts expressed there might be. She may even have remained to support Edmund's widow through the birth of her second child, such 'women's business' not meriting a mention in the chronicles of the time.

If she had any choice at all in the matter, whatever her motive, it shows a degree of courage to remain and face down a Viking army led by a young man barely out of his teens. At the time Cnut would have been a completely unknown quantity, though it is just possible Emma may have seen him during one of the London sieges, or after the Deerhurst treaty, and made some assessment of what she had to deal with. She would have been well aware that she could be regarded as a prize of war, and was possibly not at all surprised to be sent for. The surprise might have been that it was to be a Christian marriage, and even more that it turned out to be a complete success.

For fourteen years Emma had been married to a man twenty years older than her, and likely regarded as an elderly failure. By contrast, she was now the older and possibly more worldly wise of the two, with a husband maybe ten years younger and in the vigorous prime of life. England rejoiced, the army rejoiced, Gaul rejoiced, says the Encomiast, and adds that it is hard to believe the 'magnitude of delight' the couple discovered in each other. For Cnut it had been purely a political marriage, and it is interesting that his rejoicing is described as unexpected. Both motives ascribed to him – the reconciling of the English and the avoidance of any Norman challenge – were probably foremost in his mind, but clearly he got more than he bargained for, and within a short time remarkable changes were noticeable in the new king of England.

For the first year or so of his reign Cnut behaved as a conquering Viking might have been expected to behave, particularly one not entirely secure in his new role. From 1018 onwards, however, there is no more slaughter and summary 'justice' for traitors. The majority of his fleet and army were paid off and sent home to Denmark, albeit at the huge cost of £72,000 from England, and a further £10,500 from London. This sum, though, was probably the 'tribute' mentioned in the Deerhurst treaty, the interval being the time taken to raise such a large amount of money.

In 1018, too, a great assembly was held at Oxford, with representatives, both Danish and English, from all over the country. There they were probably surprised to learn that they were to be governed by 'Edgar's law', a decision which the Chronicle declares came about by agreement. This set of laws, ascribed to King Edgar the Peaceable but based on earlier codes, had been re-written and adapted by Wulfstan, Archbishop of York, for Athelred in 1008. They would be updated again by Wulfstan and issued in 1020 as Cnut's law code, covering the rights and duties of both high and low, in church and state.

The emphasis in these laws is solidly Christian, and by 1020 Cnut seems to have metamorphosed into a model Christian king, at least in England. Most of the credit for this is given to the two archbishops, Wulfstan in York and Lyfing in Canterbury, but it is likely that Emma, too, had a hand in moulding the young king. It has been pointed out that Cnut came from a land where Christianity was only just replacing older, wilder, gods. In England, though, it had been woven into all aspects of the state and its institutions for centuries past, and Emma, who had been part of that system for more than a decade, could have played a major part in guiding her new husband through its intricacies. With a political brain that matched his own, she would have pointed out that opposing the church would have led to constant struggle, while having the major clerics onside would smooth his way considerably.

One consequence of this is that the writers of the time tell us very little more about Cnut's reign in England. There were clearly no further rebellions or political upheavals. All that is recorded is his involvement in certain religious matters. Thus, in 1020 he established a church at Ashingdon on the site of his victory over Edmund, providing one of his own Mass priests to serve there and pray for the souls of all those killed on that day. In the same year a monastery was founded and generously funded at Bury St Edmunds, and even earlier, in 1018, he had provided a large sum for the rebuilding of Chartres cathedral. In all these matters and many more besides, Queen Emma seems to have had a hand. Cnut, for example, had no connection with Chartres except that his wife's brother was buried there, yet William of Malmesbury refers to a letter of thanks to the king from Bishop Fulbert, for 'pouring out the bowels of his generosity in donations'.

In 1023, considerable fuss is made over the exhumation of the body of St Alphege from St Paul's Cathedral and its re-interment as a focus for pilgrims at Canterbury. This was probably an astute political move, since London was still relatively hostile and the new Archbishop of Canterbury, nominated by both king and queen, was firmly onside. Cnut accompanied the body all the way, with Queen Emma joining him for the last part of the journey, along with 'her royal child, Harthacnut'.

By this time Emma had probably had both the children she would have with Cnut. Her daughter, Gunhilda, would have been one or two years old, Harthacnut probably nearer five. The daughter, of course, gets no mention until the time comes for her to marry, but the Encomiast falls over himself in praise for the son, whose name, he declares, means Swift or Strong Cnut. These, he says, are only some of the qualities of this child, and indeed he cannot number all the excellencies he possessed. He does, however, take the opportunity to introduce into his story the other two sons of Emma, though with an implication that they are younger than Harthacnut, and also the sons of Cnut. While the parents' unparalleled love for Harthacnut, the heir to the kingdom, made them keep this child by them, he says, they sent their two other legitimate sons to Normandy to be brought up by Emma's brother. So he dispatches them to the right place for the part they were to play later in the story, but without ever acknowledging their true situation.

It should be remembered that if Emma had put aside two sons on her marriage to Cnut, so, too, had her husband. We hear nothing about Swein and Harald, the children of Elfgiva of Northampton, at this stage, though they were almost certainly somewhere in England. It is clear, however, that Cnut had not forgotten them, and intended to provide for them in some way. As for Edward and Alfred in Normandy, though Emma has been condemned for abandoning them, it has been pointed out that, whatever decision she made in 1016, their fortunes were unlikely to have been improved.

If Cnut's reign in England was largely uneventful, he was far more active elsewhere. In 1019 he had returned to Denmark to claim that country on the death of his brother. Thorkell had been left in charge in England at the time, but two years later, for some unspecified reason, he was outlawed and expelled. He may have been the cause of Cnut taking a fleet out the following year, possibly to the Isle of Wight, but likely as far as the Baltic, maybe countering a threat from his former friend. A reconciliation took place in 1023, under the terms of which Thorkell was to be regent for Cnut in Denmark, and also would become the guardian of Harthacnut. The fact that Cnut would receive Thorkell's son in exchange suggests a hostage swap, but as Thorkell then disappears from the record we are none the wiser. Certainly, around this time Harthacnut, probably no more than eight years old, was dispatched to Denmark. His guardian after Thorkell was to be Ulf, who was married to Cnut's sister Estrith.

One Scandinavian saga implicates Emma in an attempt to make Harthacnut king of Denmark at this time. The Saga of Olaf Haraldson would have been handed down by oral tradition, before being written down in the Heimskringla by the Icelander Snorri Sturluson around two hundred years later. In places it is corroborated by other sources, but there are also many inaccuracies, and the time lapse means there was plenty of opportunity for later events to be unknowingly woven into earlier stories. This Saga claims that Emma stole Cnut's signet seal and forged letters to the effect that Cnut wanted the people of Denmark to accept his son as king. These letters were then produced by Ulf to convince the Danes that Harthacnut should be king with Ulf ruling as regent.

The story seems unlikely. Emma was doing very nicely as the wife of Cnut and should have had little reason to challenge his rule, particularly in a land far away, and in favour of a child. She would have had nothing to gain and everything to lose. Several other accounts, however, including the *Anglo-Saxon Chronicle*, claim that Ulf rebelled against Cnut at about this time, siding with Olaf of Norway and Anund of Sweden against his brother-in-law.

In 1025 they fought a battle against Cnut's Anglo-Danish forces at a place identified only as the 'Holy River'. Although Cnut suffered a defeat, this was apparently only a temporary setback. Ulf soon became reconciled, perhaps using the story above as an excuse, though nothing seems to have rebounded on Emma. A short time later, however, he was murdered while in church, it is claimed on the orders of Cnut. Clearly the king's reputation as a pious Christian monarch did not survive the journey to Scandinavia.

There is no evidence Queen Emma ever travelled with Cnut to the north. Nor did she accompany him in 1027, when he journeyed to Rome to attend the coronation of the Holy Roman Emperor Conrad II. This was part pilgrimage, part business trip. The Encomiast enthusiastically describes his humility, prayerfulness and generous gifts to churches and monasteries along the way, being an eyewitness to the king's actions at his own monastery of St. Omer. Cnut himself wrote home of the warm welcome he received from other Christian rulers, possibly the first time a Viking leader had been so feted. He also notes how he had negotiated passage for pilgrims and traders from England to Rome, free of the various tolls that had previously been demanded of them. At the same time, he established a friendship with Conrad, and arranged for his daughter Gunhilda to be betrothed to Conrad's son.

Cnut's pious pilgrimage did not blunt his ambitions to expand his Scandinavian empire. Travelling from Rome to Denmark, the very next year he deposed Olaf Haraldson of Norway, though by bribes and intimidation rather than violence. When Olaf fled, Norway came once more under the sway of Denmark, and Haakon Ericsson, son of its earlier ruler, was sent to govern on behalf of Cnut. When Haakon drowned the following year, Olaf tried to return but was killed. Then, in a startling move, Cnut sent his eldest son by his first wife to rule in his place. Young Swein could have been no more than fourteen or fifteen years old, and his mother, Elfgiva, went with him, apparently as regent or co-ruler. Certainly, the Norwegians referred to this period as 'Elfgiva's time,' rather than 'Swein's time'. It is tempting to see this as Cnut regularising his domestic affairs in England, no doubt at the urging of the church, but also, probably, at the instance of his official queen. Both Emma and Elfgiva were strong, determined women, as later events would prove, and as the queen rose in status and power, she would have been less and less likely to tolerate the presence of a rival in England.

There is never a suggestion that Emma was formally appointed regent during Cnut's long absences from England. By this time the 'ealdormen' of earlier times had become 'earls', with three in particular being especially powerful. Siward, originally from Norway, was earl of Northumbria, while Leofric, from an old

English family, held the same post in Mercia. It was the earl of Wessex, however, Earl Godwin, who was the richest and most dominant. Godwin's origins are obscure, perhaps deliberately obscured, since one story claims he was the son of a cowherd. Most likely, though, he was the son of Wulfnoth Cild, that thegn who had wreaked havoc with King Athelred's fleet some two decades earlier. It is likely Godwin fought for Athelred's son Athelstan, and probably for Edmund Ironside as well, but he must have impressed Cnut, since he is found at that king's side early in his reign. He became earl of Wessex in 1018, and soon after married Cnut's sister-in-law and the sister of Ulf, Gytha, who bore him at least nine children.

It would have been these earls, together with the senior clergy, who formed Cnut's council in England, and that council would have ruled in his absence. Nonetheless, Queen Emma clearly occupied a position of power and wealth at this time. Petitions were made through her. Charters and letters refer to grants, donations and appointments being made by king and queen together, and in many cases Emma's name as witness to a charter comes immediately after Cnut's, even before the archbishops and earls. William of Malmesbury emphasises donations to Winchester and its cathedral, given 'at Emma's suggestion', adding that she, 'with pious prodigality exhausted (Cnut's) treasures in works of this kind, while he was meditating fierce attacks on foreign lands.'

We have evidence of the partnership of king and queen in relation to one particular gift to Winchester, that of a great gold cross. The frontispiece of a book of donors to the New Minster there bears an illustration of this event. Cnut and Emma stand on each side of an altar on which stands the cross. His hand holds it, as if placing it carefully, while hers is extended almost to touch it. Size and placing are significant in illustrations of the time, and here Emma is shown of equal size with her husband and on exactly the same level. So both are equally to be regarded as donors of this great gift. It is, of course, a representation rather than a portrait, but Emma is possibly the first named woman to be depicted in this way.

It would be overly cynical to see these gifts to the church as purely political moves. The Encomiast declares that Cnut was the friend and intimate of churchmen, though he is probably going much too far in claiming the bishops regarded him almost as a brother bishop, and the monks as a fellow monk, due to his temperate lifestyle and devotion to justice and Christian charity. Nonetheless, in a highly religious age such actions did him no harm in the sight of men. Malmesbury suggests, 'Perhaps he wiped away the foul stain of his former crimes with God; certainly he did so with men,' and there seemed no reason why he should not have gone on acting as benefactor to church and country for years to come.

In 1035 Queen Emma would have been approaching her fiftieth birthday. Secure in her marriage, her wealth and her status as queen of England, she might have looked forward to a peaceful and prosperous old age. In that year, however, everything changed. First, in Norway, a popular uprising drove out Swein and his mother, replacing them with Magnus, the eleven-year-old son of Olaf Haraldson. The imposition of harsh taxes and alien Danish customs was the cause of their downfall, and it was to Denmark they fled in the autumn of the year. Then, a matter of weeks later on 12 November, Cnut suddenly died.

No cause of death is recorded for this apparently active man in his early forties, but there seems to have been no time – or possibly no inclination – to make a will or nominate a successor. The Encomiast declares he had 'arranged all matters well' before he died, but that is certainly not borne out by subsequent events. According to the agreement made with Emma before her marriage, as recorded in the Encomium, Harthacnut, now aged around seventeen years, should have been his heir, in England at least. Unfortunately, he was far away in Denmark. There was, though, another son of Cnut near at hand.

Harald, known as Harefoot, was the second son of Cnut and Elfgiva of Northampton – or so he claimed. The Chronicle declares that this was not true, and the Encomiast, too, is dismissive of this claim, under the guidance, of course, of Queen Emma. With details presumably provided by her, he says that Harald was the son of a servant, and Cnut was tricked by Elfgiva into believing the child was his, however unlikely that might seem. He had apparently been left in England when Elfgiva and Swein departed for Norway, and now, probably aged around eighteen, he laid claim to the throne. Swein was still in Denmark, where he would die the following year, but Elfgiva had almost certainly returned to England, where we now have the intriguing picture of two wives of Cnut, each a mother of his sons, opposing each other on behalf of their children, with the English crown, and their own status, as the prize.

Cnut died at Shaftesbury and was buried with full honours at Winchester, the favourite city of himself and his queen. Then, even before the Witan met at Oxford to discuss his successor, Emma took up residence in the royal palace at Winchester, with Earl Godwin as chief protector of herself and the royal treasury. At the Witan meeting, however, the Londoners, the Danes and the Mercians led by Leofric, came out for Harald. Malmesbury describes Godwin as a 'stickler for justice' for arguing against this and putting forward the claims of Harthacnut, presumably believing this was the wish of Cnut. All that was achieved, however, was a messy compromise. Depending on which account is believed, Harald was to be either regent of England until his half-brother arrived, or possibly co-ruler with Harthacnut. In either case, Emma and Earl Godwin were to hold Wessex for Harthacnut until he could leave Denmark.

Whatever the decision, it seems Harald – or possibly his mother – was not content with what he had achieved. Very soon afterwards forces arrived in Winchester to take from Emma 'all the best treasure, which she could not withhold, that King Cnut possessed'. With this treasure, it is claimed, Harald and Elfgiva now set about gathering further support through bribes distributed among the leading Englishmen. And now, according to the Encomium, a letter was sent which remains controversial to the present day.

After casting doubt on Harald's paternity and claiming the archbishop of Canterbury refused to crown him, the Encomiast gives, apparently verbatim, the content of this letter, allegedly sent by Emma to her two sons from her marriage to Athelred, who for many years had been residing in Normandy. In it the queen asks what Edward and Alfred are planning to do to claim the kingdom which is their inheritance. In failing to act, she says, they are giving support to the usurper, Harald, while the people would prefer that 'one of you' should rule. Therefore, she asks that 'one of you' should come to her quickly and privately so they can consult together as to how best to achieve that end. Furthermore, they should send back word of what they proposed to do by the messenger who delivers the letter, 'whoever he might be.'

As a result of this, both young men – Edward aged around thirty-three, and Alfred a few years younger – set out separately for England in 1036. One account claims Edward fought and won a battle near Southampton, but more likely he took a quick look, found the country hostile and retreated to Normandy. A number of accounts, however, agree on the basic outline of what befell Alfred when he landed, probably near Dover. He had travelled via Flanders where the count had suggested he take with him some part of his forces, 'as a precaution against the wiles of the enemy'. Alfred refused this offer, though, and took with him only 'a few men from Boulogne'. Making his way towards his mother he was intercepted by Earl Godwin, who conducted him to lodgings for the night. While they slept, Godwin seems to have disappeared, and Alfred and his men were taken prisoner by the forces of Harald Harefoot. The men were then tortured, killed or enslaved, while Alfred himself was taken by boat to Ely, where he was blinded so violently that he died soon after, 'nor was a bloodier deed done in this land since the Danes came,' says the Chronicle.

The Encomiast declares that the letter that set off this train of events was a forgery, sent by Harald to lure Emma's sons into a trap and dispose of potential rivals. There are certainly aspects that look suspicious – the request for 'one of you' to come, for example, as if the writer did not know or care which had precedence, the failure to name the messenger, and, especially, the instruction in the time-honoured manner of all plotters, to send in advance information as to how they meant to come. There is general agreement now, however, that the letter, or something very similar, was genuine.

Of all potential rivals, Harald probably had the least to fear from Edward and Alfred. They had been absent from England for nearly twenty years and had no known following in that land. Indeed, we don't even know if they had been in touch with their mother prior to this. Nor were they likely to be able to raise a sufficient army in Normandy, where Emma's nephew, Robert I, had recently died and his heir, the eight-year-old William the Bastard, would have his work cut out to hold on to his own lands.

On the other hand, the Encomiast has emphasised how alone Queen Emma was in Winchester. She had already been humiliated by Elfgiva, 'the concubine', and her son, and even Godwin had been unable, or unwilling, to prevent them taking away the better part of Cnut's treasure. In Denmark, Harthacnut was facing a Norwegian invasion, and had no time to spare for his mother's plight. Her daughter by Athelred, Godgifu, had recently married for the second time, her husband being Eustace of Boulogne, while her younger daughter was about to marry the heir to the Holy Roman Empire. Neither of these, however, was likely to come to the aid of the widowed queen of England. Small wonder, then, if Emma, clutching at straws, looked around for anyone else who might be able to support her. And small wonder, too, if, when faced with the consequences, she tried to cast the blame onto someone else, someone who, by the time her book was being written, was dead and disgraced.

She was, says the Encomiast, stunned with sorrow at Alfred's death, and beyond consolation. Clearly, too, she had not foreseen the defection of Godwin which happened at this time. It is tempting to wonder if her request to Athelred's sons was the spur for this. Godwin had been Cnut's man for a long time, and maybe would have preferred either of Cnut's sons to Athelred's. A less charitable view would be that he saw the way the wind was blowing and intended to be on the winning side. He would eventually serve Edward as his fourth king of England, but only when all Cnut's sons were dead.

The Encomiast is in an awkward situation in dealing with Godwin. By the time he was writing his book the earl was back in favour, but he was clearly heavily involved in the death of Alfred. All the contemporary accounts name him as a prime mover in the capture, if not the death itself. The problem is solved by declaring that he met Alfred, conducted him to lodgings and provided him with food and drink – and then never mentioning him again.

The Encomiast, incidentally, is the only one to mention a letter or summons from Emma to her sons. Such a request may have been common knowledge at the time, but it is not recorded elsewhere. Edward, of course, would know the truth of the matter, and at the time the Encomium was written Edward had just returned to England. This would provide an additional reason for Emma to require her author to clear her name, whatever the actual circumstances behind the summons.

The death of Alfred marks a significant point in Emma's fall from power. Indeed, the Encomiast seems to suggest that some thought she should take her own life at this time. This, he says, would not have been a worthy end for so great a lady, especially as it might seem she killed herself purely because of a loss of worldly power and wealth. Instead, he says, with shrewd judgement she deemed it expedient to leave England for a while. The Chronicle puts it rather more bluntly. In 1037, it says, Harald Harefoot was proclaimed full king of England, because Harthacnut had delayed too long in coming, 'and then they drove out (Emma) without any kind of mercy, against the stormy winter.'

Nor had she a ready sanctuary in Normandy at this time, making her way instead to Flanders, where Count Baldwin V received her warmly and established her at Bruges. This second exile must have been Emma's lowest point, though she seems to have been comfortably placed, and if the Encomiast is to be believed, accorded suitable honour as a royal lady. Indeed, it seems unduly churlish on his part – or perhaps on hers – to say that she accepted all that was given to her, partly with great thanksgiving, but partly indicating she was not actually in need – 'up to a point'.

If Harald and his mother expected Emma to accept her lot without a fight, they had misjudged their opponent. The Encomium suggests that many nobles had accompanied her into exile, but this seems to be wishful thinking. We hear no more of them. Instead, it was to Edward, still in Normandy, that she turned next for help. Obligingly, he travelled to Bruges to meet his mother for the first time in twenty years, but he was unable, or unwilling, to comply with her request to raise an expedition to wrest the throne of England from King Harald. He had, he pointed out, no following of his own in England, and clearly did not intend to share the fate of his younger brother. Try Harthacnut, was his recommendation, possibly with some bitterness since this young half-brother had already been made king of Denmark. He then returned to Normandy, leaving Emma, no doubt, burning with frustration.

Harthacnut was indeed her last hope, but it was not until 1039 that he came to an agreement with Magnus of Norway, leaving him free to pursue his claims to the English throne. In the meantime, Harald ruled unchallenged, though we learn little about his reign from the writers of the time. The Chronicle only records the deaths of various bishops, some trouble with the Welsh in the borderlands and a great gale. It has even been suggested that for at least part of his reign it was his mother that had the greater power, though she disappears from the records after 1036 and may have died around that time.

Finally, in 1039, Harthacnut was able to come to his mother at Bruges. That he did this instead of sailing straight to England, and with only ten ship's crews, suggests either uncertainty, or possibly knowledge that the king he sought to replace was already ill. The Encomiast inserts a divine vision into the tale of his voyage southward, which assured him that Harald would die soon, and the kingdom he rightfully sought would be his. Be that as it may, it is on record that Harald died at Oxford on 17 March 1040, at the age of around twenty-four.

It is debateable whether the Encomiast is correct in describing the nobles of England begging Harthacnut to come and rule them. The Chronicle declares he arrived with sixty ships, which seems more like an invasion than a happy homecoming. After his coronation at Canterbury on 18 June, these ship's companies all had to be paid off, which involved raising some £30,000, probably not the best start for a new, unknown monarch. Says the Chronicle, 'all were then averse to him who before had desired him.'

Harthacnut would have been around twenty-two years old at his coronation, and had been in Denmark, absorbing Danish ways, for at least fourteen of those years. Though the Encomiast claims he arranged all his affairs in peace and calm, it seems far more likely he ruled like a Scandinavian warlord, extorting tribute, sacking the city of Worcester when it resisted paying and, according to some accounts, regularly indulging himself in mighty feasts. 'He did nothing royal during his whole reign,' says the Chronicle, though the story of the exhumation and mistreatment of Harald's body, which follows this statement, can almost certainly be laid at Emma's door.

In the absence of a queen – and Harthacnut never married – Emma would have regained her status as first lady of the land, and though the Encomiast declares Harthacnut's ears trembled in horror when he was told of the death of Alfred, he had never met his half-brother, and it is far more likely to have been Emma who was determined to punish those responsible for his death. Thus Godwin, among others, was sent to London to exhume the body of the former king, which was then thrown into a sewer, dragged out again and flung into the River Thames. No doubt it was intended to remain there and wash out to sea, but London had been Harald's stronghold, and the body was afterwards rescued and buried in the Danish church known today as St Clement Danes.

We can see Emma's hand, too, behind the 'trial' of Earl Godwin, which, according to Malmesbury and John of Worcester, took place soon after the new king's arrival. Godwin was apparently required to clear himself of involvement in the death of Alfred by 'compurgation', that is, by swearing an oath himself and, if required to do so, finding sufficient others to swear alongside him. In a religious age this was no easy matter, but Godwin duly swore he had never intended the blinding of Alfred, and whatever part he had played was solely on the orders of King Harald. His restoration to favour was thus secured, helped along by the gift of a magnificent, fully manned ship for Harthacnut.

One of the more surprising actions of the new king's reign was the summoning of his half-brother Edward to end his exile in Normandy and return to England. Why he did this, and what Edward's role was to be, is not at all clear. The Chronicle, Malmesbury and John of Worcester all write as if this is simply a good-natured act, offering a home to a brother with no place of his own. The Encomium, however, written within a year of the event and at the instance of Queen Emma, declares that Edward was to be co-ruler, sharing the throne of England with a half-brother he had never met.

If this is true, it is again surely evidence of the strength of Emma's own position. Even if Harthacnut was intending to return to Denmark, as has been suggested, it can only have been Emma that pointed to the forlorn figure of Edward as a possible regent. This might have been especially attractive, though, as he had no following of his own in the country and therefore was unlikely to pose a challenge to an absent king.

Other possibilities include Harthacnut's increasing unpopularity in England, the invitation being sent soon after the sack of Worcester. A co-ruler might serve to deflect some of the anger away from their 'Viking king'. It may even be that Emma foresaw an early demise for her son, possibly due to his lifestyle or an underlying illness. In all of these cases, though, it is most likely that Emma, rather than Harthacnut himself, initiated the move that brought a rather wary Edward to England towards the end of 1041.

Whatever the intention, there is no record of Edward receiving any kind of coronation at this time. Some versions of the *Anglo-Saxon Chronicle* suggest a ritual, but a full coronation would surely have been widely recorded as such. He did not, however, remain long in this limbo state. Within a year of his arrival in England, Harthacnut was dead. According to the Chronicle, he died 'as he stood at his drink' during a wedding feast on 8 June 1042. A stroke is the most likely explanation, and though this might seem unusual at the age of twenty-four, he had been noted for the Viking habit of over-indulging in food and drink. None of Cnut's children, in fact, would live beyond their twenty-fifth birthday, though whether this was down to genetics or lifestyle is impossible to say.

The Chronicle goes on to say that 'all the people then acknowledged Edward for king, as was his true, natural right.' At that time, however, it was the coronation that made a king, and Edward's coronation was delayed by almost ten months. This suggests his acclamation might not have been entirely straightforward. Certainly, he was the only possible claimant in England at the time, but there were no doubt those who felt the Anglo-Saxon line had been terminated with Edmund Ironside, and that descendants of Sweyn Forkbeard now had a better claim. A nephew of Cnut, Sweyn Estrithsson, had been born in England, and though he had been sent to hold Denmark for Harthacnut, he was a possible figurehead for the Danish faction. That he was also a nephew of Earl Godwin might have boosted his claims, but Godwin appears to have done nothing to favour him above Edward, and, indeed, he is credited with persuading others to accept Edward as king.

The agreement made between Harthacnut and Magnus of Norway in 1039 was also viewed, by Magnus at least, as giving him a claim to the throne. They had stated that the survivor of the two should inherit the lands of the other, and while Harthacnut had probably intended that this should only apply to Denmark, Magnus – and his successors – were certainly prepared to challenge for the English throne. Since Sweyn Estrithsson was already in place in Denmark, however, and refusing to hand over that land to Magnus, each of these potential rivals took the other out of the game for the time being.

And did Queen Emma throw her weight behind her last remaining son, the 'co-ruler' she had had brought over from Normandy? It would surely have been to her benefit to do so, thereby securing her status as mother of the king, if not ensuring the continuance of the power she had enjoyed under Harthacnut. At least one account, however, declares that she attempted to rally support for Magnus, and promised to use the royal treasury at Winchester to assist him in an invasion of England. Though this is a much later account, it may be based on earlier rumours, possibly fed by what befell Emma some six months after her son's coronation.

'And soon after,' says the Chronicle, 'The king caused all the lands which his mother possessed to be seized into his hands, and took from her all she possessed in gold and silver, and in things unspeakable.' Different versions of the Chronicle give slightly different reasons for this, one linking Emma's downfall with that of Stigand, once a chaplain to Cnut and now risen to be bishop of Elmham in East Anglia. His appointment was the first recorded in Edward's reign, and, in this version, Emma is deprived of 'her' treasure, 'because she had before held it too closely'. Immediately after, Stigand is deprived of his bishopric 'and all that he possessed was seized into the king's hands,' the reason being that he was closest in counsel with Emma. Perhaps here, then, we have Emma trying to exercise powers she has had before – influencing or even making appointments, treating the royal treasure as her own – and being very sharply put in her place by a son who has no special reason to favour or indulge his mother.

In another version her downfall was because 'before that she had been very hard with the king, her son,' and had done less for him than he had either wanted or expected 'both before he was king and also since'. Here Edward is surely taking his revenge for being the queen's least favourite son. One, Harthacnut, she had intended should be king, and another, Alfred, she had earlier strenuously tried to make a saint, but she seems to have done nothing whatever for Edward. It is easy to see why, having achieved power, he might use it to humiliate her. It is interesting that in this version, he is said to have been advised by the three leading earls, Leofric, Godwin and Siward, who rode with him to Winchester, as if even now he was not entirely convinced of his ability to overrule her. William of Malmesbury, writing later, picks up this theme. Emma was punished, he claims, because she had 'for a long time mocked at the needy state of her son, nor ever assisted him, transferring her hereditary hatred of the father to the child'. He does, however, find claims she had hoarded money and given nothing to the poor unbelievable.

For whatever reason, this was a final end to the power of Queen Emma. She would live for nearly nine more years, mainly in Winchester, and though some property was returned to her, and her name is found as witness on an occasional charter, she would never again have the wealth and influence she had once enjoyed. When Edward married Earl Godwin's daughter Edith, Dowager Queen Emma was finally consigned to history.

Nonetheless, during a most tumultuous period she had proved that a strong-willed, capable woman was equal to all that fortune could throw at her, and that, given the smallest opportunity, she could grasp and exercise real power. Moreover, having achieved, as she thought, her own 'happy ever after' by commissioning the work known as the Encomium Emmae, she did her best to ensure that her version of recent events would be the one that would pass down to history.

Following her death on 6 March 1052, Emma was buried, as no doubt she would have wished, alongside Cnut and Harthacnut in the Old Minster at Winchester. Her bones were later transferred to a mortuary chest in the new Norman Winchester Cathedral, where they remained until the time of the English Civil War in the seventeenth century. At that time the various mortuary chests were broken open and the bones from all were strewn around, becoming thoroughly mixed before being replaced at random in the chests. It is only in recent years that scientific analysis has been able to establish that among these remaining bones are those of a single mature female dated to the tenth century AD. Since only one queen was listed on the chests, these are almost certainly the bones of Queen Emma. A 3D printed copy of what remains of this skeleton is now on display in the cathedral, giving this most tenacious of women a renewed presence, which she would, no doubt, thoroughly appreciate. It was no fault of Emma's that upheavals within twenty years of her death would leave herself, her sons and even the mighty Cnut, as little more than footnotes at the end of an era.

2

Matilda of Tuscany: La Gran Contessa

If Emma's power was intermittent and largely reliant on the indulgence of her menfolk, the same cannot be said of Matilda of Tuscany. Once she had entered into her inheritance, no man would ever interfere with her command of her lands and people, and, despite the misogyny of the time, she would exercise her power exactly as she thought fit.

She was descended from the Attoni, the counts of Canossa, who over several generations had expanded their holdings outward from that mighty fortress to become the most powerful lords in northern Italy. Her own father, Boniface III, had been particularly aggressive in adding to his holdings, from Tuscany through Emilia to Lombardy. By backing the candidacy of Conrad II – whose coronation Cnut attended – in the disputed election following the death of Holy Roman Emperor Henry II, he had, in addition, received as reward the title Margrave of Tuscany, allowing him considerable freedom of action in the area.

Matilda's mother, Beatrice, was the daughter of Duke Frederick of Upper Lorraine, while her maternal grandmother, for whom she was named, came from the family of the dukes of Swabia. Neither Lorraine nor Swabia was noted for its unwavering loyalty to the emperor, but on Frederick's death when Beatrice was around thirteen, she was brought up in the imperial court for a number of years, before marrying Boniface as his second wife. Matilda, born in 1046 at Lucca, was probably the youngest of the three children of the marriage, with an older brother, Frederick, and sister, Beatrice.

Unfortunately, the good relationship Boniface had had with Emperor Conrad did not continue with Conrad's son, Henry III. Henry was wary of the power and wealth the Margrave had achieved in his lands south of the Alps, which were only partly made up of imperial fiefs. In a foreshadowing of the conflict that was to occupy much of his daughter's life, however, the issue that sparked continuing resentment concerned the papacy. In 1046 there were three men each claiming to be the rightful pope. Benedict IX, of scandalous reputation, had been elected in 1032. Sylvester III had then been appointed by the Romans to replace him when he was summarily ejected in 1045, while Gregory VI, the godfather of Benedict, had apparently been nominated by Benedict himself to take over in that same year, when, having regained his office, he temporarily decided to step aside.

For Henry III, religion and the wellbeing of the church were not only personally important but also politically vital. From the time of Otto I, some hundred years before, the whole administration of the Holy Roman Empire had been based on its archbishops, bishops and abbots, and it was unthinkable that such chaos at the very top of the church hierarchy should be allowed to continue. At a council he called at Sutri, north of Rome, at the end of 1046, both Benedict and Sylvester were summarily deposed, while Gregory confessed to having paid money to Benedict on his appointment and was found guilty of simony. The best of the lot, and reform-minded, Gregory was exiled to Germany, accompanied by his chancellor, a young man called Hildebrand, leaving Sylvester to return to his former bishopric and Benedict lurking ready to do more mischief, should the opportunity arise.

At the time, Henry was formally King of Germany and King of Italy, but by a well-established tradition, he would only become Holy Roman Emperor when duly crowned by the pope. Having dismissed the three existing claimants to that office, therefore, he now took the matter out of the hands of the great Roman families who until now had done the electing, and appointed the first of four German popes, Suidger, Bishop of Bamberg, who took the name Clement II. Clement was enthroned at Christmas 1046, and immediately afterwards carried out the necessary coronation of his sponsor Henry. Unfortunately, before ten months were out Clement was dead, with some claiming he had been poisoned by Benedict.

With a measure of support from the Margrave Boniface, that disgraced pontiff now once more took the opportunity to seize the city of Rome, where he reigned – for the third time – as pope, from November 1047 to the following summer. In January 1048, however, Emperor Henry appointed another German pope, who took the name Damasus II. Unrest in Germany meant he could not escort him to Rome himself. Instead, he called on Boniface of Tuscany to do the job of evicting Benedict and installing Damasus.

The Margrave's reply provoked fury on the part of the emperor. Benedict was already enthroned and supported by the city, he claimed, and anyway, he, Boniface (now in his early sixties), was too old to start trying to chase him out. Henry's response was even more succinct – in effect, carry out my commands and get rid of Benedict or I will get rid of you. Needless to say, within a short time Boniface had assembled a force and removed the antipope, who apparently spent his later years repenting in a monastery. When enthroned in July 1048, however, Damasus II lasted only twenty-three days before dying, probably from malaria, on 9 August. By the time the third German pope in two years had been elected in December 1048, and approved by the clergy and people of Rome in February 1049, Boniface seems to have resigned himself to accepting the new pontiff, who took the name Leo IX. Nonetheless, when the Margrave was murdered while out hunting in May 1052, there were some who claimed the emperor had given at least tacit approval for his killing, and a legacy of bitterness ensued between Tuscany and the empire.

For around two years after the death of her husband, Beatrice ruled Tuscany as regent for her young son Frederick, but in 1054 she re-married. Her new husband was Godfrey, known as 'the

Bearded', and if she had been intending to provoke the emperor, she could not have done a better job. Godfrey was her cousin, and when Beatrice's paternal line ran out in 1033, his father Gothelo had become duke of a united duchy of Lorraine. On his death in 1044, Godfrey had expected to step into his shoes. Instead, he was only made duke of Upper Lorraine. In response he had rebelled against the emperor, been stripped of his duchy, and for ten years carried on a war against Henry, with Baldwin of Flanders as an ally – the same Baldwin who had earlier sheltered Emma of Normandy.

Marrying his cousin Beatrice may have been part of Godfrey's campaign, as he certainly benefitted from the wealth and strength of Tuscany. His support, in turn, bolstered young Frederick, the new Margrave. This alliance of two enemies on either side of the Alps was something the emperor could not let pass unchallenged. Crossing into Italy, Henry swiftly drove Godfrey out of Tuscany, and carried off Beatrice and the nine-year-old Matilda back to Germany. Frederick, too, might have become a captive of the emperor, but at this point he died.

The situation changed again the following year. In the process of effecting a reconciliation with Godfrey, Henry himself died on 5 October 1056. He had briefly been married to Gunhilda, the daughter of Cnut and Emma of Normandy, but his successor, the five-year-old Henry IV, was the son of Henry's second wife, Agnes of Poitou. Agnes now took on the role of regent for her son, and, as part of her policy of buying support by alliances, she quickly completed the reconciliation with Godfrey, who was then allowed to return to Tuscany with his wife and stepdaughter. For the next decade and more he would be recognised as co-ruler with Beatrice, while Matilda, now the sole surviving child of Margrave Boniface, was acknowledged as heir to all her parents' lands.

All manner of accomplishments are claimed for the young Matilda, particularly by her first biographer, the monk Donizo, whose monastery was at Canossa itself. That she was 'more learned than a bishop,' is probably an overstatement, but with her background it would be more than likely that she could speak at least some German and French as well as her native Tuscan language, which would later develop into the language of all Italy. The ability to read and write at least some Latin is also probable.

There is more dispute about various claims that she was trained in warfare and in the martial arts, in particular that she became accustomed to wearing armour, and could wield a sword and axe and use a lance. Similarly, claims that she preferred these activities to more womanly pursuits are probably made with the benefit of hindsight, after the fates had forced her life into martial channels. Certainly, in her younger days she would have had plenty of opportunity of studying at first hand the planning, logistics and strategy that went into waging war, but whether she was ever trained to take an active role, as opposed to a command position, is more debateable. Even then, her betrothal at a young age to Godfrey's son, known as Godfrey the Hunchback, suggests that the intention was for her inheritance to be merged with his, and she would have, at best, a junior role.

One thing she would have learnt from her mother and stepfather was a deep respect for the church, and an enthusiasm for the growing movement that sought to reform the worldly and decadent ways into which it had fallen. A start had been made by the line of short-lived German popes. Priestly marriage had been roundly condemned, though many priests, bishops and even archbishops still had wives, mistresses and children. Sons, sometimes coyly referred to as 'nephews', still succeeded clerical fathers, even into the higher offices of the church. Since the granting of offices of state in the Holy Roman Empire to bishops and archbishops had been intended to prevent these posts becoming hereditary, successive emperors were fully behind this reform.

Simony – making payment in return for a church office – was also condemned, and this, too, was regarded as a necessary reform. Gregory VI had been dismissed for just such a payment, however innocently made. The offices of bishop and archbishop were, of course, extremely attractive since these invariably carried with them major landholding. Such men usually lived in comparative luxury and wielded great power, not only within the church but also in affairs of state. In the past, the close relationship of church and state had been seen as advantageous to both sides. The king or emperor protected the church, and in return received the benefit of its advice, and its influence over the people. By the eleventh century, however, the boundary between church and state had become dangerously blurred. It was claimed, with apparent approval, that the pope, the Holy Roman Emperor and the Byzantine Emperor were the three heads of the world, and, as we have seen, the Holy Roman Emperor had already taken upon himself the right to appoint, or at very least to approve, the appointment of the pope.

When church leaders were also so vital to the state, it is understandable that rulers – kings and emperors – would want to make sure the posts were filled with men acceptable to them and whose loyalty could be relied on. The tradition had become established that the ruler would not only select the man to be appointed, but also invest him in office by handing over the ring and crozier that were the symbols of his ecclesiastical authority. It was this 'investiture' that now became the focus of the reform movement within the Western church, a reform that was a step too far for most monarchs, and which became the source of the violent collision between empire and papacy that was to dominate Matilda's life.

One name in particular is associated with this so-called 'Investiture Controversy', that of Hildebrand, later to become Pope Gregory VII. As a young man he had accompanied the disgraced Gregory VI to Germany and observed at close quarters the intermingling of church and state functions in that country. Returning to Rome with Pope Leo, he quickly became a leading figure in the reform movement, with a growing conviction that church and state must be separated, that kings and emperors should have no role in appointing clergy and that the pope, as head of the church, should not be answerable to any earthly power.

This growing spirit of independence was supported by many in Italy, including Beatrice and Godfrey (never notably submissive to the empire). The first, perhaps tentative, testing of the waters came with the death in July 1057 of the last German pope, Victor II, less than a year after the death of Emperor Henry III. A matter of days later, a new pope was elected by the reformists in Rome, with no attempt at consultation with the Regent Agnes in Germany. He was Frederick of Lorraine, abbot of the monastery of Monte Cassino and the brother of Godfrey the Bearded. Even now, though, as the new pope adopted the name Stephen IX, Hildebrand set off at once to seek retrospective approval from the Empress Agnes. Before he returned, however, Pope Stephen had died, having exacted a promise from his cardinals that no new pope would be elected before Hildebrand's return.

In defiance of this, the old guard in Rome quickly elected a member of a leading Roman family as Benedict X, but Hildebrand and his Tuscan supporters simply refused to accept such an election. Meeting with a group of reforming cardinals in Florence, they elected the bishop of that city as Pope Nicholas II, and Godfrey provided the army that accompanied him to Rome and forced Benedict to flee. Also in the entourage, and witness to the enthroning of Nicholas on 24 January 1059, was the twelve-year-old Matilda. It is likely that this was also the first time she met Hildebrand.

Nicholas was the second in a line of reforming popes strongly backed by Godfrey and Beatrice, and sometimes referred to as 'Tuscan Popes'. Though he reigned for only two-and-a half years, with the strong will of Hildebrand behind him, a number of significant developments took place during that time. First, it was decreed that in future the election of a new pope would be solely the responsibility of the cardinals of the church. Some vague words were included about imperial privileges, but this was clearly an attempt at a decisive break with the empire, which, at the time, was too weak to protest.

The second development was a healing of the relations with the Normans, now occupying a large part of southern Italy. These had arrived as parties of adventurers early in the eleventh century, and had gradually forced out the Byzantines and Lombards whom they had originally served. Only a few years before, Pope Leo had attempted to expel them, by agreement with the Byzantine emperor, and been soundly beaten at the battle of Civitate, following which he had been held prisoner for nine months, though treated with the utmost respect. Now, however, perhaps anticipating the coming struggle with the Holy Roman Empire, it was felt expedient to secure as much support for the papacy as possible, particularly that of the energetic and efficient Normans.

In the summer of 1059, therefore, Pope Nicholas met the two Norman leaders, Robert Guiscard (Robert the Crafty) and Richard of Capua, at Melfi, confirming the latter as Prince of Capua, and investing the former as Duke of Apulia and Calabria, and (if he could get it from the Muslims), Sicily. By what authority he did this, no-one questioned, though these lands had never been part of the Papal States. In return, however, the Normans swore an oath to be faithful allies of the pope and the Roman Church, and to render assistance whenever it should be needed.

Unsurprisingly, after this relations with the Holy Roman Empire became strained. When Nicholas died in July 1061, Hildebrand oversaw the election of another Tuscan pope, Alexander II, but disaffected bishops, particularly those from Tuscany's neighbour Lombardy, demanded that Agnes, as regent, appoint an alternative. The bishop of Parma was duly selected as Honorius II, and, despite the efforts of Beatrice to block the Appenine passes and prevent his passage, he reached Rome in April 1062. When Godfrey arrived with an army soon after, there was something of a stand-off, but the situation in Germany was now changing.

In April 1062 the eleven-year-old Henry IV was kidnapped by a faction disapproving of the policies of Agnes. Led by Anno, archbishop of Cologne, they deposed Agnes as regent and Anno took over in her place. After a certain amount of skirmishing, and on enquiry into the credentials of Pope Alexander, he was confirmed as pope by the empire, while Honorius was expelled and excommunicated.

In 1065 Henry IV was declared of age, and around this time Godfrey was finally given at least part of the duchy he craved, becoming Duke of Lower Lorraine. By now he was in his sixties and would spend most of his time in the duchy, establishing a court at Bouillon, and leaving Beatrice and her daughter with more or less a free hand in Tuscany. They were by his side, however, when he died at Verdun on Christmas Eve 1069, and though Matilda seems to have managed to put off her marriage to his son until then, she now became the wife of Godfrey the Hunchback.

Despite similarities of age and rank, it was not a successful marriage. A daughter, christened Beatrice, was born in August 1071 and died soon after, and by the end of the year Matilda had left her husband and returned to her mother in Tuscany. The Tuscan inheritance was hers by right, and she soon made it clear she did not intend to be subject to the rule of Godfrey.

Though Matilda was now twenty-six years old, Beatrice continued governing in her name until her own death in 1076, while her daughter absorbed all she could teach her and firmly resisted all the efforts of Godfrey to force her to return to her marriage. He had followed her to Tuscany and tried in vain to get Beatrice, and even the pope, to order Matilda to obey him, before finally giving up in 1074, and returning to Lorraine. He then became a staunch supporter of Emperor Henry IV.

In April 1073 Pope Alexander had died, and, in the midst of his funeral rites, Hildebrand had abruptly been acclaimed as the new pope. In his own words, the crowd 'rushed upon me like madmen ... and dragged me by force to the place of apostolic rule,' a spontaneous acclamation that was apparently well orchestrated. The fact that he was not even an ordained priest was quickly remedied, and then, under the name of Pope Gregory VII, he set about completing the reforms to which he had already devoted his life.

At the time, Henry IV was in the midst of a Saxon rebellion against his rule and in need of papal support. In May 1074, therefore, he submitted to the pope and did penance for his earlier clashes over the appointment of bishops and archbishops, and using advisors excommunicated by Pope Alexander. As soon as the rebellion was crushed, however, with the help of Godfrey the Hunchback, the relationship changed. By the time Matilda finally took over the wealth and military power of Tuscany in April 1076, it had become clear that the emperor and the pope were well on the way to a mighty trial of strength, and in the coming struggle Godfrey would be on one side and his wife firmly on the other.

As a headstrong, autocratic ruler, the twenty-four-year-old Henry would probably have provoked a showdown anyway. He immediately went back on his word, for instance, and appointed a new archbishop of Milan. Pope Gregory, however, was more than a match for him in single-minded provocation. The document 'Dictatus Papae', dated to 1075, sums up his view of the independence of the church from lay interference, and the position of the pope within it. The pope was sole head of the Universal Church, it proclaimed. He alone could make new laws for the church and appoint, depose or reinstate bishops and archbishops. He was answerable to no-one, and could also, if necessary, depose kings and emperors and free their subjects from their oaths of loyalty.

This went a great deal further than earlier popes had dared to go, and directly challenged the system by which the Holy Roman Empire was administered. If Henry could not appoint his bishops and archbishops, this, he claimed, was tantamount to handing over his entire empire to the pope. At a council at Worms in January 1076, the senior German clergy were required to sign a declaration that they no longer recognised the 'false monk' Hildebrand as pope and would no longer obey him. A similar declaration was made a little later by the bishops of Lombardy, indicating their own loyalty to the empire.

Among the accusations now made against Gregory were that he had been improperly elected and that his judgements and decrees were made in consultation with a 'senate of women', contrary to all the teachings of the early church. These women included not only Beatrice and Matilda, who were in regular correspondence with the pope they wholeheartedly supported, but also Henry's mother Agnes, who had moved to Rome, and his mother-in-law Adelaide of Susa.

Godfrey the Hunchback was present at Worms, and it is claimed he was behind the accusation also made there that Pope Gregory and Matilda were lovers. When he was assassinated a month later, some implicated Matilda in the deed as revenge for the slanders spread about her. This seems unlikely as reports of the council at Worms were slow to reach south of the Alps. In any case, Godfrey had made many other enemies in his active support of Henry against the Saxons. There is evidence that Matilda thought of retiring to a convent at this point, possibly as a result of these accusations. She was dissuaded, however, by the pope himself, who suggested she would serve God better by an active, rather than a contemplative life. In this assessment he would, no doubt, come to feel entirely vindicated.

Gregory's response to the declaration at Worms was to excommunicate not only the rebel bishops, but also the emperor himself, informing his subjects they no longer needed to obey him. Should any do so, they, too, risked excommunication, a very serious threat in a highly religious age, when to be cut off from the church and its rituals, and risk hellfire, was not a situation to be taken lightly.

Immediately, the old splits within the German empire re-opened, with a large number of imperial princes and dukes taking the opportunity to oppose Henry. At a meeting at Tribur in October 1076, he was given an ultimatum – show he was penitent, dismiss his evil counsellors and obtain absolution from the pope *in person* before 22 February of the following year, or they would depose him and elect a new king.

It was clearly their intention to prevent Henry from reaching the pope in time. With rebel sympathisers on both sides of the Alps, the passes between Germany and Italy were held against him, and in the depths of winter, it was not thought possible he could get past. Gregory, in fact, had been invited to meet the rebels at Augsburg in early February, such was their confidence that they would be crowning a new king. Henry, though, did not give up so easily.

His wife was Bertha of Savoy, daughter of Adelaide of Susa, who, since the death of her husband, had ruled Turin and Savoy along with her sons Amadeus and Peter. There was a way into northern Italy through these lands if Adelaide could be persuaded to let him through, though the fact that Henry had tried unsuccessfully to repudiate his wife some half dozen years before, probably meant there was little love lost between them. Since that time, however, Henry had learnt to rely on Bertha, and she it was who now interceded for him with Adelaide, presumably convincing her mother he was sincerely penitent. How much Henry knew of the pope's plans is unclear, but if he was to reach him before February, time was not on his side. He set out, then, in bitter winter weather, accompanied by Bertha and the youngest of their four children, Conrad, who was less than two years old. Adelaide still had to be bribed with a grant of land, but she then joined the party, along with her son Amadeus.

In the meantime, Pope Gregory had set out for the meeting at Augsburg. Most of his advisors had counselled against this, pointing out that he would have to cross hostile lands in northern Italy to get there. It was Matilda, the new de facto countess of Tuscany, who encouraged him to make the journey. With the forces now at her disposal, she was prepared to guarantee his safety to the northern edge of her lands at Mantua. From there the German princes were supposed to provide an escort for the rest of the way.

She was as good as her word, and by 8 January 1077 Gregory had been safely delivered to Mantua, only to find there was no sign of the promised German escort. Worse still, word was brought that Henry and his party were already in Italy, though no-one seemed sure of what, if any, forces he had brought with him. Once again, the pope listened to Matilda's advice. Her ancestral fortress of Canossa was nearby. Perched high on a rocky mound in the Appenine mountains, its triple-walled defences were considered impregnable. Whatever forces Henry had brought, Gregory would be safe there.

Thus it was to Canossa that the German king came to find the pope, in the bitter snowy weather at the end of January. He came not with an army, but barefoot and bare-headed, with every sign of penitence. Some sources suggest he even wore a monk's tunic and a hair shirt. There is little doubt the penitence was a sham and that both parties knew it, but it was a masterly ploy. To refuse forgiveness was un-Christian and therefore unthinkable, but to grant absolution, lift the excommunication and confirm Henry as king and emperor would be a betrayal of all those who had been prepared to back Gregory against their lawful king.

For three days Pope Gregory held out. Some sources claim Henry spent those days outside the castle gate, fasting in the snow. Others suggest he was more comfortably lodged at Bianello, another of Matilda's castles nearby. What is certain is that during this time a number of people, including Adelaide of Susa, Abbot Hugh of Cluny (Henry's godfather), and Matilda herself, mediated between king and pope. Donizo, in his *Vita Mathildis*, 'Life of Matilda', claims that it was Abbot Hugh with the king's party who persuaded Matilda to intercede for Henry, declaring, 'No-one can do it if you do not.' Eventually, pressure was put on Gregory to do what, in the end, he had to do. On 28 January 1077 the gate was finally opened and Henry was admitted to the pope's presence. What words passed between them are not recorded, but the celebration of a Solemn Mass in the castle chapel, and the giving and receiving of Holy Communion, signified to all Henry's return to the church. It was, however, a conditional return. Henry had to swear that he would meet with the pope and the German princes at a general council, when any accusations made against him would be judged by Gregory, who alone could decide whether or not he should retain his kingship. Even if he did he must in future remain obedient to the pope and co-operate in his church reforms. As to whether he had now been formally re-instated as king, this was left vague. He was not, before this council meeting, to bear any of the things that signified kingship, nor take part in administration. Nor were his subjects yet to be returned to their fealty to him. Henry, however, was fully confident he had won at least this round of the contest. 'I, Henry, king ...' began the declaration of acceptance that he signed at this time.

The meeting at Canossa was clearly not the end of this matter, in fact the supporters of both sides were outraged at what had taken place. Those backing Henry felt he had been humiliated in submitting to the pope, while those backing Gregory were furious that he had so easily forgiven him. For the next seven months the pope remained within Matilda's lands, and he did not respond to Henry's request for another meeting at Mantua, down on the plain and close to imperial Lombard territory. Nor did Henry provide the promised safe conduct to a council in Germany. His own return northwards in April 1078 was prompted by the election of Rudolf, duke of Swabia, as anti-king on 15 March, the rebellious German princes having decided not to wait for Gregory's approval. If they had expected the pope's endorsement, however, they were disappointed. He had clearly declared that he alone would decide the matter, and refused to support Rudolf until he was allowed to do so. So while civil war raged in Germany, for the next two years Gregory and Henry exchanged veiled threats – Gregory formally banning lay investiture and excommunicating the king's appointee and former chancellor, Archbishop Wibert of Ravenna, while Henry hinted at deposing Gregory and imposing an antipope of his own.

Throughout this time Matilda was still the pope's trusted supporter in northern Italy, communicating with both sides, suggesting compromise and ever ready to escort the pope to the limits of her lands, if safe conduct could be arranged for the rest of the way to Germany. It was only in early 1080 that Gregory accepted he would never get such a safe conduct and agreed to decide the matter between Henry and Rudolf in Rome in their absence.

Representatives were sent to put the case for each side, but it didn't take long for the pope to conclude that Henry had broken all the promises made at Canossa, and to formally depose and excommunicate him, recognising Rudolf as king of the Germans in his place. In reply Henry called a synod of German bishops at Brixen, and on 25 June 1080 they, in turn, declared Gregory formally deposed. They elected instead the staunch imperialist Wibert of Ravenna who took the name Clement III, a clear reference to that Clement appointed by Henry's father as the first German pope. Then, while Henry turned his attention back to defeating Rudolf, Clement himself set off for his own homeland in Lombardy, the seat of imperialist power in northern Italy.

It was clear that sooner or later Henry and Clement would attempt to seize Rome, and Gregory's immediate reaction was to try and line up as many allies as he could. To the north he could rely on the countess Matilda, who, with her lands stretching as far as Mantua, effectively blocked the traditional route from northern Italy to Rome. To the south the Normans were less reliable. Jordan of Capua, who had inherited his lands from his father Richard in 1078, had already encroached on papal territory, and though he and Robert Guiscard renewed their commitment to Gregory in 1080, Guiscard immediately left to pursue his ambitions against the Byzantine Empire.

It was to Matilda that Gregory looked, then, for the forces he would need to protect his papacy. The immediate plan was to attack Ravenna, and thus complete the blockade across the north, while re-claiming lands previously forming part of the papal states. This may have been prompted by a rebellion in Ravenna itself against the new Antipope.

On 14 October 1080 Henry fought yet another battle against Rudolf of Swabia near the River Elster. Previous battles had been indecisive, but this time Rudolf clearly won. In the course of the victory, however, he lost his right hand and suffered a mortal wound, expiring a few days later. With the loss of their leader the rebel cause fell apart. On almost the same day, close by Matilda's castle at Volta near Mantua, her forces were heavily defeated and put to flight by Lombard supporters of the king.

It is probable that Matilda was not there at the time, and her forces were reputedly well outnumbered, with some, no doubt, engaged in the Ravenna campaign. Still, it was a serious blow, and the defeat encouraged a number of cities where there was strong imperialist sympathy to rise up and expel her supporters. In particular Pisa and Lucca could no longer be relied upon, with Bishop Anselm of Lucca being driven out and forced to seek refuge with Matilda in the mountains.

By the spring of 1081, knowing that Henry was on his way over the Alps, even Pope Gregory seems to have contemplated Matilda's surrender. As one by one the cities north of the Apennines declared for the king, from Piacenza and Parma in the west, Reggio and Modena in the centre, to Ravenna in the east, it seemed impossible she would be able to hold out. Matilda, however, had other ideas. Withdrawing to her core ancestral lands on the heights, she prepared to dig in and wage something of a guerrilla war, harrying imperial forces where and when she could, and avoiding anything in the way of a pitched battle.

Henry's aim, at the time, was to reach Rome, instal his 'pope' and obtain the coronation that would enable him to call himself Holy Roman Emperor. Weakened as she was, Matilda could not prevent his march on Rome, though his diversion to Ravenna to collect Clement and his forces may have been an acknowledgement that she was not yet wholly defeated.

It was towards the end of May when he reached Rome, apparently expecting the gates to be thrown open to him. The vast majority of Romans, however, remained loyal to Gregory and the gates remained closed. Nor would the city fall easily. The whole area was surrounded by the mighty Aurelian wall, built in the fifth century and some sixty feet high. The area around St Peter's Basilica, which had been outside this wall, was now similarly protected by the Leonine wall, built in the ninth century. Though this was only half the height, encircling what had become known as the Leonine city, it was still a formidable barrier, especially as Henry had brought no siege engines with him. Quickly realising this, and realising, too, that the malarial marshes around Rome were no place for an army during the heat of the summer, Henry withdrew northwards.

He knew now he would need a larger force and a longer time-span to break into Rome, but before he returned to Germany to prepare for this new campaign, he consolidated his hold on towns such as Pisa and Lucca that had formerly been Matilda's. It was in Lucca in the summer of 1081 that she was formally declared an outlaw and her lands forfeit. Of those lands in Lorraine which she had inherited after a struggle with her husband's nominated heir, the county of Verdun had already defected to Henry. In Italy her line of Apennine fortresses was completely encircled by imperial supporters, and the lower lands were repeatedly plundered and ravaged to deprive her of resources. Matilda, though, remained defiant, marshalling her forces to hit and run, to skirmish with the enemy and to harass Henry's supply lines. Those holding her castles remained firm, and she still maintained contact with Pope Gregory and his supporters. She also established a most efficient intelligence service, and, while paying her own forces, even managed to send money to Gregory to pay for his.

Henry over-wintered in Germany, but in the spring of 1082 he was back, this time determined to besiege Rome to the end. In the course of the year he persuaded Jordan of Capua to defect, and also opened negotiations with the Byzantine Emperor Alexius Comnenus. Comnenus promised gold and men in return for Henry's undertaking that he would attack the lands of Robert Guiscard after he had taken Rome, and thus draw him away from his onslaught on the Byzantine empire. In the summer heat, once more withdrawing from Rome, though leaving behind a besieging force, Henry attacked Matilda's lands again, but with no more success than before.

By the end of that year, hunger in the besieged city was beginning to undermine loyalty. It was not until June 1083, however, that the cracks began to show. By some accounts it was the arrival of a contingent of knights from Milan that made the breakthrough, scaling the Leonine wall and opening the gate into that part of the city. Donizo, however, is adamant that a traitor let them in. However it happened, it was a mighty boost for Henry, as was the arrival of quantities of Byzantine gold. It was not the end, though. Pope Gregory was whisked away from certain capture into the nearby fortress of Castel Sant'Angelo, and across the Tiber from the Leonine City, the rest of Rome still held out.

By now papal funds were nearly exhausted and Matilda, too, was considerably impoverished, but with Henry using Byzantine gold to buy friends in Rome, something had to be done. The monastery at Canossa, like many others, had amassed a sizeable treasury, gifts made over the years by the counts and others. This was now liquidated by Matilda and sent for the support of the pope. The treasury of another monastery near Modena was treated in the same way, thus allowing Gregory to continue his defiance, and helping him to bolster his position in Rome, at least for a little longer. No wonder Henry once again spent his summer months unsuccessfully attempting to take one of Matilda's castles near Modena.

It was early in 1084, however, that the trickle of support for Henry in Rome finally became a flood. He himself had been dutifully beginning a campaign against Robert Guiscard when he received the news that Rome would at last open its gates to him and to his 'pope'. On 21 March 1084, seven years after his humiliation at Canossa, Henry, King of the Romans, and Clement his pope, marched into the city, taking up residence not in the imperial palace, but in the Lateran, the home of the pope himself. A few days later, a gathering of cardinals and Roman nobles sympathetic to the empire formally declared Gregory deposed. In his place Wibert, archbishop of Ravenna – already known to some as Pope Clement III – was elected, consecrated and enthroned with suitable pomp on Palm Sunday, 24 March. A week later Henry achieved his ambition. Crowned and anointed by his tame pope, he emerged as Holy Roman Emperor, with his wife Bertha as Empress at his side.

For Gregory and for Matilda it must have been the lowest of low points. Benzo, Bishop of Alba, writing at the time but strongly partisan towards Henry, depicts Matilda wringing her hands and weeping for her lost lands and goods. This is almost certainly overstating the case, but she was probably particularly stung by the fact that in her own beleaguered situation, she was unable to help the pope when he needed it most.

Gregory was not entirely without forceful friends, however, and Henry's and Clement's triumph would be short-lived. Within a few weeks it became known that Robert Guiscard was on his way north. Possibly stung into action by Henry's attack on his own lands in Puglia, he was coming to answer the call of his sworn ally Pope Gregory, leaving his son Bohemond behind to carry on his assault on the Byzantine lands. Despite the alliance, the Normans were still generally regarded as unruly barbarians, and Gregory's appeal to Guiscard must therefore have been seen as something of a last resort on his part.

We don't know the size of the army Guiscard brought with him. Contemporary accounts range from an unlikely 36,000 men to a paltry 4,000. Whatever it was, Henry didn't wait to find out. He had achieved his coronation and made abortive attacks on Castel Sant'Angelo and some other fortresses within the city loyal to Pope Gregory. He had no intention of fighting Guiscard in the summer heat, however, and on 21 May left Rome rather hurriedly with his wife, his army and his newly consecrated Pope Clement. The almost contemporary, though partisan, account by William of Apulia suggests the reputation of Guiscard was enough to frighten him away.

Another contemporary account, that of Geoffrey of Malaterra, gives copious details of what followed. Approaching with caution, Robert Guiscard camped for three days outside the city while reconnoitring its walls and defences. It had taken Henry a two-year siege to get in, but Guiscard managed it rather more quickly. Under cover of darkness, a party of his men simply used ladders to scale the wall near a poorly guarded gate, and once inside let their fellows in. Which of the many gates they used is disputed. Malaterra claims it was at San Lorenzo in the east, while others claim it was one of the northern gates. Modern research seems to suggest the Porta Latina in the south. Whichever it was, once inside they lost no time in marching to the bridge over the Tiber by Castel Sant' Angelo and rescuing the pope.

Again, there are different versions of how this was done. Some suggest a strategy of mass arson, followed by three days of rape and pillage, when Guiscard may have lost control of some of his men. William of Apulia concedes that some buildings were burned and the pope was 'violently freed', while Geoffrey of Malaterra describes a more clinical operation, somewhat like a commando raid, with the pope quickly installed safely in the Lateran Palace. He suggests it was a counter-attack by the Romans that led to battles in the streets and the order to fire the buildings. What is certain is that a considerable number of buildings, particularly churches, were burnt, and though to say Rome was left a smoking ruin would be overstating it, there was clearly a good deal of destruction involved.

As a result, although Pope Gregory and his champion Guiscard won a victory, in the process they lost the war. Malaterra claims the Roman nobles eventually sought reconciliation with the pope, but he no longer trusted them enough to remain in Rome. Their loyalty, says Malaterra, could only be secured with bribes – 'You threaten one man with another, and thus you fill your money bags.' By now, though, Gregory had no bribes left, and so when Guiscard departed soon afterwards, so did Pope Gregory, travelling south to the Norman capital of Salerno.

It was a bitter blow to the reform party, but not quite the final word in a tumultuous year. On the retreat from Rome, 'Pope' Clement went only as far as Tivoli, but Henry had got what he came for and was intent on returning to Germany, where Herman of Salm had been elected king in place of Rudolf of Swabia. Before he left, however, he instructed his Lombard supporters to complete the conquest of the still defiant Matilda of Tuscany. No doubt he saw this as a simple mopping-up exercise. He had been able to travel around, and even through, her lands for some time, but there was always the risk of a sudden, swift attack on his supply line, and the woman herself was a rallying point and provider of refuge for those of the reform party driven out elsewhere. Even now she was sheltering two bishops who were loud in condemning his actions, calling his pope the Antichrist. Matilda was a thorn in his flesh and had to be dealt with.

With the emperor gone, the imperialist forces were gathered under the leadership of the Bishops of Parma and Reggio, with the lay element represented by Margrave Oberto. They were, claims Donizo, a mighty force, 'shield armed and splendidly mounted', intending to devastate Matilda's lands, seize her fortresses and capture the lady herself, thus winning honours for themselves within the Holy Roman Empire. The first part of the plan went well, as in late June 1084 they entered her lands, progressing with much incidental plundering from Reggio to Modena, and meeting little real resistance. When they came to attack her fortress at Sorbara, however, they found they had underestimated their enemy.

Matilda herself seems to have been close by, and well-informed of the movements of this host, perhaps watching them from high ground. Now she determined to strike a blow that would show the imperial party that the reformers, and indeed Pope Gregory himself, were still a force to be reckoned with. We have four accounts of the action at Sorbara, one from an eyewitness, a clerk sent by Bishop Anselm of Lucca to deliver a blessing to Matilda's forces. He coyly declares that the blessing was duly delivered, 'through my humble self', sometimes translated as 'through our smallness'. At one time it was believed his name was Bardo, but now this is rejected and he remains anonymous, referred to as Pseudo-Bardo.

He implies that the imperialist forces moved faster than Matilda expected, so that she had less than a day to assemble her own men. This is backed up by another account, that of Ranger of Lucca. Both Pseudo-Bardo and Ranger were engaged in writing biographies of Bishop Anselm of Lucca, and therefore anxious to show the power of his blessing. Nevertheless, it is clear that the strategy at Sorbara was Matilda's strategy, and its success due to her direction of the men at her disposal.

By all accounts these were few, which would explain the decision to mount a dawn raid on the imperialists. Though usually referred to as the Battle of Sorbara, this seems to have been less of an open field battle and more an attack on the enemy camp, an attempt to take them by surprise when they were hardly awake. It certainly did that. Though Ranger records fierce fighting, broken spears, shattered shields and the noise of battle rising to the heavens, Pseudo-Bardo declares the imperialists 'quickly showed their backs' and fled before the onslaught. Among them went the Margrave Oberto, who 'whimpered like a nun' and ran away without honour. The casualty lists given suggest they were pursued to some effect by Matilda's cavalry, with countless numbers killed or made captive. Among the latter was the Bishop of Parma, while Donizo – writing some time later but well-placed for information – declares the Bishop of Reggio had not even time to put on his armour, and that he hid for three days among the bushes before managing to escape. The one-sidedness of the victory raises comparisons with the aftermath of Agincourt some four hundred years later, with the enemy utterly vanquished and Matilda's side reporting only three dead and some wounded. They would have been boosted, too, by the spoils of battle, the entire contents of the imperialist camp, including some five hundred horses and much armour.

It was clearly a turning point in northern Italy. Now, says Ranger, powerful Matilda, cheered by these events, gained ground, while Donizo declares 'the renowned Matilda was a terror to them all.' There would be no further attempt by the imperialists to bring her to account, and she remained not only a figurehead for the reform party, but also a channel of communication between the pope in Salerno and his supporters in the north and beyond. At one point she writes to these supporters, telling them that Henry has taken control of the papal seal and may use it to mislead, and therefore they should believe no messages that did not come through her.

While it is clear Matilda did not charge into battle at the head of her forces, still she was acting, as Pseudo-Bardo says, 'in a manner to which women are not accustomed'. There would be no more attempts to capture her, for some years at least. Instead, it was her reputation that underwent a violent assault. She had already been accused of being the mistress of Pope Gregory. Now she was referred to as his 'evil partner', a Jezebel, and variously likened to the snake in the Garden of Eden and to Eve tempting Adam astray. In this highly misogynist age, scripture was quoted to prove her a heretic, in particular the Apostle Paul's instruction that women must not usurp authority over men but must be submissive and silent. There was nothing submissive about Matilda, and she was emphatically not silent, constantly encouraging the reformers with letters and messages of hope and conviction.

While she did not write her own defence, she certainly encouraged others to do so. Bishops Anselm of Lucca and Bonizo of Sutri, who were sheltering with her at the time, both produced works justifying her actions, as did John of Mantua. They countered scripture with scripture, quoting, among others, the actions of Deborah the prophetess in the book of Judges, and replied to accusations that Matilda was a 'sower of discord' and preferred war to peace, with the idea of a 'just war'. This concept was gaining ground at the time and would find its flowering a little later in the first crusade, but Matilda may have been one of the first to be referred to as a 'soldier of Christ'. John of Mantua, in particular, declared that earthly powers were given to protect men from the devil's servants on earth, and that Matilda should not be distressed if she had to take up arms and use the sword against the opponents of the true pope, when words alone were not enough. The pope, he said, fought with the sword of heaven, while it was Matilda's job to fight with the sword of the world.

Unfortunately for her, while Matilda remained strong in the north, the reform papacy itself was rapidly weakening. On 25 May 1085 Pope Gregory died, still at Salerno, while Antipope Clement had returned to Rome the previous November. On his deathbed Gregory named a number of candidates who might be elected to succeed him, but it was almost a whole year before bishops and cardinals managed to assemble in Rome for such an election. In the meantime, one of the candidates, Bishop Anselm of Lucca, had died. The choice then fell unanimously on another, Desiderius, the immensely successful abbot of Monte Cassino. Desiderius, however, made it clear he really didn't want the job. Before he could be persuaded to accept consecration, riots in Rome forced him to flee back to his monastery, and it was nearly another year before he finally agreed to take on the role. Prince Jordan of Capua, in particular, had persistently pushed for this, Monte Cassino being within his territory and Desiderius being something of a mentor of his. Finally, in the spring of 1087, the combined forces of Prince Jordan and Countess Matilda succeeded in re-taking the Leonine city, and on 9 May Desiderius was consecrated as Pope Victor III in St. Peter's Basilica. The chronicle of Monte Cassino is clear that this was 'through the aid and power of the aforesaid countess.' He remained in Rome only a matter of weeks, however, before retreating once more to Monte Cassino, and there he died on 16 September.

His successor, who took the name Urban II, was not elected until the following March, and then in Terracina in the territory of Prince Jordan rather than in Rome, where Clement once more reigned. Urban had been Prior of Cluny before becoming Bishop of Ostia, and was committed to the Gregorian reforms, though with rather more tact and diplomacy than Gregory, whom William of Malmesbury describes as 'rather too austere towards men'.

In the north of Italy, meanwhile, Matilda's influence was spreading. With the victory at Sorbara and the continued absence of Emperor Henry, many with reform sympathies were beginning to find their voices again. It helped that a number of staunchly imperialist bishops died around this time, including the bishops of Parma and Reggio and Archbishop Tedald of Milan. Matilda, together with Anselm of Lucca before his death, encouraged the election of reform-minded bishops, though not all succeeded in establishing themselves in competition with others appointed by Henry. Bonizo of Sutri, for example, now appointed Bishop of Piacenza, took two years to enter his see, and the following year was brutally expelled, being blinded and mutilated in the process. By contrast, some imperially appointed bishops began a slow defection to the reform party. Thus, although Urban was unable to take his seat in Rome, he could travel in the north under Matilda's protection and begin to find acceptance there.

Throughout this time the emperor had been fully engaged in his German lands, with no time to spare for the challenge growing beyond the Alps. Having taken Matilda's county of Verdun, he gave it to Godfrey of Bouillon, later adding the duchy of Lower Lorraine. Lorraine had had its troubles, but it was the Saxon rebels to the east that posed the biggest problem, defeating Henry's forces on several occasions, especially when in 1086 they formed an alliance with Bavaria.

Soon after this, however, the situation began to change. Henry's eldest son, Conrad, had been left in Italy in the care of Archbishop Tedald, possibly as early as 1077. In the spring of 1087, now aged thirteen, he was recalled to Germany and crowned at Aachen as co-ruler with his father, having sworn he would never try to overthrow him. When, shortly afterwards, the anti-king Herman of Salm died, the rebels began to put out feelers for peace. It was suggested they could be reconciled with Henry if he could persuade the pope to absolve him from his often-repeated excommunication (the same proposition put to him before Canossa). Nothing definite came of this, but from now on a number of leading Saxons began to defect to the emperor.

Should Henry secure peace within his northern lands, it seemed likely his thoughts would then turn to stamping out the resurgent reform movement south of the Alps. Such a peace appeared even more likely when, after the death of his wife Bertha at the end of 1087, he became engaged to Eupraxia of Kiev, the widow of a prominent Saxon noble, Henry of Stade. At the same time he was also offering to negotiate peace with Welf, duke of Bavaria.

Whether Henry's engagement was the spur is impossible to say, but around this time Pope Urban seems to have suggested to Matilda, his staunchest supporter, that she, too, could secure a useful alliance through marriage. If Welf of Bavaria could be firmly attached to their cause, not only would this encourage Henry to remain in Germany, but Welf's extensive holdings in the southern state of Swabia would enable the blocking of the Alpine passes, thus making his passage into Italy with an army far more difficult. It was not Welf senior he had in mind as a matrimonial partner, however, but his eighteen-year-old son, later to be known unflatteringly as Welf the Fat.

Matilda was now forty-three years old. She had abandoned her first husband around the time young Welf was born and had felt no need of another at any time since. If Welf is seen as a political pawn, then no less was Matilda, and it is unlikely she would have agreed to such an arrangement for anyone other than the pope. The incentive for the Welfs, of course, was Matilda's powerful position and extensive lands in northern Italy, which would, in theory at least, be brought under their control. The Welfs had their own lands in Lombardy, with connections to the strongly imperialist Obertenghi family, this providing a further incentive for Matilda and for the pope by increasing their opportunities to spread the reform message.

Thus it was that the year 1089 saw two important weddings. On 18 August Henry IV married Eupraxia, who, on being crowned empress, took the more German name Adelaide. Soon afterwards Matilda, countess of Tuscany, was united to a man young enough to be her son. Writing some thirty years later, Cosmas of Prague gives an interesting view of the latter nuptials. According to him, for two nights after the wedding Welf refused to come to the marriage bed for fear of witchcraft. Then, on the third night, Matilda appeared naked before him, and when he recoiled, slapped his face, spat at him, called him a vile worm and threatened him with a horrible death if she should ever see him again. Cosmas also includes in his writing an earlier letter purporting to be from Matilda, proposing to Welf 'for the good of all my kingdom', and promising him castles, palaces, gold and silver. This letter is now believed to be utterly spurious, and it seems highly likely that the dramatic scenes between Matilda and her new husband are also the product of a wild imagination. On the other hand, it is more than probable that the marriage was never consummated – but then, that was never the point of it.

If it was intended to keep Henry in Germany, however, it failed. There is evidence he was already planning another expedition to Italy, though some have claimed it was this very wedding that made such an expedition essential. Like his father before him, he could not afford to have enemies on both sides of the Alps, and while his son Conrad had returned to Lombardy as his father's representative, he had not so far had much effect in curbing the activities of the redoubtable countess.

In March 1090, therefore, Henry returned to Italy. His aim was clearly to break the stubborn defiance offered by Matilda, now backed up by her new husband. Devastating their lands on the way, he made straight for Mantua, her major city north of the River Po, and in April 1090 attempted to put the place under siege. His blockade would last for the next eleven months.

It was, though, a hard place to besiege. Standing on the River Mincio, it could easily be resupplied by boat, and Donizo writes of the cunning Matilda filling the place with provisions and soldiers, while Henry was forced to spend time taking a number of her fortresses in the surrounding area to try and cut off the river traffic. Matilda, and, indeed, Welf, were within the city for at least part of the time, and a good deal of hard fighting is reported, involving both Matilda's forces and also those raised by the city itself. Had the contest been purely military, it is likely Matilda and Welf could have held out almost indefinitely, still possessing some strongholds to the south, and especially beyond the River Po. In the end, however, it became a battle for the hearts and minds of the Mantuan citizens, with Matilda offering relief from tolls and taxes, and Henry promising an even greater degree of independence.

On 10 April 1091, Mantua finally opted for Henry, surrendering the city into his hands. By then Matilda had left, withdrawing to the south and preparing her forces for the defence of lands to the south of the River Po. The loss of Mantua was a severe blow – Donizo spends some time denouncing the treachery of its citizens – but there was still no thought of giving up the struggle.

The next year and a half represent the high point of Henry's campaign in northern Italy, as he first concentrated on mopping up Matilda's fortresses north of the Po. An attempt was made to attack him late in 1091, when the countess learned he was travelling within the Welf lands between Mantua and Padua with a reduced escort. Donizo declares she sent a task force of over a thousand men, probably led by Welf, to ambush him, but their plan was betrayed. By the time the forces met at Tricontai, Henry had called up a sizeable army and Matilda's forces were routed – the second serious defeat of the year.

Henry's plans were slightly complicated by the death, in December 1091, of his mother-in-law Adelaide de Susa. The emperor immediately declared that his son Conrad should have her lands, despite her nomination of her great-grandson Peter as her heir. Conrad, who presumably until that time had been supporting his father, was thus despatched to claim the county of Turin. Adelaide had, of course, been a strong supporter of the reform party, and it seems likely that the reform message may have begun to influence the eighteen-year-old Conrad during the time he now spent in the area.

In the summer of 1092 Henry began what he surely intended to be the endgame as far as Matilda was concerned. Pushing south of the River Po, he captured and devastated swathes of land beyond the major route, the Via Emilia, and began a siege at Monteveglio in the mountains to the south-west of Bologna. This was one of Matilda's strongest fortresses, and had he been able to storm it or starve it into surrender, it would have been another major blow for the countess. Reinforced by the presence of his pope and the forces Clement brought with him, it seemed only a matter of time before the castle would fall. Resistance, however, was stubborn, the defenders even managing to pierce his blockade on occasion to resupply the garrison.

Towards the end of the summer Henry tried another approach, offering what he regarded as generous terms to the countess. He would lift the siege, he said, and restore her lands and titles, if she would only agree to recognise Clement as pope. It is notable that, although the names of Welf and Matilda appear together on documents issued around this time, with Welf's name first as tradition demanded, Henry's offer was clearly aimed at Matilda. She was the leader, the commander of her forces, and the figurehead of support for Pope Urban, still vainly trying to gain a foothold in Rome. She was the one that must be captured, killed or forced to surrender before his work in Italy could be completed. He was gambling that he had done enough damage to the lands of her vassals that their support for her had been fatally undermined. Indeed, there were some who advocated accepting his offer, but the final decision was Matilda's and, promising to compensate those of her supporters suffering for her sake, the decision was taken to fight on.

At about the same time, a sudden sortie from within the besieged fortress at Monteveglio succeeded in killing, among others, an illegitimate son of the emperor's. When the siege was then abruptly called off, it may have been an attempt to persuade the countess that Henry had become discouraged by this death. He seemed to be withdrawing towards Parma, but then suddenly turned southwards and launched an attack on Canossa itself, the very heart of Matilda's 'kingdom'. It is likely Henry believed Matilda was inside the fortress at Canossa while the bulk of her forces were elsewhere. Indeed, he was very nearly right. She was just returning from a council with her supporters, but her spies, as usual, were quick to inform her of the emperor's movements. Leaving one part of her forces to garrison Canossa, she marched with the rest to nearby Bianello, where at least some of Henry's party had been lodged during his humiliation at Canossa some fifteen years earlier. If he had intended to trap her at Canossa, he was just too late. Donizo even declares that her group, in leaving the fortress, passed within earshot of the emperor's forces, and having seen her safely to Bianello, a number managed to return and re-enter the castle even as it was being invested.

It was by now October and the mountains would soon feel the pinch of winter. Matilda, the all-important figurehead, was still free, and now Henry had a dilemma. He could besiege Canossa and risk being caught between two forces if Matilda brought up reinforcements from Bianello. Alternatively, he could follow Matilda, possibly all over a mountain range that was her own home ground, being made to look ridiculous if she demonstrated her usual skill in remaining just out of reach.

We don't know exactly what forces each could command, or even what really happened next. The only detailed account is that of Donizo, who was on the spot, being a monk in the monastery at Canossa. On the other hand, as he states that every time Henry attacked, the abbot had all his monks singing psalms and invoking saints to defend them, the likelihood is that Donizo was inside with them and not at liberty to watch what was going on outside the castle walls. He would, though, have been well placed to question others afterwards.

Donizo's story is that when the emperor attacked, a thick fog appeared around the castle. He gives no details of sorties from within, or attacks from the rear by reinforcements. The only action he describes is the unhorsing of the man carrying the emperor's banner, who, incidentally, he identifies as the son of Margrave Obert who was defeated at Sorbara. Thereupon, one lone foot soldier rushes out and seizes the banner, which seems to demoralise the emperor to such an extent that he immediately abandons the siege. Furthermore, adds Donizo, Henry retreats so fast, he is over the River Po in two days – though how he would know that is not clear – with his power evermore waning from that time on.

He is certainly correct that this second visit of Henry to Canossa was a turning point, but there must surely have been more to it than that. It could well be that while Donizo was singing his psalms some violent battle was going on outside, though he makes no mention of casualties or spoils of victory, which would surely have been apparent after such an action. On the other hand, Henry had been inside Canossa and seen its powerful defences at first hand. He may simply have realised he had no chance of taking such a place before winter set in, and withdrawn. This would not, however, explain the speed of his retreat, or the rapid decline in his fortunes thereafter. Whatever the explanation, Canossa seemed destined to be a humiliation for Henry whenever he approached it, and his failure to capture or defeat this woman who defied him must have had an effect on morale. Like the Grand Old Duke of York, he had marched his men to the top of the hill, and now marched them down again, with nothing to show for it.

Nor was Matilda resting on her laurels. Henry, and probably his mounted forces, may have speedily reached the safety of the Po valley, but the infantry would have taken longer, and again Donizo describes Matilda's army pouring down from the hills, no doubt harrying the stragglers, and swiftly re-taking all the lands they had recently lost. In one place their approach and victory was so rapid, he claims, that the castle they took was still filled with the emperor's treasures and possessions.

If 1092 ended in humiliation for Henry, the next year was even worse. There was new trouble in Germany, with Henry's appointee Frederick, duke of Swabia being challenged by a supporter of the Welfs. Part of the imperial army was dispatched to deal with this, but then Welf of Bavaria and his allies managed to close the Alpine passes against the emperor. Soon after this a number of Lombard cities, including Milan, Cremona, Lodi and Piacenza, went over to Matilda, and then, worst of all, Conrad, 'beloved son' and crowned co-ruler, defected to the enemy.

Why he did this is not entirely clear. One suggestion, backed to a certain extent by Conrad himself, is his disgust at his father's morals and treatment of his new wife. Another possibility is simply a power grab, seeing his father weakened and vulnerable, and wanting to take over the empire while there was still an empire to take. The writers of the time, however, were quite clear that the influence behind this sudden change of heart was Matilda, countess of Tuscany. He was 'won over by the persuasions of Matilda', says the anonymous writer of the Life of Henry IV, adding that she was 'the prime mover of the deed'.

Henry's initial reaction was to imprison his son, but Conrad escaped and made his way to Matilda, who quickly arranged for his coronation as King of Italy. In fact, he may have been crowned twice. One coronation took place in Milan with Archbishop Anselm, Henry's own nominated and invested archbishop, who had now defected to Matilda. The other may have been in Monza, with the ancient Iron Crown of Lombardy. Matilda and Welf attended at least one of these coronations, and Pope Urban, too, threw his weight behind this new ally.

With the help of Roger of Sicily, he had at last managed to get a foothold in Rome, and he now proposed a marriage between Conrad and Roger's daughter Maximilla, as a way of supporting the young man against his father. Conrad, he wrote, in a very business-like letter, had no resources of his own, but with Roger's resources behind him 'would be strong enough to vanquish enemies of the Holy Church of God'. The daughter was duly despatched – plus a handsome dowry – and the wedding took place in Pisa in 1095.

By the time of this wedding, however, two other marriages had come to an end. As if it was not enough humiliation for Henry to lose his son to Matilda, in 1094 he lost his wife as well. The Empress Adelaide/Eupraxia had travelled with him to Italy, but from the time of the defection of Conrad had apparently been under house arrest in Verona, the only part of Italy still open to the emperor. Henry had had a wild reputation in his youth, but the allegations made against him now smack more of propaganda than fact. Donizo, who gives details of Adelaide's rescue, draws a veil over these, saying he doesn't want his account to 'degenerate' by reciting them. He merely says that the empress came to fear her husband 'as the ewe lamb fears the teeth of the wolf'. Others, though, are not so reticent, describing orgies, the offering of Adelaide to other men, including Conrad, and even an attempt to celebrate a Black Mass on her naked body. In 1094, says Donizo, an appeal was made to Matilda for protection, and, despite the fact that Verona was in imperial hands, a company of soldiers was sent and forensically removed the empress, 'without the noise of battle'. As so many before her – archbishops, bishops, nobles, laymen and princes – she then found a warm welcome and shelter from her enemies with the countess.

It may well be in retaliation for this that, late that year, Henry tried once more to go on the offensive, putting under siege Matilda's castle at Nogara, near Mantua, which town he still held. Again, we don't know the size of the blockading force at his disposal, but we do know that the countess quickly learned of the siege, and just as quickly raised a force to relieve it. From Donizo's account it appears that, this time at least, Matilda herself led her men, and that their arrival by night at Nogara was enough to persuade Henry to abandon the siege instantly and withdraw his men in haste, leaving behind much of their equipment. He would never face Matilda again.

She had, of course, informed Pope Urban of the defection of the empress, and when he called a synod for March 1095, this would form part of the agenda. The synod was held at Piacenza, perhaps to emphasise that this was now safe territory for the reforming pope, having recently been strongly for the emperor. It was well attended, with figures suggesting over 4,000 churchmen of various ranks and some 30,000 laymen. It was held in the open air as there was no place large enough for so great an assembly. The empress was there, escorted by Matilda, and repeated the accusations she had earlier made against her husband. In this she was backed up by Conrad. Henry and 'Pope' Clement were then again formally condemned by Pope Urban, and Conrad recognised as the true king of Italy.

It was at this same synod that representatives of the Byzantine Emperor Alexius Comnenus first made an official request for help from the Western Church against the Seljuk Turks, who by now had overrun much of Anatolia. Urban had earlier made overtures of friendship to the Eastern Church, following the schism that had taken place in 1054, and he was clearly sympathetic as they emphasised the threat to Christendom as a whole, and the loss of access to the Holy Land, where, earlier, pilgrimages had been regularly undertaken. No decision was made at the time, but the pope now felt secure enough in Italy to embark on an extended tour of France. This would culminate in the Council at Clermont in November 1095, where a powerful sermon called on the West, and in particular the Franks, not only to aid the Byzantine Emperor, but to retake Jerusalem and the other Holy Places from their current rulers, who, Urban claimed, had 'laid waste God's kingdom'. The sermon was recorded by Fulcher of Chartres, among others, who would ride with the first campaign to the Holy Land and chronicle its progress. While noting the powerful response triggered by the sermon, he also describes the ongoing divisions in a church with two popes – and suggests one of Urban's motives was probably to unite Christians in fighting pagans, rather than each other.

It took some time for the Frankish army to assemble for this 'crusade' – a name only subsequently applied to the venture – and it was a year later when the pope and Matilda joined it at Lucca. Their first objective was to sweep down to Rome and definitively establish Urban in that city. The Roman supporters of Clement had been weakened by his absence with Henry, and though bribery had won over some of them, there was still resistance there to Pope Urban. Fulcher of Chartres, however, declares that now Urban was able to take control of all parts of the city associated with the papacy, 'with the help of a certain noble matron named Matilda, who was then powerful in the area'. Nonetheless, he claims the crusaders praying in St Peter's Basilica were on one occasion pelted with stones by some of Clement's supporters who had climbed into the roof.

By now Matilda was fifty years old and it seems surprising that some expected her to continue with the crusaders to Jerusalem. She may herself have considered this possibility. The situation in northern Italy was still unstable, however, as witness the attack on Nogara, and her presence was needed in the area more than ever as the political and matrimonial alliance with the Welfs, father and son, came to an end.

For the second marriage to break down in 1095 was that between Matilda and Welf the Fat. Her most devoted biographer, Donizo, ignores the marriage altogether so we have no clear information as to the cause of the split, nor, indeed, who left whom. By then Welf would have been in his mid-twenties and possibly no longer prepared to put up with this overbearing wife, who consistently seems to have relegated him to second place, particularly in the planning of campaigns and direction of forces. It may be, also, that Matilda's declared intention of handing over her lands to the papacy, rather than to her husband, meant the alliance was no longer a potential source of profit. Welf might even have wanted a younger wife who could give him children, though this idea is undermined by the fact that no application was made for a divorce or declaration of nullity, and Welf never married again. Living up to his byname 'the Fat', he is described by Archbishop Suger some ten years later as 'a corpulent man of amazing width and height and a loud voice'.

It seems more generally accepted that Matilda, as in all else, was the one that instigated the split. Possibly Welf was attempting to assert his traditional male role as ruler of his wife, and she refused to give up the independence she had possessed for decades past. It may simply be that, in this mis-matched, political marriage, she felt he had outlived his usefulness. Such a reading of the case would explain the abrupt about-face of Welf senior, who now opened negotiations with Henry with a view to reconciliation.

He, who not long before had supported Conrad and helped to bottle up the emperor in north-east Italy, now even gave up the demand that Henry should denounce 'Pope' Clement. The Brenner Pass was re-opened, and in return Welf was once more officially recognised as duke of Bavaria. Now, however, instead of calling up troops for a final onslaught on Matilda, Henry abandoned that fight and lost no time in returning to Germany. It was more than six years since he had last stood on his native soil.

The Investiture War in Italy was apparently over and the clear winner was Matilda of Tuscany. The emperor's repeated humiliations had also undermined his position at home. Alliances had to be re-made and steps taken to put right things that had gone awry. In 1098, Conrad was formally deposed as King of the Germans, and on 6 January 1099 his seventeen-year-old brother Henry was crowned in his place, he, too, swearing an oath that he would never seek to replace his father during his lifetime. Conrad retained the title King of the Romans until his death in July 1101, but by then his support had fallen away substantially. Like Welf, he had been useful in the struggle against the emperor, but with the immediate crisis over and Henry departed, he had played little further part in events.

Antipope Clement, too, had been reduced by the departure of his imperial supporter. Confined mainly to the area around Ravenna, he had been powerless to prevent Pope Urban from establishing himself in Rome. Urban's papacy came to an end, however, when he died on 29 July 1099, two weeks after the fall of Jerusalem to the crusaders, but ironically before news of that event reached Rome. Immediately, Clement mustered what forces he could gather and set out to try and regain his former glory. He got as far as Albano, some sixteen miles from Rome, before being repulsed by troops sent by Matilda and Roger of Sicily on behalf of the new pope, Paschal II, who had been elected and consecrated a mere two weeks after the death of his predecessor. The unifying zeal inspired by the success of the crusade would stand Paschal in good stead for many years, and this was the final end to Clement's dream of re-taking the papacy.

There were still pockets of imperial support resistant to reform, however, even within Rome. When Clement died in September 1100, some managed to enter St Peter's Basilica and elect a new Antipope, Theodoric, who lasted less than four months before being captured by Paschal's supporters and confined to a monastery. He was immediately replaced by another Antipope, Adalbert, who, after a similar amount of time, was handed over to Paschal following a bribe and similarly confined. Neither of these received the slightest support from the emperor himself. Nor was any fuss made when, after rumours of miracles occurring at the tomb of Clement, Paschal had his body exhumed and dumped in the River Tiber. It was not until 1105 that another antipope appeared. Then, dissatisfaction with Paschal's apparent favouring of certain Roman families led to the election of a worthy Roman priest who took the name Sylvester IV. After a number of violent street battles, he, too, was ejected from Rome and languished without imperial support until 1111, when the emperor briefly found a use for him. By that time, though, the empire had a new ruler.

At the end of 1104 the young Henry, crowned for nearly five years, grew tired of waiting for his father to die and abruptly deserted him, apparently for the reform party within Germany. His excuse was his father's repeated excommunication, and some suggest he had been influenced by reformers in the more rebellious regions. If so, this was a very temporary conversion, and it seems more probable it was simply a ploy aimed at winning substantial support. In 1105, he appealed to Pope Paschal to be absolved from his oath to his father, promising in exchange to support the pope and promote the church, even to the extent of abandoning investiture.

With Paschal's backing he quickly won the support of the Saxons and Swabians, and also that of Welf the Fat who had succeeded his father as Duke of Bavaria a few years before. By the end of the year the emperor was clearly losing ground to his son. A meeting was arranged with a view to a reconciliation, though it is not clear whether it was the father or the son who requested it. It was to take place at Mainz on 21 December 1105, but the younger

Henry intercepted his father on his way there the day before. In a letter to King Philip of France Henry IV describes how, when he saw his son, he was overcome by paternal affection and sorrow, and throwing himself at his feet, he begged him not to dishonour his name by taking up arms against his own father. With all appearances of contrition and regret, the younger Henry seemed completely reconciled, but, says his father, 'spurning all natural affection, he conspired against my life … and had no scruples in employing force and deception to achieve his ends.' The emperor was conducted to a nearby castle, since, apparently, the Archbishop of Mainz would not entertain an excommunicant within his city. There, it quickly became apparent that he was a prisoner, and on 31 December he was forced to abdicate in favour of his son. The new Henry V was duly crowned a few days later by the archbishop, who nonetheless delivered a warning that, if he did not prove to be a just leader for the empire and for the church within it, he would end like his father. In fact, the elder Henry managed to escape in February of that year, and was gathering support to fight his son when he fell ill, dying at Liège on 7 August 1106. 'Never in history,' says Donizo, 'was human pride and abuse of power … punished by more cruel degradation.'

The mood throughout the empire and beyond was generally one of relief. The new king of Germany and Italy was a young man in his early twenties. He had promised, and now repeated his promise, to be loyal to Paschal and to the church. It was a time, too, when solutions were being found to the problem of lay investiture. In England, for instance, Pope Paschal had recently given his blessing to an arrangement threshed out between King Henry I and his famously devout Archbishop Anselm. Hopes were high that a similar arrangement might finally put an end to the feud between the pope and the Holy Roman Empire.

After the turmoil of earlier times, the turn of the century was a relatively quiet period for Matilda, enabling her to begin to repair the damage done to her land and people. She is credited with founding, building or re-building some hundred churches throughout the area, many of them as stopping places for pilgrims on the way to

Rome, and many still in use serving local communities. Among the monasteries greatly enhanced by her contributions are those of San Benedetto Polirone near Mantua, and Donizo's own monastery of St. Apolonia at Canossa. The situation of her lands meant there was a constant stream of travellers passing through, from England, France and Germany, on the way to Rome. For many of them, including Archbishop Anselm on his journey to Rome in 1103, she provided an escort, his meeting with the 'famous Countess Matilda' being recorded by his companion and biographer Eadmer. Her relationship with the new pope was perhaps not as close as with Popes Gregory and Urban, but he had been a follower of Gregory VII and continued his reform policies, corresponding regularly with the countess and sending her Cardinal Bernard of Vallombrosa as a legate to Lombardy and personal counsellor.

At this time, an important project was the founding and support of a school of jurisprudence at Bologna, the earlier one at Ravenna having come under the jurisdiction of Clement. As head of her feudal lands Matilda had often presided over her own court, though latterly this duty had more and more been delegated to judges in the different towns, the countess merely giving approval to their judgements. The school at Bologna was intended to collect and promote the principles of Roman law, which were in danger of becoming lost or watered down by outside influences.

While this, then, was generally a time of peace and recovery, the years did not pass wholly without incident, particularly in formerly imperialist areas. It was only in 1101 that the town of Ferrera was finally returned to Matilda's rule, and the nomination of Bernard as Bishop of Parma in 1104 led initially to trouble. Some disparaging remarks he made about Henry IV and Antipope Clement in a sermon went down badly in the town that was Clement's birthplace, and which had earlier been staunchly imperial. According to Donizo, rioting ensued and the bishop was seized and imprisoned. The appearance of Matilda at the head of an army, however, quickly drew out envoys suing for pardon and peace, and, after some negotiations and the intercession of the bishop himself, order was restored.

By this time Matilda was approaching sixty years of age. She was once again the most powerful ruler in northern Italy, already la Gran Contessa, but she had no heir. There is some evidence that, for a time, she contemplated a young Florentine, Guido Guerra, inheriting her title, but a stronger though equally contentious case can be made out that she intended everything to go to the papacy.

A charter dated 17 November 1102 purports to confirm an earlier gift to the papacy made at the time when Gregory VII was pope, the charter for which had been lost. In this new charter, for the removal of all doubt, Matilda donates to the papacy all her goods and property, held now or to be acquired in the future, whether acquired by hereditary right or otherwise, both in Italy and on the other side of the Alps in Lorraine. The gift, she says, is made for the benefit of her own soul and the souls of her deceased parents, and the charter is signed in the manner commonly employed by the countess, 'Matilda, by the grace of God, if she is anything.'

There is, indeed, no record of an earlier charter, if one ever existed, though if it did it would add another reason for the furious attacks on Matilda by Henry IV, since many of the lands she seemed to be giving away would have been imperial fiefs, and not hers to dispose of. It has also been argued that the 1102 charter itself, existing only in the form of a copy, was a later forgery, made at the time the papacy was disputing ownership of her lands with the empire. In favour of this it must be said that, from the date of the earlier claimed gift even up to her death, Matilda continued to treat the lands in question as if they were still wholly hers to enjoy and to deal with. An alternative suggestion is that the charter was made at this time, and specifically refers to an earlier purported gift in order to prevent her estranged husband Welf – now supporting the emperor against the reform party – from claiming any part of her extensive domain. Whatever the truth of the matter, it seems clear that events a few years down the line brought about a change of heart in the countess, and, whether or not the charter was specifically revoked, an entirely different disposition of her property.

For the first few years of the reign of Henry V, while he secured his position in Germany, it seemed that peace might finally be achieved between empire and papacy. The potential for further conflict soon appeared, however. Henry's aim, of course, was to be crowned by the pope as Holy Roman Emperor, while Paschal was determined his earlier promises of loyalty should be turned into reality. It soon became apparent, though, that Henry needed the right of lay investiture just as much as his father had, and, taking advantage of the pope's apparent willingness to negotiate, he continued the practice, despite a number of warnings. He seemed to believe that as long as they continued exchanging envoys, he could behave with impunity. In the end, though, when Paschal made it clear there would be no coronation until the practice ended, Henry set out in person for Rome in the summer of 1110.

He had recently become formally betrothed to the eight-year-old daughter of Henry I of England, who had himself negotiated a settlement of the Investiture Controversy for his kingdom. The young bride had brought with her a large dowry, and with this money the German Henry had equipped an army of some 30,000 men to accompany him to Italy, believing such a show of force might 'persuade' the pope to be more flexible in his negotiations.

It was presumably as part of this show of force that any sign of opposition along the way was ruthlessly crushed, including at Matilda's castle of Nogara. Nor did the army refrain from acting as armies did at the time, taking what they needed from the surrounding land and trampling anything in their way. One account, though, declares that Henry avoided damaging Matilda's cultivated land. He was, no doubt, aware of the benefits to be gained from her goodwill.

In view of the assault on her castle, it seems surprising that Matilda made no attempt to hinder Henry's passage. Some have put this down to her advancing years and a wish to avoid further conflict. She had, after all, spent some twenty years fighting the young man's father. Alternatively, she may, like many others, have simply decided to remain neutral, awaiting the outcome of the meeting between king and pope. She had been encouraging a reconciliation, and when she met Henry at Bianello in November 1110, may have seen enough in his demeanour to make her believe it was imminent.

Initially it seemed she was right, although the abbot and chronicler Suger who was contemporary with these events declares Henry was only pretending when he proclaimed peaceful intentions, and that he made all sorts of promises, not fearing to deceive the pope, the whole church or, indeed, God himself. In February 1111, Pope Paschal and Henry V announced they had come to an agreement that satisfied both of them. Henry would give up the right to lay investiture, and in return all the lands previously given by the empire to the church would be returned to him. To an outside view, if they were dealing honestly this no doubt seemed eminently reasonable. It was, after all, these lands which gave power and wealth to the church leaders, who thus had to be under imperial control.

What was not taken into account, however, was the fury of the German bishops and archbishops who were about to be stripped of their temporal powers. When the terms were read out to them in Rome, on the occasion which should have seen the crowning of the emperor, chaos ensued. The ceremony was abruptly cancelled, whereupon Henry renounced the agreement and seizing the pope, numerous cardinals and others, carried them off to imprisonment in fortresses outside Rome.

In earlier times we might have expected Matilda to intervene once again to rescue Paschal. Now, however, the only move she made was to send a request for two of her own bishops, those of Reggio and Parma, to be released, which request was immediately complied with. Possibly she had heard that Robert, Prince of Capua, was mounting a rescue attempt with three hundred knights. This was turned back short of its objective, however, and Paschal and his companions remained imprisoned.

Nor was it a gentle imprisonment. The elderly pope himself was roughly treated, and by one account became so ill his fellow prisoners feared for his life and urged him to concede whatever Henry demanded. At the end of two months, he gave in. On 12 April 1111 Paschal announced the granting of a 'privilege' to

Henry, allowing him to continue lay investiture throughout his empire. He also took an oath never to excommunicate him, or take any other action against him in reprisal for his recent treatment. The following day Henry was duly crowned Holy Roman Emperor.

Once again there was an outcry. Some were outraged at Henry's use of force against the pope, others that Paschal had given in so quickly and so completely. It may have been that Matilda fell into the latter camp. Certainly, when Henry left Rome shortly afterwards, he was received as a guest at Canossa and remained there a full three days before travelling on to Germany.

What they actually discussed in that time we don't know, since they apparently discoursed in private. Donizo tells us they came to a firm agreement, but not what it comprised, other than that Matilda was named 'Imperial Vicar and Viceregent of Italy', possibly in gratitude for her apparent acceptance of Henry's new arrangement with the pope. It has also been speculated that, at this time, she made Henry heir to her lands. He certainly seemed to believe that was the case when he claimed them later.

Whatever Matilda's reasons for her pact with Henry – possibly she felt she could be a channel for more peaceful exchanges between empire and papacy – she kept out of the furore that blew up concerning the emperor's 'privilege'. Almost at once this had been denounced by Archbishop Guy of Vienne, later to be pope himself, and it was condemned and declared void by a Lateran Council the following year. Paschal himself accepted this verdict and effectively withdrew the claimed 'privilege'.

By this time well into her sixties, however, Matilda was becoming increasingly ill and frail. To a large extent the love and loyalty of her vassals enabled her to administer her extensive lands in peace. There is no doubt, though, that her formidable reputation helped. When, in the summer of 1114, rumours reached Mantua that she had died, this still rebellious city rose up and claimed an independence that had been promised by Henry IV many years before. Even before this time it had caused problems, harassing Matilda's vassals and interrupting navigation on the nearby River Po.

Matilda had indeed been seriously ill that year, but news of the Mantuan revolt seemed to revive in her the spirit of the Matilda of old. Rising almost from her sickbed, she is said to have declared, 'The time has come for Mantua to perish.' Summoning a sizeable army, she herself led it towards the city, intending to place it under siege. Once again, her reputation preceded her, and, discovering the countess was still very much alive, the Mantuans were quick to sue for peace. Amid pledges of future loyalty, she was eventually welcomed into the city at the end of October, thereafter travelling to her favourite monastery, the nearby San Benedetto Polirone, to give thanks.

It was her last campaign. Through the following spring and summer, her longstanding illness steadily weakened her, and she finally passed peacefully away on 24 July 1115. According to Donizo, her last words as she kissed a crucifix were, 'Oh Lord Christ whom I have served so well, serve me now.' She was buried, much to Donizo's disappointment, not at Canossa but at San Benedetto, where a handsome tomb was erected for her, though this was not to be her last resting place.

After her death her legend lived on down the centuries. She is believed by many to have been the inspiration for 'Matelda', the flower girl in Dante's *Divine Comedy*, who leads the author from Purgatory to Paradise. This depiction in turn inspired the great painters of the Renaissance, Botticelli, Da Vinci and Michelangelo. In the opening of Condivi's contemporary biography of Michelangelo, the great artist even claims descent from the counts of Canossa, and the 'memorable deeds' done by Matilda in her lifetime are duly acknowledged.

At the time of the Counter-Reformation in the sixteenth century, when the Catholic Church began to fight back against the Protestant Reformation begun in Germany with Martin Luther, Matilda once again became a figurehead for those supporting the papacy. Her role in the humiliation of Emperor Henry IV at Canossa was first depicted in paintings, and then, in 1633, Pope Urban VIII himself paid for her remains to be brought to Rome. At first they rested in Castel Sant'Angelo, while a magnificent tomb commissioned by the pope was prepared for her by Bernini in S. Peter's Basilica itself. In 1645 she was re-interred in this new tomb, the first monument ever erected in St Peter's for a person who was neither a saint or a pope. She was, said Pope Urban, an illustration of how princes may protect and support the Holy See, and, no doubt, he hoped she would serve as an inspiration to others.

Honoured in her own land, Matilda has been largely forgotten elsewhere, even by those who still refer to a 'Walk to Canossa' as a symbol of humiliation. In her own time, she was called everything from whore to heroine. What is clear, though, is that she was a woman of singular determination, utterly devoted to the support of the papacy and the very necessary reform of the church, and with considerable skills of administration and command. In times of war, she was, almost alone, true to the cause she believed in, marshalling armies, directing battles and sieges, fortifying castles and laying down intelligence networks, and all with a flair and degree of success equalling, if not excelling, any other commander of her time. She provided sanctuary to the victims of war and a rallying point for all, on both sides of the Alps, who believed in the need for reform. Moreover, in times of peace she was a builder, a patron of arts, a sponsor of learning and a generous benefactor to causes of all kinds.

She was undoubtedly a strong woman, probably a stubborn woman, but, according to Donizo at least, with a 'graciousness which endeared her to everyone'. Above all, though, she was without doubt the most influential woman of her time. The figure sculpted by Bernini that stands atop the tomb in St Peter's remains defiant to the end, guarding the papal tiara and key which she carries. Beneath, the inscription describes her as 'a woman with a man's soul' and 'a champion of the Apostolic See', but perhaps the inscription on her original tomb at San Benedetto comes closest to the truth, describing her simply as 'invincible'.

3

Matilda the Queen and Matilda the Empress

The year 1125 was a significant one for two young women named Matilda. In that year one became a wife and the other a widow. Of the two, Matilda of Boulogne, the new bride, had had the more peaceful existence up to that point. By contrast, the English Matilda, daughter of King Henry I, though only a few years older, was already an empress, much travelled and with considerable experience of tangled international affairs. They were first cousins through their mothers, but they would probably never have met each other, and, though they wouldn't have known it at the time, their futures were to become inextricably linked.

As is often the case with women of the time, we have no precise date for the birth of Matilda of Boulogne. Estimates vary from 1105 to as late as 1113, though the latter is less likely. Reasonable probability would put it between 1105 and 1110. She was the first, and, in the event, the only child of Eustace III, Count of Boulogne, and Mary of Scotland, sister of Queen Edith/Matilda of England. As such she was nobly descended on both sides. On her father's side she could claim descent from Charlemagne, while her maternal grandmother, Margaret of Scotland, was already venerated as a saint, although her actual canonisation would come later. Margaret, in turn, was the granddaughter of Edmund Ironside, briefly king of England, and a link to the old royal house of Wessex.

Nor was the glory all in the distant past. The father of Eustace had fought for William the Conqueror at the battle of Hastings and had later been rewarded with substantial lands in England, known as the Honour of Boulogne. Eustace himself had been a crusader, answering the call of Pope Urban at Clermont and travelling to the east with his younger brothers Godfrey of Bouillon and Baldwin. *Their* mother was the sister of Godfrey the Hunchback, and thus, briefly at least, sister-in-law of Matilda of Tuscany. The presence of Godfrey of Bouillon with the crusading army was thus an additional reason for the Tuscan Countess not joining them on the road to Jerusalem, especially as the Emperor Henry IV had given him her county of Verdun, and other of her lands in Lorraine.

After distinguishing himself at the sieges of Antioch and Jerusalem, and at the battle of Ascalon that followed, Eustace had returned home leaving both brothers behind, Baldwin as Count of Edessa and Godfrey as 'Defender of the Holy Sepulchre', effectively king of Jerusalem. It was after this that Eustace married Mary of Scotland, a marriage at least partly engineered by her sister Edith, following her own recent marriage to King Henry I of England. Eustace was by then in his early forties at least and Mary around twenty, a situation that was not unusual at the time. With his illustrious forebears and siblings, no doubt Eustace hoped for a male heir to carry on his line, and he was probably disappointed by the arrival of Matilda, particularly when it later appeared she would be his only child. As such, however, she would become a most desirable heiress.

A similar disappointment was probably the initial reaction of Henry I of England when his own daughter Matilda was born in February 1102. Even more than Eustace, he needed a male heir. He had had the crown of England for barely eighteen months, following the death of his older brother William Rufus. That death, though apparently a hunting accident, would later be claimed as murder, with Henry pencilled in as the organiser, if not the actual perpetrator. It certainly fell very conveniently for him, as his eldest brother, Robert Curthose, was even then on his way back from the crusade, covered in glory and with a new and wealthy wife. Well before Robert reached his duchy of Normandy, however, Henry had been crowned and anointed King of England, and Robert's rather feeble challenge for the throne in July 1101 was bought off with the promise of a pension of 3,000 marks a year. Nonetheless, the birth of a male heir would have helped secure Henry's position.

Though he himself had been born in England, and his wife Edith, now known as Matilda, represented the old line of Wessex kings, the Norman Conquest and its bloody aftermath was still within living memory, and the promise of a smooth succession uniting old and new bloodlines would have greatly enhanced his situation. As it was, he would have to wait more than a year for a son, christened William. Within that time Robert, too, would have a son, also christened William and known as 'Clito', or 'throneworthy'. The fact that both boys were named after their grandfather the Conqueror was a clear statement of intent, and the battle for the English throne would continue until, in 1106, at the battle of Tinchebrai in Normandy, Robert was decisively defeated and taken prisoner. He would remain in comfortable confinement in various strongholds of his brother for the rest of his life, though young William Clito was allowed to remain free, a concession Henry would come to regret.

While all this was happening, there was, of course, no mention of Matilda in the English chronicles, girls only entering the record when the question of their marriages arose. For Matilda this occurred when she was only six years old. Late in 1108, Henry V, King of Germany and Italy, having disposed of his father two years before, was casting around for a wife who would bring him sufficient wealth to make him secure in those lands, and to enable him to put pressure on Pope Paschal to crown him Holy Roman Emperor. Henry of England, with the resources of England and Normandy at his disposal, was a wealthy man with an eminently eligible daughter. True, she was still a child, but heirs were not a pressing issue for the German king in his early twenties, while money was.

Initial negotiations were begun in 1108, with the English king prepared to offer a dowry of 10,000 silver marks with his daughter, gaining in return the prestige of becoming father-in-law to the Holy

Roman Emperor. For the German Henry there was an additional incentive to make this match. Already at loggerheads with the pope over lay investitures, he could point to the settlement of the issue recently made with the English king as a model for his own case, and especially so if he was married to that king's daughter.

The contemporary chronicler Henry of Huntingdon declares that the English court held by Henry I at Whitsuntide 1109, was one of 'extraordinary magnificence'. No doubt the intention was to impress the envoys sent by the German king. These were 'remarkable for their great stature and splendid attire' and came 'demanding the king's daughter in marriage for their master'. It would not, of course, have been expressed as bluntly as that, and clearly the details had already been worked out. Now, though, the betrothal was formally agreed and oaths were sworn on both sides.

Matilda herself would not have been present at court, but a few months later the royal child appeared with her parents at a council at Nottingham, and by the New Year all was ready for her departure to Germany. In the interim the vast dowry had been accumulated, causing the *Anglo-Saxon Chronicle* to complain about the distress felt through the country 'from the taxes which the king raised for his daughter's dowry'. Then in February 1110, a few days after her eighth birthday, 'the king sent his daughter with manifold treasures over the sea, and gave her to the emperor.' Thus it was Matilda of England who became the child-bride of Henry V of Germany, and it was her dowry that paid for his expedition to Rome later that year, which, to his ultimate satisfaction, resulted in him being crowned by the pope, albeit after his scandalous kidnapping of the pontiff.

Matilda, of course, was far too young to be legally married at once, but having met her future husband for the first time at Liège, the pair then exchanged betrothal promises in person at Utrecht on 10 April 1110. Three months of progress around the country followed. Then, on 25 July, Matilda was formally anointed and crowned Queen of the Germans and Romans at Mainz. The ceremony would have been an ordeal for the eight-year-old, who, in her formal robes, was carried throughout by Archbishop Bruno of Trier. The majority of the attendants who had accompanied her from England had already been dismissed with generous gifts and sent home, the intention being that she should grow up surrounded by the language, customs and culture of the land which was to be her future home. After the coronation, therefore, she was handed over into the care of Archbishop Bruno who would be responsible for her upbringing for the next few years.

Returning from his adventures in Rome the following year, Henry may have been misled by his pleasant sojourn with Matilda of Tuscany into thinking all would now be well in his realm. If so, he was quickly disillusioned. The so-called 'Privilege' of investiture, granted under duress by Pope Paschal, was immediately denounced by the church, with protests led by Archbishop Guy of Vienne. Once again, clergy and princes in Germany split on religious lines, some supporting the pope and some the emperor. In March 1112, Paschal confirmed the findings of a Lateran synod that the Privilege was indeed invalid, though he held back from pronouncing Henry excommunicated. This was enough, however, to cause the emperor's long-time chancellor and advisor, Archbishop Adalbert of Mainz, to split from the imperial party. He was promptly accused of stirring up rebellion and plotting against the emperor's life and was imprisoned.

In the midst of all this turmoil, on 7 January 1114 Matilda was finally married to the Emperor Henry V. He was thirty-two and she still a month short of her twelfth birthday. The wedding was a lavish affair, attended by countless archbishops, bishops, dukes, abbots and lesser nobles and clergy. It was probably intended to be a unifying event but in fact had the opposite effect. Hardly was it over before the rumbling unrest turned into violent rebellion.

In a little over a year, defeat in two battles and the defection of Archbishop Frederick of Cologne led to the complete loss of Saxony and the release of Adalbert, while in the spring of 1115 Frederick's formal pronouncement of the pope's sentence of excommunication on Henry paved the way for further revolts. Very few, chiefly Swabians and Bavarians, were now attending the emperor's courts, and though a reconciliation of sorts was then achieved, it was clear that only a proper settlement with the pope was going to bring about peace in Henry's troubled lands. Thus, at Christmas 1115, Henry, Matilda and his reduced court celebrated the feast at Speyer, while Adalbert and his more numerous supporters met at Mainz, a clear illustration of the continuing breach between them. The death of Matilda of Tuscany some months before, however, had now given Henry the perfect excuse for a return to Italy.

In his eagerness to secure the lands which he claimed the countess had willed to him, the emperor and his wife travelled to Augsburg early in the New Year, crossed the Brenner Pass as soon as it was possible to do so, and reached Italy in March 1116. It was Matilda's first and only visit to the country, but she was destined to spend some time there. The forces accompanying the royal couple were considerably fewer than on Henry's previous visit, but, whatever the actual intentions of Countess Matilda, he had little difficulty in obtaining possession of her lands, while at Canossa the new young Matilda was warmly welcomed in place of her namesake.

A year was then spent consolidating the imperial hold on northern Italy, with popularity bought, in the towns especially, by the granting of privileges. In view of the ongoing troubles north of the Alps, Henry was determined to have a secure power base to the south. When he finally set out for Rome in March 1117, his forces were considerably supplemented by men from this area.

He claimed he wished only to negotiate with the pope, but Paschal was not prepared to undergo another of Henry's 'negotiations'. As a parting shot the emperor was excommunicated all over again, then Paschal fled to Monte Cassino, sending the Archbishop of Braga, Maurice Bourdin, to speak to Henry on his behalf. Bourdin is described by the contemporary chronicler William of Malmesbury as 'a man whom anyone might highly reverence,' except, apparently, for his boundless ambition, '... nor would he have hesitated to purchase the holy see, if he could have found as desperate a seller as he was a buyer.' Henry seems to have read his man very well. We cannot know what he offered him, but it was clearly enough. Within a very short time Bourdin had switched sides.

Though the way to St Peter's was blocked by Paschal's supporters holding Castel Sant' Angelo, at Easter 1117 the royal husband and wife, together with their tame papal legate, crossed the Tiber by boat. Then, on 23 March, Easter Sunday, Henry and Matilda were crowned emperor and empress by Archbishop Bourdin. Henry, of course, had been previously crowned by Pope Paschal, and Matilda had been anointed and crowned as queen, but this was almost certainly the only occasion on which she was crowned as empress. Perhaps she didn't know that the coronation should have been performed by a reigning pope to make it 'official', or perhaps she felt it came within the powers of a papal legate. Perhaps she didn't care. Whatever the truth of the matter, she immediately adopted the title 'Empress' and clung to it for the rest of her life.

The withdrawal of Henry and Matilda to northern Italy allowed Paschal to return, and Bourdin was promptly excommunicated. The emperor still seemed keen to negotiate a proper settlement, but before any progress could be made Paschal died on 21 January 1118, thus paving the way for further divisions. Within days a successor was elected, taking the name Gelasius II. He was a former monk of Monte Cassino and had already given sterling service in reforming the administrative work of the papacy. He had no time to settle in, though, before, in his own words, 'the sovereign emperor, coming by stealth and with unexpected haste to Rome, compelled us to depart the city.' Henry was coming again to 'negotiate', but Gelasius was having none of it. The emperor, he said, 'demanded peace by threats and intimidation', and, when he found the pope would not comply, 'intruded into the bosom of the church, the bishop of Braga'. Bourdin, indeed, was now to be Pope Gregory VIII, at least according to the Holy Roman Emperor, who declared the election of Gelasius invalid. As a result, both he and his 'Antipope' were immediately excommunicated, and far from settling the unrest in Germany, it now became considerably worse.

Matters became so pressing that Henry was forced to return to Germany. Matilda, however, still less than seventeen years old, was left behind in Italy to act as regent for her husband. With the aid of a chancellor she seems to have filled the role admirably. For more than a year she held courts, gave rulings and administered the territories under her control to the apparent satisfaction of all concerned. William of Malmesbury, writing a little later in England, declares she 'resembled her father in fortitude and her mother in sanctity ... nor was it easy to discern which of her good qualities was most commendable.' He was, of course, writing to please her half-brother at a time when Matilda was striving for even greater glory.

By the time she re-joined her husband late in 1119, matters in Germany had become more stable. There was, too, a new pope following the death of Gelasius. The election of Archbishop Guy of Vienne as Callixtus II might have been calculated to challenge the emperor. He was, after all, the orchestrator of outrage concerning Henry's so-called 'Privilege'. In the event, though, he proved more than ready to negotiate, and the matter might have been settled at a council held at Rheims in October 1119 but for the emperor's blundering. The chronicler Orderic Vitalis must have been there, for he writes, 'In fact we found that the emperor had come to the place of meeting with a great army, and as if he was about to fight a battle.' Callixtus promptly left, and 'with grief', pronounced a renewed sentence of excommunication against Henry and his 'Antipope'.

It seemed clear to all, however, that it would only be a matter of time before a settlement *was* reached. Henry had already withdrawn his support from Gregory VIII, who was then rapidly turned out of Rome, pursued to Sutri and taken prisoner. The ambitious Maurice Bourdin would spend the rest of his life in a monastery known as 'The Den', a virtual prison for recalcitrant clerics. It took several more years, however, for the investiture dispute to be finally brought to an end by the Concordat of Worms, a compromise similar to that achieved by Henry I of England, which was eventually agreed between pope and emperor in September 1122.

The youth of Matilda and the long separations from her husband had given little opportunity for producing the necessary heir, a matter which now assumed some importance. By this time Henry had turned forty, and though Matilda was still young, it seemed imperative that a son and heir should be born soon. The German princes had always insisted that kingship was an elected rather than an hereditary position, and though Henry was the fourth of his line, without a direct male heir there was every chance he would be the last. Still, though, no child was born to the imperial couple.

In England Henry I had a similar problem. His only legitimate son, Matilda's brother William, had drowned in a shipwreck off the coast of Normandy in November 1120. The king, a widower, had quickly married again, Adeliza of Louvain being his young bride, but by now he was in his fifties, and though he had a number of illegitimate sons, there was no sign of a new legitimate heir. To make matters worse, William Clito, the son of his brother Robert Curthose, was now a grown man and laying claim to Normandy at least, if not to England as well. There had already been one rebellion in that duchy in favour of Clito, which had been backed by King Louis VI of France. While diplomacy had robbed them of allies, it was Henry's success at the Battle of Brémule in 1119 which ended the conflict, albeit only for a time.

It was diplomacy, too, that had won for Henry papal acceptance of his rule in Normandy, following the Council at Rheims in that same year, and he may well have felt scorn for his son-in-law the emperor, who had so damaged his own chances at that time. After the drowning of his heir, however, some of Henry's diplomatic achievements began to unravel. He had gained the support of the powerful Fulk of Anjou, for example, by arranging for his son William to marry Fulk's eldest daughter. The County of Maine was her dowry, along with a number of important castles on the Norman borders, which Henry immediately garrisoned with his own men. When she became a widow soon afterwards, Henry was happy to return her to her father, but flatly refused to return her dowry. Fulk promptly married a second daughter to William Clito, and it took Henry a considerable amount of money and argument to persuade the church to annul the marriage on the grounds they were too closely related – ignoring the fact that the relationship was exactly the same as in his own son's marriage.

Had Empress Matilda produced a son he would certainly have been claimed as heir to England as well as to the German empire. Failing that, Henry's closest male relatives were his nephews, William Clito, whom he would never have acknowledged as heir, and the sons of his sister Adela of Blois, William, Theobald, Stephen and Henry. Adela had been a widow since 1102 when her husband Stephen Henry of Blois had been killed in the Holy Land. Since then she had been administering the county of Blois and the family's other lands, first as regent for her son William, and later, when for some reason William was deemed unsuitable, for Theobald.

Adela was Henry's favourite sister, and, with far more resources than she, it is likely he undertook to help advance the prospects of her sons wherever he could. William had already been set aside, Henry had entered the abbey at Cluny as a child oblate, and Theobald was clearly going to inherit his father's lands. So it was Stephen that came to Henry's court, probably around 1110, to join a group of young men – including David of Scotland, younger brother of King Alexander of Scotland – who all hoped to win the king's favour and gain advancement. Stephen was probably in his mid-teens at the time, and over the next few years would be knighted by Henry, given the title and Norman lands of the Count of Mortain, and a little later, a major landholding in England comprising the Honour of Eye and the Honour of Lancaster.

This generosity to his nephew has led some to believe Henry was marking down Stephen as a future heir. It should be remembered, though, that all this took place before 1120, at a time when Henry had an heir of his own, and that these honours were as much to Henry's advantage as Stephen's. Mortain was on the southern borders of Normandy, and its possession by Stephen would encourage him and his brother Theobald to guard it against their unruly neighbour, Fulk of Anjou. Similarly, having two of the major Honours in England in the hands of a friendly nephew would prevent any challenge to the king from an over-mighty noble outside the family.

A major landowner, and one with royal connections, must, of course, have a suitable wife, and there is some suggestion that it was around this time that Stephen was betrothed to Matilda of Boulogne. Once again, it is likely Henry had a hand in this. Boulogne had long been an ally and was well placed both for the promotion of the increasingly important English wool trade, and as a check on its neighbour Flanders, which regularly allied with the king of France. There was no question of an immediate marriage, of course, as Matilda would have been at most ten years old and was probably much younger.

As well as his nephews Henry had a number of illegitimate sons, the eldest of whom, known as Robert of Caen, had fought alongside his father at the battle of Brémule. At that time he was around thirty years old and, having married the foremost heiress in England, was a significant landowner in the Welsh Marches, with a son of his own. It is possible Henry considered making him his heir after the catastrophe in 1120. His own father, the Conqueror, had, after all, been illegitimate. In the end, though, he decided against, and making Robert earl of Gloucester a year or two later was less a step towards the throne than a putting in place of a reliable protector for any heir that might then be produced by his new wife or his daughter the empress.

Perhaps in expectation that a son of his might later become king of England, Emperor Henry clearly grew more supportive of his English namesake in the early 1120s. There is evidence, too, that Empress Matilda tried to visit her father at this time but was not permitted to cross hostile Flanders in order to do so. In 1124, a German army threatening France prevented the French king from supporting a rebellion in Normandy, which his English counterpart was then able to crush. This was to be the last campaign of Emperor Henry V, however. He was probably already suffering from the cancer that would kill him, and though he held on until the spring of 1125, it was now fairly clear that there would be no heir in Germany, either for the emperor or the English king.

Early in 1125, with the blessing of King Henry of England, Stephen of Blois, Count of Mortain, married Matilda of Boulogne.

Immediately afterwards, her father, Eustace, now in his seventies, abdicated and retired to a monastery. Thereafter, Stephen and Matilda ruled jointly as count and countess of Boulogne, a situation Eustace confirmed a little later, saying 'I gave my patrimony with Matilda, my daughter.' Before the end of that year he, too, would be dead.

The marriage, although arranged for political purposes, would become a strong and loving one, a true partnership indeed. Stephen was universally recorded as handsome, athletic, good-hearted and generous, though with an indecisive streak and given to occasional acts of recklessness. Matilda was calm, level-headed, diplomatic but determined, making up in decisiveness what her husband lacked. It seems fairly clear that she was the cleverer of the two, and that Stephen came to rely on her completely for advice and encouragement. Both had been brought up to be pious, were well-educated and appreciative of the arts, and Stephen in particular had had his strong, capable mother as an example of women's ability to take a full part in the affairs of the world.

There was, of course, an age difference which must have been at least ten years and may have been as much as fifteen. We can't know how old Matilda was when she married, and nor are the births of their children any guide since only two can be dated with any accuracy. Her daughter Marie is variously claimed to be the first or the last child, born as early as 1126 or as late as 1136. At least one and probably two sons were born before 1131, followed by a daughter, Matilda, around 1133, and a son, William, late in 1135 or early 1136.

Again, the marriage and the extent of their joint lands in England have prompted some to see Stephen as a natural heir to Henry. It seems unlikely, however, that they had any such pretensions at the time. If Henry was looking to nephews, Theobald of Blois was the elder brother, and perhaps it is significant that when his eldest son was born in December 1127, he named him Henry. By contrast, the first two sons of Stephen and Matilda were named Eustace and Baldwin, both strongly connected to the County of Boulogne, and with no precedent in England.

Within a few weeks of Matilda of Boulogne becoming a wife, her namesake in Germany became a widow. The Holy Roman Emperor Henry V died at Utrecht on 23 May 1125 and, according to the contemporary Orderic Vitalis, 'On his deathbed he bequeathed the emblems of imperial power to the Empress Matilda.' It is extremely unlikely he meant to imply she should take actual power in the empire. Without a son she had no claim even to a regency role. More likely he meant her to hold the regalia until his heir was duly elected, maybe hoping she could use her diplomatic skills to ensure the choice would fall on his preferred candidate, his nephew Frederick of Swabia. Even in that, however, he was thwarted. His long-time opponent Adalbert, Archbishop of Mainz, by some means persuaded Matilda to part with the regalia, and then convinced the very willing German princes that the election was wholly in their hands. In the event, Lothair of Saxony was elected, the man who had led the rebel army that had defeated Henry in 1115. The victory of the emperor's enemies seemed complete.

In that atmosphere there was no place for Matilda, though, according to Robert Torigny writing a little later, 'The people of (Germany) wished to keep her among them.' Matilda herself was reluctant to leave. The German empire was all she had known from childhood upwards, and she had enjoyed wealth, prestige and power for more than a decade. There was one, though, who viewed her widowhood at the age of twenty-three as nothing less than a heaven-sent opportunity – her father, Henry of England.

William of Malmesbury says Henry 'recalled' his daughter. Without husband or son, he was once again her natural guardian in the eyes of that age, and though she came reluctantly, come she did, first to Normandy to meet her father and then, in September 1126, to the England she had not seen for sixteen years. She brought with her only her own jewels and regalia, two crowns and a precious relic, allegedly the hand of the Apostle James, which had been part of the German Imperial Treasury and would now be transferred to Reading Abbey, founded by her father.

In England she was virtually a stranger, but Henry didn't wait long before unveiling his plans for the future. Malmesbury claims these were the result of 'long continued deliberation'. Immediately after his Christmas court, at a fully attended council held in January 1127 he announced that Matilda was to be his heir, and furthermore that he required all present, clergy and laity alike, to swear an oath that they would accept her as sovereign. Both William of Malmesbury and John of Worcester give full accounts of this occasion, though the accounts differ slightly as to the oath sworn and its importance. Malmesbury makes the oath conditional. Matilda is to be heir only if Henry produces no legitimate male heir of his own, an event becoming increasingly unlikely. He also describes how Henry's chief minister at the time, Roger, bishop of Salisbury, though clearly disapproving of the whole plan, had to read out the oath, justify it by reference to Matilda's lineage on both sides, and then administer it to everyone present. There was, he claims, a 'singular dispute' between Robert, Earl of Gloucester, the king's natural son, and Stephen, Count of Boulogne, his nephew, as to which had precedence in taking the oath. In the end, he says, Robert deferred to Stephen who went first, followed by all the nobility in order of rank.

According to John of Worcester, the succession was only one of many matters discussed at the council and he gives it far less emphasis. He suggests it was put forward as 'the king's wish' that Matilda should succeed him, 'with her lawful husband, if she had one', that this was discussed and that all then agreed and swore the oath the king required. Unlike Malmesbury, he does not suggest they were 'compelled' to take the oath, or, like the *Anglo-Saxon Chronicle*, that they were 'caused' to do so. He, too, reports a dispute between Robert and Stephen but puts a very different gloss on it. According to John they were competing, not to be first but to be last, with Robert declaring that Stephen 'should do this first' as he was 'sitting at the king's right hand'.

There is enough similarity between the accounts, however, for us to be sure that, whether compelled or consenting, eager or reluctant – and there were probably some of each – all who were considered 'persons of note' within the kingdom swore an oath in January 1127 to accept Matilda as heir. The only woman recorded as an oath-taker was Henry's new wife, Queen Adeliza. We cannot know, therefore, if Matilda of Boulogne was present on this occasion, or, indeed, if she and the empress ever met. If, as has been suggested, her son Eustace was born about this time, it is possible she had remained in Boulogne.

Whether Henry felt any measure of security after this oath-swearing is not clear, but it had consequences that, perhaps, he had not foreseen. For several years Louis VI of France had taken no interest at all in the affairs of William Clito, possibly thinking Henry might, in the end, be forced to acknowledge him as his heir. Now, however, he took up the young man's cause with energy and determination. In a very short time Clito was married to Joanna de Montferrat, the half-sister of Louis's own queen, and set up with lands along the border with Normandy, including Pontoise, Mantes and 'all the Vexin' – a territory long disputed between France and Normandy – if he could get it. A few months later, following the assassination of Charles the Good of Flanders in March 1127, Louis inserted Clito as Count of Flanders, overriding the claims of the other possible candidates, William of Ypres and Thierry of Alsace. Now for the first time the young man had a power base and resources of his own, and, with sympathetic Norman lords flocking to join him, posed a real threat not only to neighbouring Boulogne, but also to Henry's control of Normandy itself.

Through the early part of 1127 the English king's main pre-occupation seems to have been arranging a marriage for his new heir, Matilda. Only John of Worcester had mentioned that she might have a husband when she inherited the kingdom, but the idea of a woman ruling without one would have been seen as a dangerous innovation at the time. On the other hand, a great deal might depend on who that husband was to be. Roger of Salisbury later claimed he had only sworn the oath accepting Matilda as heir on the understanding that he and the nobility would be consulted on the matter, and that their consent would be a prerequisite. In the event, Henry seems to have consulted nobody but himself.

His purely political aim was to renew the alliance with Fulk of Anjou, which had been so disastrously lost following the death of his son. Anjou was a powerful state that, although theoretically subject to the overlordship of France, had shown considerable independence in recent wars, sometimes supporting Louis and William Clito, and sometimes providing the momentum to turn matters in favour of Henry. It might be thought that the relationship between the two leaders was irretrievably broken down, but following a visit to the Holy Land some years before, Fulk had now received a proposal that made him receptive to Henry's overtures of peace. Baldwin II, King of Jerusalem, now in his mid-fifties, intended his daughter Melisende to be his heir. Like Henry, he believed she would need a suitably powerful husband to support her in this role, and, having been impressed by Fulk on his earlier visit, he now suggested the count would be the perfect candidate. As negotiations with Baldwin progressed, Fulk became anxious to secure an equally strong alliance for his own son, Geoffrey, who could then become Count of Anjou in his place. It was exactly this alliance that Henry of England was now offering.

Of course, in this purely business deal no-one consulted the couple whose futures were most involved. At the time negotiations began, Geoffrey was thirteen years old. We are not told his reaction, but Matilda seems to have made her objections clear. Letters tentatively dated to the time suggest she threatened to refuse the match. In reality, though, she had little choice but to swallow her pride and go along with her father's wishes. In May 1127, the twenty-five-year-old former queen and empress was escorted to Normandy by her half-brother Robert of Gloucester and another of Henry's favoured young men, Brian fitzCount. There she was betrothed to Geoffrey, the son of a mere count and a boy little more than half her age. Henry and Fulk had achieved their alliance, but the prospects for a strong and happy marriage were very poor.

By this time William Clito, with the help of Louis of France, had got control of most of Flanders. Henry's early tactic of backing William of Ypres as a rival had failed to pay off, his man being quickly defeated and taken prisoner. Now he tried another angle, forbidding the export of English wool to the important Flemish cloth towns such as Bruges, Ypres and Lille. In addition, some accounts say that in the summer of 1127 he directed Stephen of Boulogne to make war on Clito, though Orderic Vitalis, writing in Normandy, has a different version. He claims it was William Clito who invaded Boulogne in order to force Stephen to acknowledge his overlordship. In doing so he 'laid waste his territories with fire and sword in the most cruel manner'. Stephen's response was probably a disappointment to Henry. There was no great battle, and though, no doubt, he defended his lands, nothing notable is recorded in the chronicles of the time.

According to Vitalis it was Clito's own actions in over-zealously pursuing and punishing those responsible for the assassination of his predecessor, which, together with Henry's economic sanctions, began to turn the Flemish against him. Henry found a new champion in Thierry of Alsace who over a period of time, with English money and English promises, won over many of the major towns. By the spring of 1128, Clito was appealing to Louis for help, but this, too, was short-lived as Henry briefly moved an army onto French soil threateningly near Paris. As soon as Louis retreated from Flanders, however, the English king returned to Normandy where he had more pressing business.

On 10 June 1128, Geoffrey of Anjou was knighted by Henry, still two months short of his fifteenth birthday. A week later Geoffrey and Matilda were married in the cathedral at le Mans, and as Fulk immediately began preparing to hand over to his son, Henry no doubt felt satisfied he had achieved all he had aimed for: not only the alliance he wanted, but also the prospect of a grandson to inherit his crown. 'Howbeit,' says the *Anglo-Saxon Chronicle*, 'this (marriage) displeased all the French and the English.'

Anjou was a traditional enemy of Normandy, and many Norman lords did not relish the prospect of an upstart Angevin count ruling over them. Theobald of Blois, who had served Henry loyally for more than a decade, would also have seen his slight prospect of a crown disappearing. In England, too, there was much talk of being tricked into the oath of allegiance to Matilda and muttering about the secrecy of the whole affair. William of Malmesbury declares that no-one had known of Henry's plans apart from Robert of

Gloucester and Brian fitzCount, and that he himself had heard Roger of Salisbury declare himself freed from his oath by this marriage.

Among those displeased must also be counted Matilda herself. When a few days after the wedding William Clito won a resounding victory against Thierry of Alsace, she might have conceded that the alliance, and hence the marriage, was a necessary evil. Only weeks later, however, Clito was wounded during an assault on a castle. Gangrene quickly set in and he died on 28 July 1128. With him died all focus for rebellion, both in Flanders and in Normandy, and, no doubt, in Matilda's mind at least, all justification for her marriage.

Early in 1129, Fulk of Anjou left for Jerusalem, and shortly afterwards Matilda, too, left Anjou to take up residence in Normandy. She had shown little interest in her new husband's county, rarely witnessing charters and shunning the title 'countess', but it is not entirely clear whether she walked out or was thrown out. It is possible the marriage had not been consummated and she was hoping for an annulment. If so, she would be disappointed. On the other hand, her dowry was to consist of a number of strategic castles in southern Normandy, none of which had yet been handed over, nor had Geoffrey's future role in England or Normandy been clarified, so it may have been Geoffrey who lost patience and ejected his wife.

Matilda remained in Normandy for more than two years, and though Henry was also in the duchy for part of that time, there is no record of him pressuring his daughter to return to her husband. The king is not noted for his soft-heartedness, so we can only speculate why this should be. Did she flatly refuse and threaten to enter a convent? Was he having second thoughts about the wisdom of the marriage? Was it, in fact, safer for Matilda to remain in Normandy while Geoffrey put down a series of revolts in Anjou? We have no record of communication between Henry and Geoffrey at the time, though he did visit Theobald of Blois. He also entertained the new pope, Innocent II, at Rouen, and it was only after this, in the summer of 1131, that he returned to England, taking Matilda with him.

Something had clearly changed, possibly advice from the pope, or maybe a spirit of reconciliation between the parties themselves. In September 1131 a great council was held at Northampton and there it was decided that Matilda must return to her husband. Robert of Torigny, writing later but possibly having actually met Matilda, declares that Geoffrey had 'claimed her'. It is William of Malmesbury, however, closer both in time and distance, who emphasises something else that, according to him, happened at this council. 'The oath of fidelity to (Matilda) was renewed by such as had already sworn ... and also taken by such as hitherto had not.' This oath, then, was taken not only after the marriage, but after it had been confirmed by the council. It seems likely that Henry had heard of the earlier grumbles about the marriage and intended to close every loophole, though, significantly, the oath contained no mention of the future role of the young Count of Anjou.

Geoffrey, at least, seems to have decided to make the best of his marriage. He sent an impressive escort to bring his wife home and received her 'with the pomp worthy of such an illustrious princess'. Perhaps this helped to reconcile Matilda to her lot, for her first son was born on 5 March 1133, not only an heir to Anjou but also, at last, a male heir for Henry, now in his sixty-fifth year. Needless to say, the child was christened Henry. Some accounts suggest his grandfather was present for the child's christening at Le Mans, while his father stayed away. On the other hand, most agree that the king did not leave England until early August – accompanied by earthquakes and other omens – and it is unlikely the christening would have been delayed that long.

King Henry was certainly on hand for the birth of Matilda's second son, born at Rouen on 3 July 1134 while she was paying an extended visit to her father. By all accounts it was a difficult birth and for a time it was feared she would die, though she was never sufficiently feeble to prevent her arguing with Henry about where she should be buried.

It has been suggested that Matilda spent this long time in Rouen in order to be tutored by her father in the niceties of ruling England and Normandy. If that is the case, perhaps she disagreed about that as well, for the cosy family relationship seems to have broken down soon after, when she returned to her husband. According to Robert of Torigny, Henry intended to return to England in 1135 to deal with trouble on the Welsh border. Instead, he was detained in Normandy 'in consequence of various disputes which arose between himself and the Count of Anjou, originating in the artifices of his daughter'.

Matilda's offence most likely consisted in siding with her husband in demanding the handover of the castles that formed her dowry. In addition, there is a suggestion that she – and possibly Geoffrey, too – wanted an oath sworn by the Norman lords similar to that already sworn in England, and possibly some transference of power itself in the duchy. Orderic Vitalis is perhaps unfair in claiming 'Geoffrey of Anjou coveted the vast wealth of his father-in-law,' but closer to the mark in saying Henry 'had no inclination to allow anyone, while he lived, to have any pre-eminence over himself, or even to be his equal'.

For the whole of the summer and early autumn he patrolled the borders of Normandy, strengthening castles and taking lands from lords of doubtful loyalty. Then, late in November, he took a break to go hunting in the forest near Rouen. On the evening of Monday 25 November, after a day's hunting, he ate a meal of lampreys – a meaty type of fish – despite Torigny telling us, 'His physician had forbidden him to eat of this dish.' Almost immediately he fell ill, throughout the week he steadily worsened, and on the following Sunday, 1 December 1135, he died.

In the days before his death there was time for the major nobles of England and Normandy to gather round the king. His son Robert of Gloucester was there, together with William of Warenne, the mighty Earl of Surrey, and the Beaumont twins, Robert of Leicester and his brother Waleran de Meulan with extensive estates in Normandy. Rotrou of Perche was there, another Norman lord, who had married Henry's illegitimate daughter, and there, too, was the Archbishop of Rouen to hear Henry's last confession. Conspicuous by his absence from this little group was Stephen, Count of Boulogne. For some time now he had been seen less frequently at Henry's court, no doubt kept busy (and apparently content) with his county of Boulogne and huge estates in England. In December the same year, his wife Matilda was in the last stages of pregnancy, and good family man that he was, perhaps he did not want to leave her. Or maybe there was another plan forming in his mind.

At the king's deathbed, one question hovered over all. Now it came to the point, who would actually succeed this mighty king, the 'invincible monarch, the wise duke', as Vitalis calls him. William of Malmesbury had no doubts. When the question was put to him, he says, the king 'awarded all his territories, on either side of the sea, to his daughter, in legitimate and perpetual succession'. This would have been entirely consistent with his earlier policies and no-one present sought to challenge it. Stephen of Boulogne, however, had other ideas.

Henry died on the Sunday night, and by the following Thursday Stephen and a relatively small retinue had landed in England. He was refused entry to Dover and Canterbury, each held by Robert of Gloucester, but instead made for London where he had a house of his own. There it was that he first laid claim to the English crown. He had, no doubt, been brought up with the tale of how Henry himself had taken advantage of his brother's death, and the absence of major nobles, to seize the crown. Now the situation was very similar. Henry had made for Winchester and the royal treasury, but Stephen's power base was in London and its surrounds. In addition, his role as Count of Boulogne would have had influence with the Flemish and English merchants of the wool trade based in the city.

We don't know on what basis Stephen staked his claim. William of Newburgh later pointed out that not only was he breaking his oath by claiming the crown, but he was not even the legitimate heir, his brother Theobald having a prior claim even if the Empress Matilda was set aside. On the other hand, a chronicle kept at Ely, known as the Liber Eliensis, states that a royal steward, Hugh Bigod, was later prepared to swear on the holy gospels that on his deathbed Henry had nominated 'my most dear kinsman, Stephen' to reign after him – this despite the fact that Hugh was not actually there, and that this startling change of policy was not mentioned by any who were.

On whatever basis, and entirely without precedent, a council of Londoners now took it upon themselves to claim 'as their undoubted right and especial privilege' the power to nominate a new king, and Stephen was thereby acclaimed, 'by common consent'. This is recorded by an anonymous author in a document known as the Gesta Regis Stephani – the Deeds of King Stephen – which also reports an astonishing amount of 'fake news' surrounding the occasion. Thus, according to the Gesta, the death of King Henry was followed by a period of utter chaos, when people fought and rioted and committed all manner of heinous crimes against each other, while even the wildlife of the country was affected, with birds and wild animals suddenly disappearing. It was from this chaos that Stephen rescued them, says the Gesta, and he was hailed as a saviour. Given that less than a week had passed between the king's death and Stephen's arrival, however, this whole tale seems unlikely in the extreme, but the rumours must have been widely enough spread to be repeated, albeit in a less dramatic form, in the *Anglo-Saxon Chronicle*.

With London secured, Stephen now had to win over two most important institutions: the church, and the administration established by King Henry and run so efficiently by Roger of Salisbury. In both cases he was most effectively assisted by his brother, Henry of Blois, who had some years earlier been appointed Bishop of Winchester, with the approval of the king. Bishop Henry it was who arranged the handing over of the royal treasury to Stephen, and who did much to overcome the initial scruples of William Corbeil, the Archbishop of Canterbury. On the other hand, Roger of Salisbury was already minded to break his oath, and readily accepted Stephen as king. Robert of Torigny seems to regard it as a divine judgement on both these clerics that the archbishop died within the year, while the death of Roger of Salisbury would be brought about by the very king he helped to the throne.

No time was lost in getting the crown on Stephen's head, the belief at the time being that it was a coronation, and especially the anointing, that made a king, rather than any right of inheritance or nomination. At the latest he was crowned and anointed by the archbishop in Westminster Abbey on 22 December, though there is some confusion about the exact date. Around the same time, at home in Boulogne, the Countess Matilda was safely delivered of a son, who, emphasising the new royal connection, would be christened William after his conquering great-grandfather.

By coincidence the other Matilda was also pregnant at the time, though in the early stages, and possibly feeling the common effects of those early months. Nor was she in any position to influence events in Normandy or England. Still at loggerheads with her father, she was far away in Anjou when he died, and Stephen was probably well on his way to England before the news reached her. She and Geoffrey had by now achieved a partnership that might be termed 'supportive indifference'. She still took little part in affairs in Anjou, and he, perhaps in deference to her feelings, was known to refer to her in charters as 'daughter of the King of the English and former wife to Henry, Roman Emperor', rather than using her current title of 'Countess of Anjou'. The fact that he was known as 'Geoffrey the Handsome' and, at twenty-two, had a fine, athletic figure, seemed to matter little to the former empress, nor the fact that he was growing into a shrewd and capable ruler. Matilda's ambitions in England were almost certainly solely for herself and her sons, while Geoffrey never seems to have aimed higher than Normandy.

Normandy was certainly the first target. As soon as news of Henry's death reached them, the long-disputed castles in the south of the duchy were taken over. According to Vitalis, 'Geoffrey of Anjou ... sent forward to Normandy his wife Matilda,' though doubtless she was equally eager to secure these important fortresses. Argentan, Domfront and Exemes were handed over immediately, while William Talvas, a descendant of the Montgomery family and ally of Geoffrey, also reclaimed his ancestral castles at Sées and Alençon, which Henry had confiscated.

Geoffrey's own foray into Normandy was not so successful. In attempting to spread out from these secure bases, his Angevin forces aroused the fury of their traditional Norman foes. Vitalis claims they were initially given a cautious welcome, but then accuses them of violating churches and cemeteries, where, no doubt, valuables had been taken for safekeeping, and committing 'many cruelties'. They were then driven out by the Normans, he claims, with the serious loss of some seven hundred men, and, having retreated to Anjou, 'after being sharply punished at the point of the sword, had no desire to repeat the experiment'.

The Normans were probably encouraged in their resistance by what was happening elsewhere, for by now it was clear that even those lords present at King Henry's deathbed were preparing to break their sworn oaths. They had accompanied the old king's body as far as Rouen and were awaiting a change in the winter weather to allow them to travel with it across the sea to Reading Abbey, where it would be interred. In the meantime, a meeting was held at nearby Neubourg where it was decided, possibly in the absence of Robert of Gloucester, to offer the crown to Count Theobald of Blois. The count had already travelled to meet them to accept this honour when news was brought from England that Stephen had pre-empted his brother and was either already crowned or was about to be crowned, depending on which account is believed. Since most lords had lands in England as well as Normandy, it was then resolved to accept this fait accompli and acknowledge Stephen as both king of England and duke of Normandy. Theobald thereupon took himself off in something of a huff to consult with Louis of France and, far from opposing Geoffrey's incursions into Normandy, signed a truce with him that would last for some months.

Stephen was clearly going to face no immediate opposition in Normandy, but others were not so easily won over. King David of Scotland may have felt himself in an awkward position. Like the rest, he had sworn to accept the empress as Henry's heir, but he was uncle to both her and to Matilda of Boulogne. In the event, late in December 1135 he chose to invade England, ostensibly in fulfilment of his oath, though some have accused him of simply intending to grab what he could of the northern lands. Within a few weeks he had taken a great swathe of territory, from Carlisle and its environs in the west, through to Newcastle in the east, with the castles of Carlisle, Norham, Wark, Alnwick and Newcastle now under his control. When Stephen appeared with an army early in February 1136, however, he was immediately prepared to negotiate.

The chronicler Richard of Hexham, close in both time and distance, describes two characteristics of Stephen that would become even more apparent in the coming years. He had, he says, 'firm courage' in the face of challenges, but 'smiled at ... the loss of worldly possessions ... as if he did not feel them'. Both traits were shown here as Stephen, who had been prepared for a fierce battle, now cheerfully gave away Carlisle – in effect the whole of Cumberland – to David's son Henry, along with David's own earldom of Huntingdon, with Doncaster thrown in as a make-weight, and half a promise to add Northumbria later. In exchange the castles at Wark, Norham, Alnwick and Newcastle were returned, but no homage was demanded from David, and the rights of the empress were not mentioned.

By Easter 1136 Stephen must have felt he was well on top of the situation. His wife Matilda had joined him and was crowned as Queen of England on Easter Sunday, 22 March. Early in the year he had presented his case to Pope Innocent, including, apparently, the claims of violent disorder after the death of Henry, and had received in return a letter addressed to 'Stephen, illustrious king of England'. It should be mentioned that Pope Innocent himself faced a challenge from an antipope, Anacletus, at the time, and was equally anxious to secure Stephen's support.

Best of all, in Stephen's view, soon after Easter he was joined by Robert of Gloucester, who had returned to Normandy after Henry's funeral in January without offering homage to the new king. If it seems surprising that such a major figure should break his vow to his half-sister, Malmesbury offers us his reasoning. Staying in Normandy at the time, he says, would harm himself without benefitting his sister, whereas in England he might be able to persuade others to her cause, 'to convince them of their misconduct and recall them to wiser sentiments'. Malmesbury says he puts nothing into his chronicle which he is not able to confirm for himself through a reliable source. In this case, however, the only reliable source would be Robert himself, to whom the work is dedicated. So it may be that – as with Queen Emma's Encomium – this is the view that Robert of Gloucester wanted recorded for posterity.

Be that as it may, he now submitted to Stephen and joined his court on its way to Oxford. There the king triumphantly issued his coronation charter, promising freedom to the church and peace and justice for all.

Robert was kept at court for some time, either because the king was so delighted to have secured his submission, or because he still doubted his loyalty. Even when, soon after, trouble broke out in Wales, Robert and his fellow Marcher lords, of equally doubtful loyalty, were not permitted to go and deal with it. As a result, the greater part of formerly Norman Wales, including Ceredigion, Carmarthen and Glamorgan, was lost, chiefly to the benefit of Owain Gwynedd in central and northern Wales, and Gruffydd ap Rhys and his sons in the west – another loss of worldly possessions Stephen seemed not to feel.

There was trouble in Normandy, too. A dispute initially over an inheritance soon led to a split on factional lines, with the over-enthusiastic actions of some supporting the king's lieutenant, Waleran de Meulan, driving others into the Angevin camp. Again, a decisive appearance by the king might have rallied support for him in the duchy and ended once and for all any challenge on behalf of the Empress Matilda. Stephen wavered, thought of going, and then went instead to put Exeter under siege, to teach a lesson to a minor lord, Baldwin de Redvers, who had defied orders to come and do homage. Even when that siege was successful, Stephen's leniency allowed Baldwin and his men to depart unpunished and with their arms. de Redvers promptly took up the empress's cause in the Cotentin area of Normandy, attacking and plundering all who supported the king.

Through the summer of 1136 Empress Matilda herself was based at the fortress of Argentan, where, on 22 July, her third son was born. Like the son of the other Matilda born a few months earlier, he was christened William. His birth, however, meant that for much of this crucial period the empress herself was unable to take an active role. Her recovery this time must have been quicker than the last, though, for when Geoffrey launched another attack on Normandy late in September of that year, Matilda was not far behind.

In nine days of rapid movement and violent attack, Geoffrey stormed up the west of the duchy from Argentan to Lisieux. He had with him a large army and the backing of, among others, William of Talvas and Duke William of Aquitaine, and he seems to have expected that others would flock to his support along the way. Some did, and six castles were taken or handed over in that time, but it soon appeared, at least according to Vitalis, that the majority who joined him were simply 'reckless thieves ... and sturdy plunderers ... assembled like kites from all quarters ... for no other object than pillage, slaughter and conquest'.

Finding Waleran and his army lurking near Lisieux, there was no attempt to put the place under siege. Instead, Geoffrey retreated to another castle, Le Sap, and on 1 October, in the course of investing that castle, he was badly wounded in the foot. The following day Matilda arrived with reinforcements, one account claiming she rode with them on horseback, possibly even wearing some form of armour. If so, she was a brave woman, having given birth a matter of weeks before.

The gesture was in vain, however. Close to the action in his monastery at St. Evroult, Vitalis gives a vivid description of the retreat from Le Sap which now took place. The Angevins, he says, had 'gorged themselves with crude eatables ... and suffered so severely from diarrhoea that, leaving foul tokens of their passage along the roads, numbers of them could scarcely crawl home'. Geoffrey himself lost his baggage in an ambush at a river crossing, and for a second time made an ignominious departure from Normandy. His thirteen days in the duchy had won him, says Vitalis, 'not the dominion but the eternal hatred of the Normans'.

Before Easter the following year, Stephen and his court finally put in an appearance in Normandy. Bishop Henry of Winchester had gone before him, some say to smooth the way for him, while others claim he was expecting to be appointed Archbishop of Canterbury, in place of William Corbeil who had died the previous year, and he wanted to be nearer to the pope in readiness to receive his pallium. If the latter is true he was destined to be disappointed, but his diplomacy in Normandy probably secured a warmer welcome for his brother when he arrived in the Cotentin in March 1137. Queen Matilda accompanied him, along with their eldest son Eustace – never, in the chronicles, referred to as Prince Eustace – who was probably by then around ten years old.

One who did not accompany them was Robert of Gloucester, and again William of Malmesbury offers a reason for this. He claims Robert took the opportunity of remaining in England to size up the support for his sister in the country, and to arrange 'what he conceived proper to be done afterwards', that is, when he returned to his real loyalty and openly declared for the empress.

Stephen's Easter court, held at Évreux, was a splendid affair, the counterpart to his Easter court at Westminster the year before, but this time intended to impress any Norman lords who might be wavering in their loyalty. A number did, indeed, present themselves and do homage. It was a time, too, for Stephen to make up with his brother Theobald, who, says Torigny, 'was angry that ... Stephen ... should obtain possession of the crown, which he said belonged to him'. Afterwards the whole court, now including Theobald and Robert of Gloucester, moved to the border to meet with the ageing Louis of France. At this point Stephen was formally invested as Duke of Normandy, though the homage due was performed not by Stephen but by Eustace.

While this was going on, Geoffrey of Anjou was hovering at or near the Norman border, apparently in full expectation of a major battle to win or lose crown and duchy once and for all. Stephen, too, seems to have anticipated such a confrontation, having assembled a large army at Lisieux ready to march on Argentan. A considerable part of this army was made up of Flemish mercenaries led by William of Ypres, who had been serving Stephen for some time. The Norman lords, according to Vitalis, were jealous of the favour shown to William and the Flemings, and 'took every means of privately annoying (them)', matters coming to a head when the army had barely left Lisieux. The flashpoint, a barrel of wine allegedly stolen by a Fleming, was blown out of all proportion, and thereupon the army disintegrated, the Norman lords leading their forces away and refusing all attempts by the king to persuade them to return. Humiliated, Stephen was forced to agree a truce with Geoffrey, paying him 2,000 silver marks, effectively to go away for at least a year.

As if that was not bad enough, it was at this time, too, according to William of Malmesbury, that the English king attempted to deal with the suspect loyalty of Robert of Gloucester. An ambush intended to dispose of the earl failed due to Robert receiving a warning, and when challenged about this Stephen tacitly admitted being behind it, though promising such a thing would not happen again. Needless to say, when the court abruptly returned to England in November 1137 Robert remained in Normandy, pondering his future.

One reason given for the court's return is the sudden death of one, or possibly two, of the children of Stephen and Matilda. Their daughter Matilda would have been around five years old, and the son, Baldwin, probably a little older. Both apparently died in the royal apartments in the Tower of London, possibly of the same illness, and both would be interred at Holy Trinity Priory at Aldgate in London. With another daughter, Marie, having already taken the veil, this left just the two sons, Eustace and William, as potential heirs to England, Normandy and Boulogne.

Trouble in England, and another threatened invasion by David of Scotland, may also have influenced the sudden return, and would account for Stephen stripping Normandy of all its major nobility. Just two inexperienced leaders were left, with instructions to put an end to the continuing troubles in the duchy, described by Vitalis as 'blows mutually given by the swords of her own sons'. In the event they proved quite unequal to the task.

The Gesta Stephani likens Stephen's position in 1138 to that of Hercules, lopping off the heads of the hydra, and 'as fast as one of its heads was lopped off more sprung forth.' Some of his troubles were of his own making, such as the attempt to give Bedford castle to the youngest Beaumont brother, which led to a winter siege. Others might be put down to letters written by the empress to David of Scotland, and to others in the country possibly identified by Robert of Gloucester as potential supporters.

The immediate result was another surging Scottish invasion in the first weeks of the year, led by King David and his son Henry. With an army made up of Scots, English, Normans, wild Picts from Galloway and even Germans, they rampaged across the northern lands as far as the River Tyne before being chased back to Scotland by Stephen, who paid like for like in plundering David's southernmost lands. The English king dared not stay long, however, seeing doubtful loyalties everywhere, and even a threat of invasion from the continent. His Easter court that year was held at Northampton, and there he decided to divide his forces.

Waleran de Meulan and William of Ypres were dispatched to Normandy where it was rumoured Robert of Gloucester was preparing to switch his allegiance to his sister's cause. The elderly Thurstan, Archbishop of York, was told he must guard the north with whatever resources he could find, while Stephen himself would travel west to the Welsh Marches, where a concentration of those likely to support Robert were already disgruntled by the loss of lands in Wales. The most surprising role, however, was that handed to Queen Matilda. Dover Castle, a mighty fortress guarding an inviting entry point for an invasion, was still in the hands of Robert of Gloucester and well garrisoned by his men. It was to be Matilda's job to take this castle by storm or siege and ensure in future it was held for the king.

She set about it with admirable clarity. Her forces were led by one Faramus, a second cousin through an illegitimate son of her grandfather's, but it is clear the planning and direction of the operation were entirely the queen's. Putting Dover under siege on the landward side, she called up her countrymen of Boulogne to blockade the port and thus cut off all chance of supply or aid by sea. By the end of August Dover was starved into submission, and Faramus was installed as its new commander.

This was a time of the greatest success for Stephen. He had failed to take Bristol Castle, held for Robert of Gloucester by his eldest son William, though he had mopped up lesser castles in the area. He had then failed again at Dudley. At Shrewsbury, however, he had stuck to his task in besieging the fortress, taken it in the end by storm, and hanged a considerable number of the defenders, even some of the highest in rank. A few months earlier, following a siege at Hereford, Stephen had once again allowed the rebel leaders to depart unharmed, leading the Anglo-Saxon Chronicle to note, 'he was a mild man and a soft and a good,' but 'he did not enforce justice.' This sudden change from his usual leniency, however, brought about the immediate surrender of Dudley, and may have influenced the outcome at Dover. At almost the same time the Scots were heavily defeated at the Battle of the Standard, where the English army, inspired by Archbishop Thurstan, slaughtered may thousands. King David managed to escape 'through the woods and thickets' to Roxburgh, while it is claimed his son Prince Henry limped into Carlisle days later with only one companion.

So far Stephen had satisfactorily dealt with the many-headed hydra, but already he would have known that this was only the beginning. Shortly after Pentecost he had received a formal defiance from Robert of Gloucester, that most correct of noblemen, renouncing his fealty to Stephen whom he now accused of unlawfully taking the English kingdom from its rightful heir. Already the major Norman castles of Caen and Bayeux were being held on behalf of the Empress Matilda, and Stephen could now expect an invasion of England itself would soon follow. To a cool head it would, therefore, seem imperative that peace should be secured in the north, lest the king should find enemies at both ends of the country. In the event it seems clear that the cool head belonged to Queen Matilda, who now swapped her successful role as military leader for a more usual queenly function, that of diplomat and peacemaker.

In September 1138 a papal legate, Alberic, Bishop of Ostia, arrived in England. Ostensibly he was there to ensure that all now acknowledged Pope Innocent as head of the church, Antipope Anacletus having died in January of that year. With the pope's authority behind him, however, he could also do much towards securing peace between enemies. Late in the year he met David of Scotland at Carlisle, the Scots having previously acknowledged Anacletus and, as well as gaining his acceptance of Pope Innocent, he managed to negotiate a truce between English and Scots to last until November 1139. Stephen, though, was reluctant to turn this truce into a peace treaty.

The chronicler Richard of Hexham declares it was Queen Matilda, 'warmly attached to her uncle David of Scotland and his son Henry her cousin', who now 'persisted night and day' in raising the matter with her husband. She also had long and earnest discussions with Alberic, and when eventually agreement was reached in April in 1139, it was Matilda who travelled to Durham to sign it, alongside her cousin Henry. Only then did the two come south to Nottingham where Stephen confirmed the treaty, creating Prince Henry Earl of Northumbria, and receiving in exchange a promise of peace and loyalty from David and Henry to last for their lifetimes.

Not only did this secure the northern borders and alienate one of the empress's chief supporters, it also had an effect on the outcome of the case Empress Matilda now presented to the pope. To her and to her representative, Bishop Ulger of Angers, this case must have seemed unanswerable. Not only was she the legitimate hereditary heir to the English crown, but Stephen himself had acknowledged her as such and sworn a sacred oath to support her claim. The reply to this on Stephen's behalf was completely unexpected. Matilda, he said, had no right to the throne as her parents had not been legitimately married. Her mother, he claimed, was, in fact, a nun. In truth the wife of Henry I *had* been brought up in a convent, but full investigation before her marriage had found she had never taken any vows. Unfortunately, Bishop Ulger had not been briefed on this, and as he floundered, Pope Innocent accepted a report from Alberic on Stephen's support for the church and peace-seeking ways – along with some handsome gifts from Stephen himself – and confirmed him as the rightful king.

He would not, perhaps, have been quite so convinced of Stephen's credentials as a true son of the church if he had delayed his judgement for a few months, for in June of that year there occurred in England what Robert of Torigny later described as 'a transaction of unprecedented infamy'. At the time Bishop Roger of Salisbury was still at the heart of the English administration, a system he himself had devised. His nephews Alexander and Nigel were respectively bishops of Lincoln and Ely, and his son, also Roger, was the king's chancellor. The family had not only become immensely powerful under Henry, but also possessed great wealth and a number of fine castles, including that at Devizes, regarded as the most magnificent in Europe. Needless to say, this had excited the jealousy not only of the nobility but of the king himself, who had rapidly run through the treasure left by his thrifty predecessor on the throne.

Only a few years before Roger of Salisbury had helped Stephen to a crown, but now rumours began to spread that he was preparing to back an Angevin invasion. As the court assembled at Oxford in late June 1139, an incident was manufactured between some of the bishop's followers and those of Waleran de Meulan. Stephen immediately arrested Bishops Roger and Alexander who were already in Oxford, and demanded they hand over their castles. Bishop Nigel fled to Devizes where, after a short stand-off and a threat to hang the son of Roger of Salisbury, he, too, was arrested and imprisoned. Then, says the Gesta, all the castles and the arms and treasures found therein were surrendered to the king, and the bishops themselves, 'humbled and mortified, and stripped of all pomp and vain glory, were reduced to a simple ecclesiastical life'.

There was, of course, an outcry. William of Newburgh, writing later, declares that Stephen had become 'so depraved by evil counsels' that he 'sullied his royal character with an indelible stain'. These evil counsels were most unlikely to have come from the calm, long-sighted and pious Queen Matilda. At the time she was probably engaged in matters relating to her county of Boulogne, and in negotiating with the new French king, Louis VII, for the marriage of her son Eustace to his sister Constance. This marriage duly took place early in the following year, facilitated, according to Torigny, by the treasures Stephen had taken from the bishops.

Nor would the counsels have come from Bishop Henry of Winchester. Earlier the foremost advisor of the king, he had been rapidly eclipsed by the newly powerful Beaumont family with their allies the de Clares. The previous Christmas he had been passed over for the coveted post of Archbishop of Canterbury, though he had retaliated by persuading the pope to appoint him papal legate, and, in announcing that senior appointment now, he convened a church council to bring his brother to task for his treatment of his fellow bishops. Henry, of course, had castles and wealth of his own to defend. The outcome of the council was, however, indecisive, with some accounts saying the king admitted his guilt and others denying it. The bishops were, indeed, released – though Roger of Salisbury died soon after – but castles and treasure remained firmly in Stephen's hands. Within a very short time, though, the matter became almost an irrelevance, for shortly after the council broke up came the long-awaited arrival of the Empress Matilda.

Stephen must have thought he was well prepared. He had recently placed reliable, newly appointed earls in strategic places around the country – Waleran de Meulan as Earl of Worcester, for example, William of Aumale as Earl of York, and two members of the de Clare family, Gilbert fitz Gilbert and Gilbert fitz Richard, as earls respectively of Pembroke and Hertford. He himself was hovering near the south coast, and yet was unable to prevent what was not so much an invasion as an infiltration.

On 30 September 1139, the Empress Matilda and her brother Robert of Gloucester, sailing inland a few miles up the River Arun, landed at Arundel where they were immediately welcomed into the impressive castle by Matilda's newly re-married step-mother Adeliza. It was later claimed that Adeliza had invited her, but if so it was in the role of peacemaker rather than in defiance of her new husband, William d'Aubigny, who had recently been created Earl of Sussex, and who was, and always would be, loyal to Stephen. Indeed, it was not an army that arrived, merely an escort of around 140 horsemen, and Stephen was nowhere around.

An impressive number of decoy actions – at Dunster in Somerset, at Marlborough in Wiltshire, and, most seriously, by Baldwin de Redvers at Wareham and Corfe Castle in Dorset – had drawn him away, and by the time news reached him and he hastened to Arundel, Robert of Gloucester had seen his sister safely established there and slipped away to Bristol. By one account Robert went via Wallingford to brief his great friend Brian fitzCount who had obtained that fortress by marriage. By another, not completely implausible, he met with Bishop Henry on the road, came to an understanding with him, and was permitted to go on his way. The good bishop then proceeded to Arundel. There, Stephen was dithering as to whether or not he could besiege the empress, who had committed no act of war against him, and who was a guest under the protection of the former queen. Bishop Henry advised against. While he was besieging Arundel, he pointed out, Robert of Gloucester might raise forces against him and win victories somewhere else. Accepting this advice, King Stephen immediately provided an escort for Matilda to join her brother in Bristol. Typical of the king's own chivalrous nature, the more hard-headed Vitalis promptly condemns this as an act of 'great simplicity or carelessness' at a moment when the king could easily have 'nipped the growth of malignancy in the bud' for his own welfare and the security of the kingdom.

It is likely both sides overestimated the support the empress would get from the English kingdom once she arrived. Within a short while she had secured the royal castle at Gloucester as a residence, and she had three strong, capable leaders in Robert of Gloucester, Miles, the castellan of Gloucester, and Brian fitzCount. No other major lord rushed to submit to her, however, and it was clear there was going to be a struggle, either for her to gain the crown or for Stephen to succeed in ejecting her.

It is at this point in his chronicle that Henry of Huntingdon inserts an elegy bemoaning the fate of the country in a period later labelled 'the Anarchy'. He concludes, 'All hell's let loose and chaos reigns.' In fact, the chaos took some time to build, and hell was let loose rather slowly, but since neither side felt strong enough to risk all on a single confrontation, the war was instead a matter of picking off castles here and there, sieges and sudden flare-ups, and especially devastation of the lands of one's opponents to weaken them and discourage others from rebellion. It was the latter policy, a standard tactic at the time, that caused most damage to the land and harm to the ordinary people, leading the *Anglo-Saxon Chronicle* to bemoan that 'the land was all ruined ... and it was said openly that Christ and his saints slept.'

Not all the country was equally affected. For the most part, the south-west and Welsh Marches were firmly held for the empress, while London and the south-east were equally solid for Stephen and his queen. Between the two, the Thames valley suffered repeatedly, while other areas such as Cornwall and East Anglia, though subject to brief violent rebellions, were for the most part uninvolved in the conflict.

Initial attacks focussed on outlying castles of the enemy, with Stephen unsuccessfully attacking Wallingford and Trowbridge, and Robert of Gloucester sacking Worcester. Then, surprisingly, in the summer of 1140 a peace conference was called, mediated by Bishop Henry in his role as papal legate. It may have been a lack of resources – both sides were chronically short of funds – or a rash of opportunistic lords trying to seize castles for themselves, that brought the parties to the negotiating table. Either way it was a failure. With Queen Matilda representing her husband, and Robert of Gloucester representing the empress, the issue seemed to move on quite quickly from who would wear the crown now, to who would inherit it in future years. Both sides had sons, and though the empress was inclined to let the church decide the matter, neither Stephen nor Queen Matilda would consider disinheriting Eustace. 'They wasted words and time to no purpose,' says Malmesbury, and though Bishop Henry then visited Louis of France and Count Theobald – both interested parties – and returned with some unspecified proposals, ultimately there was no agreement and no peace. Indeed, the conflict was rapidly heading towards its most violent phase, though this came about almost by accident.

At the end of 1140, two half-brothers, Ranulf of Chester and William of Roumare, gained possession of Lincoln castle by a trick and ejected Stephen's garrison. The situation was a strange one. Lincoln Castle had two keeps. One was clearly a royal castle, but the other had belonged to Lucy of Bolingbroke, the mother of both these adventurers. According to Malmesbury, Stephen had then visited the castle and not only approved their possession of 'Lucy's Tower', but granted further lands to Ranulf and made William Earl of Lincoln.

Over Christmas, however, he seems to have changed his mind. Perhaps he was persuaded by others he had given away too much. Some claim it was the citizens of Lincoln who asked for his aid. Whatever the reason, early in the New Year he arrived outside Lincoln with a besieging force, surprising both brothers who were within the castle with their families. William of Roumare remained there, but Ranulf of Chester managed to slip away to seek help from the most powerful man he knew, his father-in-law, Robert, Earl of Gloucester.

To Robert it was a God-sent opportunity. No doubt Ranulf reported the size of the force accompanying the king, and the earl immediately called up all those supporting the empress to march with him to Lincoln. His army eventually included not only Miles of Gloucester and Brian fitzCount, but a group referred to as 'the disinherited' and even a number of Welsh princes.

For some reason Stephen seemed to doubt their resolve, and even though warned of their approach, he failed to call for reinforcements. On the morning of 2 February 1141, however, it became quite clear the army of the empress meant to seek a battle. It was the Christian feast of Candlemas, and both the Gesta and Robert of Torigny describe how, when Stephen was in church that morning, the candle he was handing to the bishop broke and was extinguished as he placed it in the bishop's hand. 'The king took this as a sign that his own power was broken.' Once again Stephen was urged to retreat. Not only were his men outnumbered by the approaching forces, but it was a holy day and should be a day of peace. The king would have none of it. Years before, his father had been shamed for fleeing the battle of Antioch in the Holy Land. Today Stephen would stand and fight.

Stand he did, too, fighting on foot among the infantry, while the royal cavalry were quickly routed, and the mercenary force led by William of Ypres was similarly put to flight by Ranulf of Chester and the Welsh. At that point William himself decided the battle was lost and 'deferred his aid for better times', taking the rest of his men away from the field of conflict. With the whole of Robert's army now closed in around him, still, says Robert of Torigny, 'King Stephen kept his ground like a lion, standing single-handed in the field.' It was, he adds, 'no easy matter to take him prisoner'. Even when, as Malmesbury reports, he was struck on the head and fell stunned to the ground, still he refused to surrender to anyone other than Robert of Gloucester himself.

The royal prisoner was quickly taken to Gloucester to his cousin Matilda, empress, but not yet queen, even though she now held her usurper captive. Prisoner he might be, but he had been anointed king and there was no precedent for undoing that sacred anointing. Even as she consigned him to imprisonment at Bristol – hopefully lifelong imprisonment, like their uncle Robert Curthose – Matilda would have known she had a long way to go before she could replace him on the throne.

The first step was to win over the church, a step made easier by the disaffection of Bishop Henry from the royal cause. As papal legate it was also his duty to try and achieve peace in the kingdom. A meeting was arranged, to be held at Wherwell, near Winchester, on 2 March. As a result of this the bishop swore to receive Matilda as sovereign and remain faithful to her, while she, on the other hand, promised him a free hand in church appointments, and that 'All matters of importance in England … should await his decision.' Both promises were conditional, but they seemed to restore Henry to the pre-eminent position he had once held under his brother and since lost. The title initially bestowed on Matilda was 'Lady of the English', a rather ambiguous title harking back to

Anglo-Saxon times. It fell far short of 'Queen', and though Matilda was immediately afterwards put in possession of the royal castle and treasury at Winchester, and 'proclaimed sovereign lady and queen' in the market place there, she still had more hurdles to cross to achieve the throne.

The first was the reluctance of Theobald, the new Archbishop of Canterbury. He could not, he said, change sides and support Matilda without beforehand consulting the king. A visit was arranged, and Stephen, regarding his fall from grace as God's judgement, at once gave permission to those who had sworn fealty to him to go back on their oaths. A similar argument was then put to the church council called by Bishop Henry, as papal legate, immediately after Easter. One of those present at that council was William of Malmesbury, and we have the details directly from him.

Stephen had been 'allowed to reign', claimed Bishop Henry, in order to give peace to the country when Matilda had delayed coming to claim her crown. He had, however, broken all the promises he had then made to the church, though Henry himself had tried to remonstrate with him. It was therefore God who had allowed his defeat at Lincoln, and thus Matilda should now be supported in replacing him. Those who agreed with this, says Malmesbury, now 'becomingly applauded', while others remained silent. No-one, however, went so far as to protest.

Mindful, no doubt, of Stephen's own election, Bishop Henry had also summoned a delegation of Londoners to come to Winchester, probably expecting he would be able to persuade them to approve his plans by some similar eloquence. There, however, he had sadly misjudged the situation. London was Stephen's territory, and his queen Matilda was by no means ready to give up the kingdom so easily. Even as the bishop was repeating his earlier arguments to the delegation, an envoy from the queen appeared. Malmesbury names him as Christian, 'if I rightly remember,' and he carried a letter from Queen Matilda which he now presented before the whole company. After the first glance Bishop Henry refused to read it, so Christian himself boldly read it aloud. In the letter the queen entreated them all to release King Stephen from prison and restore him to his throne, particularly addressing the assembled clergy and especially Henry himself, 'the brother of her lord'.

The Londoners may already have been aware that the queen was preparing to fight for her husband, and the production of this letter at that precise time may well have been calculated to stiffen their resolve. In the event, with the bishop dismissing out of hand the queen's request, they politely informed him they would report his arguments to their fellow Londoners, and then withdrew. It would, in fact, take a great deal more work, on the part of the bishop and especially Robert of Gloucester, before the Lady of the English would be permitted anywhere near their city.

If the victory of the empress's forces at Lincoln worked only slowly to advance her cause in England, it was far more effective in Normandy. As soon as news of the battle was received, Geoffrey of Anjou sent to the Norman lords demanding they hand over their castles to him. After a brief pause while they once again failed to interest Theobald of Blois in his brother's cause, very many of them did. Significant among them were Bishop John of Lisieux and the Beaumont twins, Robert of Leicester submitting on behalf of himself and his brother Waleran, who was at the time in England. Robert himself would soon return to England, but Waleran, whose main estates lay in Normandy, would replace him in that duchy, and take up the sword on behalf of Geoffrey as enthusiastically as he had previously supported Stephen. By Easter 1141, all of Normandy to the west of the Seine was firmly under the control of the Count of Anjou, though it would be a few years more before he was finally recognised as its lawful duke.

Meanwhile, the empress was creeping step by step closer to a crown. Before Easter, Oxford had surrendered to her, followed soon after by Reading and Bedford. Devizes was taken, and in May 1141 King David of Scotland, who alone had kept his original oath of allegiance, deemed it safe to join her court. The Gesta calls those submitting 'a servile and despicable crew', but concedes that the greater part of the kingdom now acknowledged her. When, just before midsummer, London finally agreed to admit her, and she came with a great procession to Westminster, only Kent was still solidly holding out for King Stephen. In that county William of Ypres was earl in all but name, and now his discretion at Lincoln paid off. Offering his backing to Queen Matilda, he began collecting an army for her, both English and mercenary, while she drew on her own lands in England and Boulogne for further support. In the meantime she continued to try what diplomacy could do, as these forces prepared for action.

At Westminster Matilda, Lady of the English, was anticipating an early coronation and handing out rewards to her faithful followers in the form of earldoms. Among them the ever useful Baldwin de Redvers became Earl of Devon, while another, Reginald de Dunstanville, became Earl of Cornwall. According to the various chronicles, however, she was not able to match her namesake in terms of diplomacy. Even William of Malmesbury suggests matters might have been better left to the 'moderation and wisdom' of Robert of Gloucester, while others suggest that, coming so close to a crown, the empress became haughty, arrogant and 'elated with insufferable pride'. When envoys from Queen Matilda came begging for Stephen to be set free, and promising he would then abdicate in her favour, become a pilgrim or possibly even a monk, her answer, says the Gesta, was framed in 'words of cruel and shameful abuse'. The same source relates how she imperiously demanded from London an immense amount of money by way of taxation, and when the Londoners asked for time to pay, raged at them that they had paid enough to Stephen to weaken her, and so had no excuse for refusing her in her turn.

It is hard to tell if these accusations are simply the misogyny of the times. Being ruled by a woman in her own name was a novelty, and with the example of her father and her first husband before her, the empress may have felt it more appropriate to command rather than request. Nevertheless, it did her little good at the time. Not only were the Londoners 'dissatisfied', Bishop Henry had also been offended by some of her appointments, notably that of a new Bishop of Durham made without consulting him. Her sharp dismissal of his sister-in-law the queen's pleas for her husband also rankled, as did her abrupt refusal of his own request that Eustace take over his father's counties of Boulogne and Mortain. It is possible he was already in contact with Queen Matilda at this time, as her forces gathered outside London, laying waste to the lands all about as a spur to return the Londoners to their first loyalty. When the blow fell on 24 June 1141, the bishop was certainly more than ready to separate himself from the Lady of the English.

On that day, so the Gesta tells us, the empress had just sat down to dinner at Westminster when the bells in the city of London began to ring. It was a call to arms, and soon an angry mob came pouring along the road towards the royal palace. Thereupon the empress 'fled shamefully with her retinue', if we believe the Gesta, leaving everything behind them, even the food on the table. William of Malmesbury describes a more ordered retreat, but even he concedes it was a hurried departure, and they left behind much that was promptly plundered by the mob.

Some, says the Gesta, thought only of their own necks and disappeared to their estates, while the Lady of the English, together with Robert of Gloucester and some others, made their way to Oxford. Bishop Henry took the opportunity to make for Winchester and the fortifications of his Wolvesey Castle next to the cathedral. Soon he was meeting Queen Matilda secretly at Guildford, and shortly after was spreading complaints that the empress had not kept her promises to him.

It was no doubt rumours of these complaints that brought Robert of Gloucester to Winchester to see for himself what was going on. What he saw prompted the return of his sister to the royal castle on the hill, but, claims the Gesta, as she and her retinue entered the town by one gate, Bishop Henry departed by another. Now as Wolvesey Castle was put under siege, Winchester itself was to become a battleground, with great swathes of the city between the royal castle above and the episcopal castle below burnt to the ground. In the course of this conflagration, the great jewelled cross atop a nearby abbey, presented by King Cnut and Queen Emma, appeared to weep before falling from its place. Different chronicles declare that Bishop Henry later used the jewels from this cross to pay his men, or possibly simply kept them for himself.

The empress had brought a sizeable force with her, along with David of Scotland and many earls, longstanding and recently created, who had regrouped with her at Oxford. Another was now added to their number, Miles of Gloucester becoming Earl of Hereford, while Geoffrey de Mandeville, Earl of Essex, a recent addition to her backers, had additional honours heaped on him to keep him on her side. When the siege began on 2 August 1141, it seemed at first as if it would only be a matter of time before Wolvesey fell and they could once again turn their thoughts to London and a crown. Bishop Henry, though, had other ideas. He immediately called on Queen Matilda for help, and now she and all those still loyal to King Stephen came swiftly to the rescue. As well as William of Ypres and his mercenaries, she had the forces of the earls of Surrey, Northampton and Arundel and those from her own lands. What tipped the balance in their favour, however, was a force of a thousand Londoners, presumably militia, summoned and led by the queen herself. With all these at her command the city of Winchester was completely encircled, and suddenly the besiegers within had become the besieged. It was, says the Gesta, an unprecedented situation. 'All of England was there in arms.'

Unprecedented, too, was this stand-off between the queen and the empress. Never before or since have two royal ladies faced each other at the head of armies, with the crown of England as the prize. There would be no battle between them, however, simply a grinding siege that ran on through August and into September. The queen's army had the advantage. Regularly re-supplied themselves, they patrolled all the roads around Winchester and cut off all aid for those within the walls. Nevertheless, a few recent converts of the empress, Geoffrey de Mandeville among them, managed to slip over those walls and re-join their friends in the service of the queen.

By the middle of September the plight of the besieged was becoming desperate. A force under John Marshal was sent out to try and secure Wherwell, either to break the circle or simply as a diversion. Though it failed to take the place, it did just enough to draw away William of Ypres and give a slim chance of a successful breakout. Thus, on the morning of 14 September the gates of the city were suddenly thrown open – one account says on the orders of Bishop Henry – and the whole army from within marched out with the empress at their head.

John of Worcester suggests this was a ploy on the part of the bishop, who intended to attack and take the empress prisoner. Others say it was a planned escape, and only the sudden return of William of Ypres destroyed the good order of the retreating column. Fearing just such an eventuality, Robert of Gloucester had set his sister at the front, closely guarded by Brian fitzCount and Reginald de Dunstanville, while he himself brought up the rear with a force of some two hundred horsemen, 'who had spirit enough not to be alarmed at a multitude'.

The sudden arrival of Queen Matilda's forces 'pouring in upon them from all sides in countless numbers', quickly turned the retreat into a rout. The priority, of course, was to get the empress away, and she and her escort fled at full speed to Ludgershall. Only pausing there to take a fresh horse, she then mounted 'male fashion', so John of Worcester claims, and galloped another twenty miles to Devizes. Even that was not deemed safe enough. With the empress exhausted by now, she was then carried in a litter – he refers to it as a 'hearse' – 'ignominiously enough, to the city of Gloucester'.

Behind her she left utter chaos, described in such detail by the Gesta writer that he must have been there. While Robert of Gloucester fought a sterling rearguard action at the crossing of the River Test at Stockbridge, as many as possible escaped as best they could, leaving behind them a trail of belongings and scattered valuables immediately looted by their pursuers. Even the Archbishop of Canterbury and his fellow bishops had 'their horses and clothes carried off, or barbarously torn from them'. Among the escapees were Miles of Gloucester and John Marshal, while David of Scotland fled from England for the third time in a matter of years.

Not so lucky, overwhelmed and made captive at the river, was Robert of Gloucester. He was immediately handed over to William of Ypres, and consigned to Rochester Castle where, in contrast to

King Stephen, now held in chains, his imprisonment seems to have been of the more open variety. Nonetheless, Queen Matilda now had a bargaining chip of her own in her fight to free her husband – though Robert himself insisted an earl was in no way equal in value to a king.

While this balance continued, some even saw prospects for peace, though there never seemed much real chance of that. For over a month, envoys passed between queen and empress, with the usually pro-Stephen Gesta bitterly complaining of 'each betraying much arrogance in negotiating'. In the end, all that could be arranged was a prisoner swap. On 1 November Queen Matilda and her sons arrived at Bristol where they were to remain as hostages while Stephen was freed. The king then travelled to Winchester where Robert was brought. William of Malmesbury reports the two men having a 'friendly interview', where Robert, having resisted both bribes and threats to make him change sides, was never likely to accept Stephen's urging to do so. Robert, in turn, left his son William as hostage at Winchester and rode to Bristol where the royal hostages were duly released, and finally William himself was freed to join his father.

For Stephen there was now a need to wipe out the ignominy of his captivity and re-assert his kingship, and this was done at a full re-crowning, carried out at Canterbury the following Christmas. There, too, Queen Matilda received a golden crown, and afterwards Stephen issued a coin to mark the occasion, showing himself and his wife side by side, clearly an indication that he knew to whom he owed his restored majesty. Earlier, Bishop Henry had called yet another church council to try to explain away his rapid changes of allegiance through the year. The same arguments were used as on the previous occasion. Matilda had broken her promises to the church, and even threatened his life, and thus had proved herself unworthy. 'I do not say that this speech was kindly received,' says Malmesbury, 'though certainly no-one opposed it' – no-one, that is, except an envoy sent from the empress who, while contradicting everything the bishop said, seems to have made little impression on his listeners.

Both sides, though, were exhausted after the turmoil of the previous year, and something of a lull set in. In the spring, Stephen and his queen set off northward, possibly on a progress, or maybe intending to re-assert their dominion over regions that had recently been neglected. He got no further than Northampton, however, before he was taken so seriously ill that for a time his life was despaired of. Once again Queen Matilda quietly assumed control, watchful lest her namesake took advantage of the situation to launch another bid for the crown that had so nearly been hers.

Indeed, at this time the empress did move her court back to Oxford, a clear statement that she had not abandoned her cause. On the way, however, a council of war was held at Devizes and it was decided a greater weight of numbers was needed to deliver a knockout blow to the royal cause. A message was sent to Geoffrey of Anjou to come and support his wife in England, but Geoffrey demanded they send him Robert of Gloucester, whom he knew and trusted, to discuss the matter before he would consider the request. Robert himself was reluctant, pointing out the perils of the journey and the weakness of the empress's party in England in his absence. It may have been the king's illness that finally persuaded him to risk it, but before he left he did much to improve the fortifications of Oxford, intending to leave his sister in an impregnable position at this furthest outpost of her lands while he was away.

By the time Robert finally left at the end of June 1142, Stephen was very much recovered, enough, indeed, to take back control from his queen, who also left the country at this time to make a visit to Boulogne and hold her court there, the first for some years. The fact that she took her son Eustace with her gives some support to the claim that he had been knighted and created Count of Boulogne the previous Christmas. At the very least, Eustace, now aged around fifteen, was being shown to the nobles of Boulogne as their future ruler.

When Robert eventually reached Normandy, surviving a violent storm on the way, he found Geoffrey more inclined to use his services in that duchy than to send aid to his wife in England. Now in his late twenties, the count of Anjou had matured into a shrewd and cautious campaigner. Always more concerned with Normandy than England, he no doubt reasoned that this, too, was part of his wife's inheritance, and that it was better to secure one part completely than fail in both by overstretching one's resources. Through summer and early autumn, therefore, Robert assisted in victory after victory, and when he returned to England in October, he took with him, not Count Geoffrey, but his son, the young Henry, then nine years old.

By that time he was urgently needed at home. Stephen had apparently come out of his illness 'waking to life and new activity', and determined to conquer his opponent once and for all. First, Wareham was seized, the port most conveniently used by the followers of the empress, then, on 26 September, Oxford itself was attacked. Well protected by rivers, with the crossings over the Thames securely held against him, Oxford did appear at first sight to be impregnable, so much so that the garrison of the empress felt able to jeer at the king as he rode the far river bank.

He took some time to reconnoitre the surroundings, however, and found – or, some say, was shown – another place where a force of men could cross the river. This ford was deeper and more difficult, but it was here that Stephen eventually launched his assault, 'swimming rather than wading across', attacking the garrison in their flank and taking them completely by surprise. As these defenders fled back through the town walls, they had no time to close the great gates behind them before the royal army was pouring through. The Empress Matilda was quick enough to escape with some of the garrison to the safety of the castle, but all the rest of the town was swiftly occupied by Stephen. And having got into the castle, Matilda was now unable to get out again.

The siege began on 26 September and, for once, was pursued by Stephen with the utmost determination. While the loyal followers of the empress gathered at Wallingford, a few miles away, they felt quite unequal to the task of tackling the king, now securely within Robert of Gloucester's fine new fortifications. Even when Robert himself returned from Normandy, they were still gathering forces and pondering their approach when Matilda took matters into her own hands.

Just before Christmas, on a freezing night with deep snow around and more falling, she was let down on ropes from the castle tower, crossed the frozen Thames, and, wearing white and accompanied by only three men, passed through the royal guard posts and so away. Blinded by the snow, only one man saw her go, says the Gesta, and he was bribed to silence. Then she and her companions walked more than six miles through ice and snow, finally reaching the safety of Wallingford. Even the Gesta writer was impressed. 'I have never heard of any woman having such marvellous escapes from so many enemies threatening her life, and from such exceeding perils.' Stephen, too, must have been impressed, for when the garrison surrendered immediately afterwards, he allowed them all to go freely away.

The following year Stephen himself had a lucky escape, very nearly trapped by Robert of Gloucester at Wilton near Salisbury, as he had been before at Lincoln. This time, however, Stephen did not stand and fight, he and Bishop Henry slipping away in the chaos as William Martel fought a fierce rearguard action to enable his escape. Martel was taken prisoner and had to be ransomed, the price being Sherborne Castle, which then became an important and strategic guard for the empress's lands in the south-west.

By now it seemed clear that, though each side could win skirmishes and take castles, neither had the strength for a knockout blow. In the midst of all this, law and order was the chief casualty. While the south-west was firmly ruled by the empress, and the south-east by Stephen and his queen, other parts of the country went their own way. Great lords fought each other, and lesser lords tried to emulate them. As the Anglo-Saxon Chronicle records,

> Every rich man built his castles … and they filled the land full of castles … and when the castles were finished, they filled them with devils and evil men… Then was corn dear, and flesh and cheese and butter, for there was none in the land – wretched men starved with hunger … never was there more misery.

It didn't help matters that, in 1143, each side lost a significant supporter. For the empress the death of Miles of Gloucester in a hunting accident was a serious blow. His son Roger inherited his lands and earldom, but he was by no means as committed to her cause as his father had been. For Stephen the loss was Pope Innocent, who died in September of that year. His successor, the short-lived Celestine II, was much less inclined to approve the actions of the English king, and, indeed, Stephen was to fall out with a number of popes in the coming years, particularly over the appointment of an Archbishop of York. The immediate consequence in 1143 was that Bishop Henry ceased to be papal legate, and thus lost his superiority over Archbishop Theobald of Canterbury.

At this time, too, Stephen's own jealousy of the wealth accumulated by his earls and suspicions as to their power did his cause no favours. Over the next few years, in quick succession, the earls of Essex, Chester, Hertford and Pembroke were deprived of some or all of their castles, in almost every case the procedure being the same as for Bishop Roger and his family earlier in the reign. Rumours of disloyalty were spread, the earl was arrested and held until the castles were delivered up, then released after taking an oath of future loyalty. None of it won any long-term benefit for the king. Geoffrey de Mandeville, earl of Essex, for example, immediately took himself off to terrorise the fenland of north Norfolk, until fatally wounded attacking one of the king's fortifications. Ranulf of Chester, only recently reconciled with Stephen, finding himself similarly accused, on his release made alliance with David of Scotland – with whom he had previously been at loggerheads over lands around Carlisle – and moved firmly to the side of the empress. At the same time, mistreatment of the Earl of Hertford, who had been a hostage for Ranulf, brought the de Clare family, including the Earl of Pembroke, into conflict with the king, and again castles were confiscated, in particular Pevensey Castle, which was now given to Eustace.

Throughout this time, as Stephen was drawn from one part of the country to another, Queen Matilda remained based in and around London, a steady presence, and a check on her husband's administration and that of her own estates in the area. It was through her influence, too, that a marriage was arranged between her younger son, William, and the daughter and sole heiress of William of Warenne, Earl of Surrey. This took place in 1147, and when the earl was killed the following year on crusade in the Holy Land, William became a very wealthy young man.

By this time Stephen had been king of England for more than a dozen years. He was now in his fifties, and Empress Matilda was forty-four, and despite the king's maladroit handling of his nobles, the idea of simply replacing one with the other was ceasing to be the major issue. Now more and more the argument revolved around who of the younger generation would succeed to the throne. Eustace was around twenty years old. He had been married for seven years to Constance but there were no children and, says the *Anglo-Saxon Chronicle*, 'she had little bliss of him.' Indeed, he seems even at that age to have been building up a poor reputation. Writing after his death, the same Chronicle declares, 'He was an evil man, and did more harm than good wherever he went.'

While Stephen and Queen Matilda clearly regarded Eustace as heir to all their possession, the empress, on the other hand, had no intention of abandoning her claim to her father's throne. If she could not wear the crown herself, as seemed increasingly likely, then it must go to her eldest son, and in contrast to Eustace, young Henry seems to have made a good impression on everyone.

Recalled to Normandy in 1144, he had spent time being tutored by his father in his future obligations. In 1147, however, without the knowledge or permission of either parent, the fourteen-year-old had assembled a band of mercenaries solely on the promise of plunder to come, and brought them to England on a reckless expedition that could have gone badly wrong. After suffering two swift defeats at the hands of Stephen's castellans, he then appealed to his relatives to pay off his men so he could depart. Empress Matilda flatly refused to do so, and when Robert of Gloucester also turned him down, with astounding cheek he turned to the king for funds. It is entirely typical of Stephen that he paid up, though probably his aim was to get rid of this loose cannon causing trouble in his kingdom. A rumour that had preceded the boy, however, insisting he had brought with him thousands of men to win the kingdom for his mother, had probably given the king a frightening vision of the future.

In October of 1147, the cause of the empress was fatally weakened by the death of her greatest champion, Robert of Gloucester. The following February, bowing to the knowledge that she herself was never likely to wrest the crown from Stephen, she finally returned to Normandy, where, some years before, Geoffrey had completed his conquest and been recognised as duke. No doubt Matilda was now grateful for his single-mindedness. Rather than returning to live with her husband, however, she set up her own establishment at the palace built by Henry I next to the Priory of Notre-Dame du-Pré, near Rouen. She and Geoffrey were, though, united in one aim – to put their eldest son Henry onto the throne of England.

Already known as Geoffrey Plantagenet from the sprig of broom, the 'planta genista', he wore in his helmet, Geoffrey of Anjou seems always to have recognised that his gains were made on behalf of his wife and, particularly, his son. There was every intention to hand over to the boy as soon as he reached a suitable age, but before Henry could become a duke, he first had to be knighted. Louis of France was never going to oblige, but David of Scotland was more than willing.

Early in 1149, therefore, with rather more discretion than on his previous visit, Henry landed in England and made his way quietly to Carlisle. There, says the chronicler John of Hexham, 'King David entertained him with great respect and sumptuous provision of costly munificence,' and on the feast of Pentecost, 22 May, he was made a knight. Assisting at the ceremony was Earl Ranulf of Chester, and the chronicles contain several different versions of a plan for the earl, King David and young Henry to launch an attack King Stephen immediately after. The plan came to nothing, but by the time Henry was returning to his mother's supporters in the south, the king probably knew of his whereabouts, drawn north to York, either on suspicion of Henry's presence or for reasons of his own. Several attempts were made to intercept him, and Eustace, too, became involved, setting ambushes on the approaches to Bristol which Henry was able to avoid. Strenuous attempts were then made to ravage the lands around Devizes and Marlborough, either to draw him out to fight, or maybe to drive him away. The supporters of the empress were not prepared for a confrontation at this time, however, and in January 1150 Henry returned to Normandy. Immediately, Geoffrey of Anjou handed over the duchy, and at seventeen years of age Henry Plantagenet became Duke of Normandy.

It now became the prime concern of Stephen and Queen Matilda that their own son should be formally recognised as heir to the English throne. There was a tradition in Normandy for an heir to receive homage and fealty in the lifetime of his predecessor, but, in the fewer than one hundred years since the Conquest, this procedure had never been adopted in England. Henry I had tried it for the benefit of his daughter, but without success, and, probably bearing that in mind, Stephen wanted something more for Eustace, nothing less than a full coronation and anointing by the Archbishop of Canterbury.

His chances of achieving this would have been higher had he not so completely fallen out with church and pope. As well as the ongoing wrangle over the Archbishop of York, he had now alienated Archbishop Theobald and, a few years previously, the country had been placed under an interdict, meaning the English people no longer had access to the church's sacraments. This, a most severe sanction, had followed a fairly pointless trial of strength between the king and his archbishop. In March 1148, Pope Eugenius had called a church council to meet at Rheims. Stephen had decided Theobald should not attend, but in defiance of the king the archbishop hired a fishing boat and crossed the Channel in order to do so, whereupon he was effectively exiled. As if adding insult to injury, when a vacancy for bishop of Hereford arose in the course of the council, Pope Eugenius appointed a replacement, Gilbert Foliot, without even consulting the king.

Once again it was Queen Matilda who smoothed the way to a reconciliation, first arranging for Theobald and Gilbert to be housed at St. Omer in Boulogne, then assisting in their return to the castle at Framlingham in Suffolk, under the protection of Hugh Bigod. Finally, in November, after further negotiations, and with Gilbert swearing fealty to the king, Theobald was able to return to Canterbury, though very little minded to give in to Stephen's future demands.

At this time, too, Queen Matilda was very much involved in overseeing the building of a new abbey at Faversham in Kent. Founded jointly by king and queen in 1148, they intended this to be the final resting place for themselves and future rulers from their dynasty. It was planned on a grand scale. The abbey church itself was to be over 360 feet long, with cloisters to match, and numerous outbuildings covering many acres of land. In fact some eighty years later, long after the deaths of its founders, it was still not complete and the church had been shortened by nearly a third. When Archbishop Theobald returned to England, one of his first acts was to consecrate an abbot for this new monastery, no doubt as a gesture of good will towards the king and queen. When he was then asked to crown Eustace, either there or at Westminster, however, he flatly refused. Pope Celestine had earlier forbidden this 'novelty', and the archbishop would not go against such a firm ruling.

Of course, the other way of ensuring the succession of Eustace was to dispose of his rival in Normandy. Louis of France was already smarting from the transference of the duchy without his permission. Nor could he tolerate the idea that the upstart Duke Henry might become king of England. It was easy, therefore, to make an alliance to attack Normandy – easier by far than actually to achieve their objective of defeating and removing its new duke. The co-ordinated attack – Eustace in the north-east and Louis in the south – had barely got underway in the summer of 1151 when Louis fell ill. A truce was arranged, which soon became a peace treaty. Eustace had to withdraw, and Geoffrey of Anjou and his son travelled to Paris, where Henry was officially recognised as Duke of Normandy and performed homage to Louis at a rather ill-tempered meeting with the French king. Also present at that ceremony was Louis's already estranged wife, Eleanor of Aquitaine.

Then, early in 1152, Theobald, Count of Blois and brother of King Stephen, died. This reminder of his own mortality spurred the king to even greater efforts to have his son recognised as heir to his throne. At his Easter court he persuaded some of the nobles to acknowledge him as such, possibly even swearing fealty, but when again he demanded that Archbishop Theobald should crown him, he was once more refused. Not only did the archbishop repeat the pope's prohibition, but this time he added the reason for it, that Stephen had obtained his crown wrongfully by breaking his oath to King Henry. For a brief time Theobald and his fellow bishops were imprisoned, until the outcry, and probably the queen's intervention, caused their release.

There was more than one notable death in 1152, however, and the second would be a far greater loss to the king than the first. Soon after the Easter court broke up, Queen Matilda paid a visit to a friend and former member of her household, the Countess of Essex, at Hedingham Castle in that county. While there she fell ill with a fever which rapidly worsened. Stephen and Eustace hurried to her bedside, but by then she was beyond all help, and a few days later, on 3 May, she died. She was buried, with full pomp and honours, in her new abbey church at Faversham, far sooner than anyone had expected such a royal burial at that place. The epitaph over her tomb, no doubt approved by her grieving husband, read, 'If any woman deserved to be carried by the hands of angels to heaven, it was this holy Queen.' Sadly, that tomb – along with those of her husband and son – was destroyed at the time of the Dissolution of the Monasteries in the sixteenth century. Reputedly the bones of all three were thrown into the river nearby, but afterwards rescued and reburied in the Church of St Mary of Charity, where a canopied tomb remains, the only memorial to this most gracious and capable of women.

And now Stephen, already deprived of the companion who had advised, sustained and supported him through all his troubled times, may have become aware that the tide in England was turning

Corfe Castle. Athelred, first husband of Emma of Normandy, became king of England after his half-brother Edward was murdered here in 978. This violence cast a blight on his early reign, while, later, repeated Viking raids darkened it further. (Author's collection)

The approach to Poole Harbour. In 1015 Cnut, son of Swein Forkbeard, invaded England with a Viking army through this harbour on the south coast. (Author's collection)

Left: St Mary's Priory Church, Deerhurst, Gloucester. On an island in the River Severn near this Saxon church at Deerhurst, King Edmund Ironside and Cnut made a peace treaty, agreeing to divide England between them. Only weeks later Edmund died, leaving Cnut to claim the entire country. (Author's collection)

Below left: On the death of Harthacnut, Emma's least favoured son, Edward, son of Athelred, became king. He ruled England for twenty-four years, and would later become known as St Edward the Confessor.

Below: Godbegot House, Winchester. This house stands on the site of Emma's manor house where she lived in retirement until her death in 1052. She was buried in Winchester Cathedral, where her bones have recently been identified. (Author's collection)

Canossa Castle, high in the Apennine mountains, was a mighty fortress, the seat of the counts of Tuscany. It was also the site of the monastery of Sant'Apollonio, where the monk Donizo wrote his *Vita Mathildis*, the Life of Matilda of Canossa. (Fabiour under Creative Commons 4.0)

Above: Humiliation at Canossa. In 1077 Emperor Henry IV came barefoot to Canossa with his wife and child, to save his throne by reconciling with Pope Gregory VII. Tradition states he was forced to wait outside in the snow for three days before being admitted. He was, though, only twenty-six at the time, not an old man as depicted here, and nothing suggests his wife and child waited with him.

Left: As a champion of the papacy, Matilda of Canossa was greatly honoured at the time of the Reformation in Europe. Her remains were removed from their original resting place at San Benedetto di Polirone to this magnificent tomb by Bernini in St Peter's, Rome. (Bede735)

Above: Seal of Emperor Henry V. The Empress Matilda married Henry just before her twelfth birthday, and two years later accompanied him to Italy, where, after driving out Pope Paschal, they were crowned by the papal legate Archbishop Bourdin, who would later be installed as 'Antipope' Gregory VIII. Matilda remained for some time in northern Italy as regent for Henry.

Below: The drowning of Empress Matilda's younger brother William off this rocky coast at Barfleur left her as heir apparent to England and Normandy. (Author's collection)

Above: In 1138, Queen Matilda successfully besieged Dover Castle, regaining it for King Stephen after a rebellion in favour of the empress. (DeFacto)

Left: Norman keep at Arundel Castle, Sussex. In September 1139 Empress Matilda arrived in England to claim the throne. She was sheltered by her stepmother Adeliza of Louvain at Arundel Castle before travelling on to Bristol and Gloucester. (Author's collection)

Below left: In 1141, Lincoln Castle was the scene of King Stephen's greatest defeat, after which he was taken prisoner and held for nearly a year at Bristol Castle. (Dmitrij M. under Creative Commons 2.0)

Driven out of London in June 1141, Empress Matilda based herself at Winchester Castle, besieging Wolvesey Castle in the town below. This belonged to Bishop Henry of Blois, who had reneged on a promise to support her against his brother the king. Queen Matilda then brought up an army to besiege the besiegers. In September Empress Matilda managed to break out, fleeing to Gloucester, but leaving her chief supporter Robert of Gloucester as a prisoner of the queen. (Author's collection)

King Stephen was held prisoner at Bristol Castle until he was exchanged for Robert of Gloucester in November 1141. Queen Matilda was herself briefly held here as part of the complicated prisoner exchange. (Author's collection)

Above: St. George's Tower, Oxford. Taken by surprise in September 1142, Empress Matilda became besieged at Oxford Castle. Just before Christmas she managed to escape, being let down on ropes from this tower, and making her way through the snow to Wallingford. (Author's collection)

Left: King Stephen and Henry II from a thirteenth-century chronicle. In 1153, King Stephen and the empress's son Henry were forced by the English nobility to make terms for an end to the civil war. Henry was adopted as Stephen's son and heir. When Stephen died less than a year later, Henry became King Henry II of England. (Courtesy of the British Library under Creative Commons 4.0)

Both Queen Matilda and her husband Stephen were interred at Faversham Abbey which they had founded. Bad feeling between town and abbey caused the abbey church to be razed to the ground after the Dissolution of the Monasteries. The royal tombs were destroyed and the bones thrown into Faversham Creek. It is claimed they were rescued and re-interred in this, rather plain, empty tomb in the nearby Church of St Mary. (Author's collection)

At Clermont in November 1095, Pope Urban II called for Western Christians to retake Jerusalem from the Muslims who, it was claimed, were preventing Christian pilgrims from visiting the holy places. Baldwin of Bourg, together with his relatives Godfrey de Bouillon and Baldwin of Boulogne, was among the group from Boulogne who answered the call.

The Melisende Psalter. It has been suggested that this exquisite little prayer book was given by Fulk of Anjou to his wife Queen Melisende as part of their reconciliation in the mid 1130s. (Courtesy of the British Library under Creative Commons 4.0)

Presentation of Christ in the Temple from the Melisende Psalter. Christ is held by Simeon; the Prophetess Anna holds an open scroll. (Courtesy of the British Library under Creative Commons 4.0)

Above: Church of the Holy Sepulchre, Jerusalem. The rebuilding of this church was commissioned by Fulk and Melisende, but the queen supervised its completion and re-dedication after her husband's death. (Gerd Eichmann)

Right: Byzantine Emperor John II Comnenus. (Courtesy of the Directorate of Hagia Sophia Museum)

This later Ottoman structure stands on the site of the older Tower of David, where Melisende was forced to shelter when her son, Baldwin, demanded to take over government of the kingdom. Later reconciled with him, Melisende continued influential in her retirement at Nablus.

The Souk, Jerusalem. The earliest souk (covered market) in Jerusalem was commissioned by Melisende. (Hynek Moravec)

Melisende was buried alongside her mother, Morphia, in the Church of the Assumption, Jerusalem. (Courtesy Avi Nahmias, available from https://commons.wikimedia.org/wiki/User:Avin)

Left: Eleanor of Aquitaine as pictured in her psalter. (Courtesy of the Koninklijke Bibliotheek under Creative Commons 4.0)

Below: Following her divorce and re-marriage to Henry II of England, Eleanor became Queen of England and Duchess of Normandy. Domfront Castle was a favourite residence, and these figures at the site celebrate the lively court of the times. (Author's collection)

It is likely Eleanor had already planned to live separately from Henry, with her own court in her own duchy, before the king fell for Rosamund Clifford. Tradition declares Henry installed Rosamund as his mistress in 'Rosamund's Bower' within a maze at Woodstock Palace, Oxfordshire. No trace of that has been found, but the pool shown here is claimed to be Rosamund's bathing pool. (Author's collection)

For most of the time, throughout the fifteen years between 1174 and 1189, Eleanor was imprisoned in the castle at Old Sarum. Occasionally allowed out to provide a figurehead for some policy of Henry's, she was only finally released when her son Richard became King Richard I on the death of his father. Throughout his reign, and through the early years of the reign of King John, Eleanor continued to wield great influence. (Author's collection)

Finally retiring to Fontevrault Abbey in France (above), Eleanor died there in April 1204 and was buried alongside her husband Henry II, with her favourite son, Richard, at their feet. The bodies were removed during the French Revolution, but the effigies of king and queen remain (below). (Jean-Christophe Benoist and Adam Bishop under Creative Commons 3.0)

against him. The great lords, sick of this prolonged struggle, were making agreements among themselves not to fight each other, or, if required to do so by a liege lord, to put in as little effort as possible. There was a feeling of tolerating the king until he should be gone, and then looking forward to a new era. Eustace himself, now named as Count of Boulogne, seems to have had no partisans of his own. He, too, had lost his fiercest champion with the death of his mother.

As far as the empress and her son in Normandy were concerned, the endgame might already have begun but for two unconnected delays. First, on 7 September 1151, Geoffrey of Anjou had died quite suddenly from a chill caught while swimming in a cold river. He was buried at St. Julien's Cathedral in Le Mans, but whether the empress attended the funeral, or what her thoughts may have been on the passing of this unwanted husband, we have no record. It seems doubtful that she ever fully appreciated the contribution of Geoffrey to her cause, or his magnanimity in handing over to his son the duchy he had spent so much time and effort in gaining. Henry's own plans for an invasion of England were, of course, immediately put on hold, as he took possession of his father's lands in Anjou and spent time in making sure there would be no sudden challenges in Normandy.

Then, in March 1152, a church council at Beaugency in France finally put an end to the marriage of Louis of France and Eleanor of Aquitaine. The divorce terms provided for her to take back that duchy which was her own inheritance, and she set off at once for her homeland. There, at Poitiers, as previously arranged, she was joined by Henry Plantagenet. Their wedding, on 18 May, was a quiet one, carried out, according to William of Newburgh, 'not very splendidly ... but with guarded prudence', discretion being absolutely necessary in the circumstances. At the time Henry was still relying heavily on his mother for advice, but it seems likely she was as much in the dark as everyone else as to his marital intentions. Once again, her reaction is not recorded.

When news got out, Louis, says Robert of Torigny, 'became incensed against the duke'. He quickly gathered another alliance against him, not only Eustace, this time, but also the new Counts Theobald of Blois and Henry of Champagne, and even Henry's own brother Geoffrey, who was apparently aggrieved at not inheriting Anjou from his father. Henry, meanwhile, having spent barely two weeks with his new bride, was already at Barfleur, once again planning his invasion of England.

'Nearly all the Normans now thought that Duke Henry would speedily lose the whole of his possessions,' writes Torigny. Instead, clearly well tutored in military matters by his father, Henry quickly rallied, and by the autumn had defeated his brother and brought all but Eustace to a truce. It was probably Matilda, however, receiving desperate messages from her supporters in England, who now advised him that he was more urgently needed in that country, while such a campaign would have the additional benefit of drawing Eustace himself back across the Channel to defend his inheritance.

In England Stephen had launched his own attack against the party of the empress, seizing Newbury and putting Wallingford under a most severe siege. Brian fitzCount had died some years before, and the new castellan had sent to Normandy the traditional appeal that, unless help was received soon, that precious fortress would have to be surrendered. Accepting his mother's advice, therefore, and dividing his forces, Henry left Matilda as his regent in Normandy, with the newly tamed Geoffrey as her military commander, and arrived in England early in January 1153.

He had not the largest of armies – some 140 knights and 3,000 men – and made no attempt to lift the siege around Wallingford. Instead, gathering the earls still loyal to his mother, he attacked Stephen's outlying castle at Malmesbury. The king arrived soon after, with his son and a large army, but then, says Henry of Huntingdon, with each side drawn up in battle array along the banks of a river, God intervened. 'For the floodgates of heaven were opened,' and with the elements, he claims, favouring Henry's side, not only rain but sleet and snow drove into the faces of Stephen's men, until 'the king could no longer endure the severity of the weather,' and withdrew to London.

The suggestion in the Gesta is that it was not only the weather that discouraged Stephen but his lack of faith in the men alongside him. He may well have been right. Within a few weeks Southampton had surrendered to Henry and the Earl of Arundel was making friendly overtures. A meeting was then held at Stockbridge between Henry, some of his chief men, and the major clerics of southern England including the Archbishop of Canterbury and Bishop Henry. It seems likely some sort of truce was put in place here, for afterwards the rivals remained studiously apart for an extended period. Stephen appeared intermittently at the siege of Wallingford, while Henry settled first at Gloucester, where he received the latest and most prominent defector to his cause, Robert of Leicester. He then toured the Midlands with this new friend, and, as if that defection was not enough, dealt another blow to Stephen when Warwick Castle was handed over to him by the wife of Earl Roger of Warwick, the earl apparently dying of shock when told the news.

It was August when Henry finally came to Wallingford to try and raise the siege, but now both parties discovered how far events had moved on. Stephen brought up an army, says Huntingdon, 'assembling the whole force he could muster throughout his territories.' A major battle seemed imminent, and then 'the traitorous nobles interfered.' The armies simply refused to fight. Between themselves, with the help of 'certain religious persons', these nobles thrashed out terms for a truce which was intended to lead to a lasting settlement. Then the king and the duke were 'reluctantly compelled' to agree. One requirement was that Stephen and Henry must meet face to face to arrange for further negotiations, which they did, though with a river running between them. Then both sides withdrew.

The person least happy with all of this was, of course, Eustace, whom nobody had bothered to consult. Seeing himself as the sacrificial lamb, he immediately took himself off to demand money from the abbey of Bury St Edmunds. Being refused, he plundered the abbey lands, sat down to feast off his plunder and promptly died. It was seen as the judgement of God, and few, apart from his father, seem to have lamented when he was buried alongside his mother at Faversham.

The majority regarded it as the removal of an obstacle in the way of peace. Work was quickly underway to hammer out a treaty acceptable to both sides, with Archbishop Theobald and Bishop Henry – the latter possibly appeasing his conscience – as chief negotiators. The resulting agreement would almost certainly have been vetoed by Eustace and by Queen Matilda, but with his younger son showing no interest in anything other than the county of Boulogne, Stephen's ambitions now seemed to run no further than his own lifetime. Thus, on 6 November 1153, in the cathedral at Winchester packed with clergy and supporters of both sides, Stephen officially adopted Henry as his heir 'by legitimate right', while Henry did homage to Stephen as king and liege lord, swearing to honour and protect him according to the agreement between them.

'What boundless joy, what a day of rejoicing,' cries Henry of Huntingdon, and no doubt there was equal delight in the palace at Rouen when the news was brought to Empress Matilda. It would be several months, though, before she would see her victorious son, who first shared a Christmas court and then a short progress with Stephen. When he returned in March 1154, however, she was able to hand back his duchy intact, despite repeated attempts by Louis to infiltrate border areas.

If she ever felt jealous that her son had achieved so easily what she had striven for so hard and for so long, she would no doubt have consoled herself with the faith he clearly put in her judgement, and the way he continued to look to her for advice. She was, for some time, his first choice as regent in Normandy whenever he was away from the duchy, and thus she remained at Rouen in 1154 when, following the unexpectedly early death of Stephen, he travelled to England for his coronation. And when on 19 December, in Westminster Abbey, Henry was crowned King of England by Archbishop Theobald, it was with the gold crown Matilda had brought with her from Germany so many years before.

Only once would she return briefly to England, to attend a Great Council meeting at Winchester in 1155. There she strongly advised against a proposed expedition to conquer Ireland, and, as usual, her advice was accepted by her son. Sadly, he did not accept her advice in 1162 when appointing Thomas Becket, his friend and chancellor, as Archbishop of Canterbury. Her experiences of conflict between church and state in Germany no doubt led her to advise against the move, but this time she was overruled. The disastrous consequences troubled the last years of her life and were still unresolved when she died at Rouen on 10 September 1167.

In accordance with her wishes she was buried with all honour at the monastery of Bec-Hellouin in a marble tomb commissioned by her son. Ironically, this was destroyed by English soldiers in the army of Henry V in 1421. Some of her bones were identified and interred in a new coffin in 1684. Lost in the destruction caused by the French Revolution in the eighteenth century, this coffin was later re-discovered and buried in the cathedral at Rouen – where her father had always wished her to be buried. Her original and famous epitaph, however, has been remembered down the years. 'Great by birth, greater by marriage, greatest in her offspring, here lies Matilda, the daughter, wife and mother of Henry.'

And namesake, too, of that other Matilda who *did* become queen of England. They have often been viewed as opposites – Matilda of Boulogne gentle, wise, dutiful and diplomatic, and the empress fierce, haughty headstrong and unreasonable. Much of this, however, may be down to the entrenched views of society at the time. Certainly, as the dutiful wife of Emperor Henry, the Empress Matilda was known as Matilda the Good. Only when she was claiming a throne for herself, rather than for a husband or son, were these insults attached to her, and then mainly by her opponents. Matilda of Boulogne, however, acted throughout in the interests of her husband, and this was seen as entirely praiseworthy. Thus, when the queen was described as having 'masculine firmness', this was meant as a compliment, while saying the empress lacked 'the gentleness of her sex' was clearly the opposite.

What both Matildas shared, however, perhaps sheathed in one and nakedly apparent in the other, was a steely will and a courage in action well beyond the ordinary. As allies they would have been truly formidable, and it seems more than merely unfortunate that fate chose to pitch them against each other as enemies.

4

Melisende of Jerusalem and Her Family: The Women of Outremer

The common view of the crusades is that they were a series of wars between Christians and Muslims for possession of the 'Holy Land', where Jesus Christ lived on earth. Indeed, the word 'crusade' itself is a much later invention, derived from the 'cross' worn on the garments of the Christian campaigners, and has since become attached to any kind of moral enterprise. Like many common views, however, this is a vast over-simplification of the situation on the ground at the time of the 1st Crusade in the late eleventh century.

The city of Jerusalem, in the heart of the Holy Land, was of course the original focal point of Christianity, though after its sacking by the Romans in AD 70 and subsequent persecutions, few Christians remained there. The apostles, the followers of Jesus, had, however, obeyed to the letter his command to 'make disciples of all the nations' and the faith had been firmly planted all over the region and beyond. Through the Roman provinces of Syria and Egypt, to Ethiopia, Persia and India, towns, cities and indeed kingdoms had converted to Christianity within a few hundred years of the crucifixion of Christ. The church in Egypt, later known as the Coptic Church, even claimed to date from that earlier time when the Holy Family sought shelter there from the wrath of King Herod, with a monastery sited at the place where, it was claimed, they had lived. Alexandria claimed conversion by St Mark from

AD 61, and Antioch by the apostles Paul and Barnabas even earlier. The Book of Revelation, attributed to John the Divine and written around AD 95, was addressed to the 'seven churches in Asia', there was a Christian church in Edessa before AD 201 and Armenia claimed Christianity as the state religion from around AD 300.

The journeying of Paul, the 'Apostle to the Gentiles', through Greece and eventually to Rome around AD 60, perhaps inevitably moved the focus away from Palestine for the first time. Rome was then the centre of the Western World, and thus gave the greatest opportunity for spreading the new religion as widely as possible. Its position as the new focal point of the *Christian* world was also secured by the martyrdom of Paul and also of St Peter during the persecutions of Nero in the AD 60s. Peter had, after all, been named by Jesus himself as the 'rock' upon which his church would be built, and all subsequent popes – good and bad – would draw their authority from that statement.

For several centuries, then, Jerusalem remained almost peripheral to Christianity. Destroyed as a Jewish city, it was partly rebuilt and dedicated to the god Jupiter by the Emperor Hadrian, but both Jews and Christians were banned from its precincts. Then in AD 312 the Roman Emperor Constantine underwent his conversion to Christianity, leading first to tolerance of the religion, and later to its adoption as the state religion of the Roman Empire. In AD 326 his mother Helena visited Jerusalem, and the site of the crucifixion and the tomb of Jesus were 'discovered', no doubt with the help of Christians from the local area to whom the tradition had been passed down through the ages. The Church of the Holy Sepulchre was built and Jerusalem once again became a focus of religious activity.

With Christianity no longer a persecuted sect but the official religion of the empire, there was now felt to be a need to define exactly what was to be believed, the basic tenets and dogma of this newly acceptable faith. Inevitably over the centuries differences had arisen in the rites and customs of widely separated churches, and arguments now began over words and translations. They were all followers of Jesus Christ, but, as the twentieth-century poet

Ezra Pound wryly observed, 'They'll no' get him a' in a book, I think, though they write it cunningly.' Fierce debates over such matters as the Trinity, the nature of Christ and the status of the Virgin Mary, at a series of officially sponsored councils in Nicaea, in Constantinople and in Chalcedon, did little for the unity of the growing church. In Egypt, in Syria, in Antioch, Armenia and Edessa, churches clung to their own traditions, some tolerated and others declared heretical, and many rejected the doctrines now adopted by the 'imperial church'.

The movement of the capital of the empire from Rome to the ancient city of Byzantium by Constantine provided further scope for division. For a time re-named Constantinople, its enhanced status and the closeness of its bishop to the emperor threatened to detract from the authority of the bishops of Rome, the successors of St Peter, who increasingly drew their support from the Frankish peoples occupying Western Europe. Once again, differences grew up in practices, traditions and even the dates of important feast days, and though for a while the bishops of Rome and Constantinople were regarded as equal leaders of the church, the claim to supremacy of the Roman bishops, now called 'popes', contributed to a decisive split in AD 1054 which has persisted to the present day.

The fall of the Roman Empire in the West late in the fifth century left the Eastern Empire, soon referred to as 'Byzantine', successor to the provinces of the Middle East. Efforts to unite the area as 'one state, one religion' were thwarted, however, first by Persian inroads, and then by the appearance of a new religion with a new force behind it, the Muslim Arabs.

Early in the seventh century the Prophet Muhammad, a native of Mecca in the Arab Peninsula, received a series of revelations from Allah, which, it was claimed, refined and perfected the beliefs held first by Jews and then by Christians. At first fighting to establish this new religion within their local area, from the time of the death of Muhammad in AD 632 his followers surged out to conquer all the neighbouring lands. Within a few decades, Persia, Mesopotamia, Syria, Palestine and Egypt had been added to this Arab-Islamic state. The belief that in the course of his ascension to heaven Muhammad had travelled from Mecca to Jerusalem and there conversed with Abraham, Moses and Jesus, made that city the third holiest for Muslims, after Mecca and Medina where the Prophet himself had lived. Jerusalem was duly captured from the Byzantines in AD 638.

The Islamic religion was no more proof against division than Christianity, however. In AD 661, Ali, the Prophet's cousin and last of the 'Rightly Guided Caliphs', died, the caliph being the chief religious and civil leader. A split now appeared between the Umayyads, a rival clan who took power and appointed a new caliph, and a minority group who felt that only a direct descendant of the Prophet should become caliph. In time the majority group became known as Sunni Islam, and the minority Shia Islam. To a large extent, in the early years at least, these two groups co-existed fairly peacefully, but differences in belief and practices developed, and such differences were always a good excuse for aggression on the part of those ambitious for land or power.

Over time, as attitudes hardened, the Sunni capital moved from the Arabian Peninsula, first to Damascus and then to Baghdad in Mesopotamia. By the tenth century the Shi'ite group, known as Fatimids after the Prophet's daughter Fatima, ruled most of north Africa and the Middle East, with power centred on Egypt. With the resurgence of the Byzantine empire at this time, the Holy Land in Palestine became something of a borderland between the three powers, frequently raided and squabbled over, but containing elements of all – Christians, both Greek and Syrian, Sunni and Shi'ite Muslims, together with pockets of surviving Jewish settlement. To the north, Anatolia, Cappadocia, Celicia, Armenia, Syria, Edessa and parts of Mesopotamia were ruled, nominally at least, by the Byzantine empire.

The picture changed once again with the arrival of the Seljuk Turks around the middle of the eleventh century. Sweeping down from the steppes of central Asia, they rapidly infiltrated the Sunni Muslim world, adopting the religion and replacing the secular leadership of the sultans. With the zeal common in new converts, the Seljuks rapidly won victories against the Byzantines and

Fatimids as well, displacing Armenians and taking Jerusalem in the early 1070s. By the 1090s the Great Seljuk Empire covered Persia, Mesopotamia, most of Anatolia, Syria and Palestine, before internal divisions weakened its powerful thrust.

Until the coming of the Seljuks there had been little organised opposition to Christians wanting to visit the holy places in Palestine. Such pilgrimages had been relatively common, the arduous journey representing a supreme penance for serious sin. The brother of King Harold of England and the father of William the Conqueror had both undertaken such a pilgrimage, though neither had survived the homeward journey. There was even a 'Hospital' or hostel established in Jerusalem to cope with the steady trickle of pilgrims. Now, however, with the borders of the Byzantine Empire pushed back to the Bosphorus, both pilgrims and empire felt themselves under attack, and it was their appeals for help that led to Western Christians being pitched for the first time into the rich mixture of religions, nationalities and cults that made up the peoples of the Holy Land.

The appeals were made to one man who, more than any other, shaped the character of what was later called the First Crusade. He was Pope Urban II, himself in the midst of his struggle against the Holy Roman Emperor and an Antipope. Barred from Rome, it was at Urban's synod held at Piacenza, under the protection of Matilda of Canossa, that the messengers of Byzantine Emperor Alexius Comnenus made their appeal for assistance against the Turks. No doubt they expected the authorisation of a small body of reinforcements to be under the command of the emperor. Urban, however, had other ideas.

There had been wars aplenty among the peoples of Europe, and battles between his own supporters and those of the Holy Roman Empire. While war in general was condemned as sinful, Pope Gregory had earlier fostered the idea of a 'just war', a war fought from the right motives and for a good purpose, along the lines laid down by St Augustine of Hippo centuries before. Indeed, at the time Matilda of Canossa was being called a 'soldier of Christ', and fighting had already pushed back the Muslims in Spain and Sicily. If the war-like tendencies of the European peoples could be harnessed for a similar 'just war', a number of benefits might be achieved. Peace might reign in Europe, the Byzantine empire could be aided, the Holy Land might be opened up once more to pilgrims – and the position and prestige of the sometimes beleaguered pope who inspired such a war might be made significantly more secure.

The Council at Clermont summoned by Urban in November 1095, was thus a call specifically to the Frankish people to use their swords against the enemies of Christ rather than each other, and to hurry to the aid of fellow Christians, not on the fringes of the Byzantine empire, but in the Holy Land itself. Similarly, although Urban had previously worked to establish friendlier relations between Rome and Byzantium, he was never specific as to his plans for the Holy Land, and the implication seems to be that he always intended any gains in that area to owe allegiance to himself rather than to the Byzantines. The unique selling points of his call to arms were the twin prospects of achieving control of the holy city of Jerusalem, coupled with the promise that such a military pilgrimage would gain for the participants a complete forgiveness for all earlier sins, especially sins of violence.

On the preaching tour preceding this council the ground had been carefully laid for what Pope Urban clearly envisaged as a single army, ultimately answerable to himself. Thus, immediately afterwards, Bishop Adhemar of Le Puy came forward to be appointed papal legate for the expedition, while count Raymond of Toulouse committed himself to leading the papal army. Urban had pitched his appeal so widely and so well, however, that it was answered by a number of other groups, each under its own leaders. Among these were to be found enemies of Byzantium, in the form of Bohemond of Taranto and his nephew Tancred, and an enemy of the pope himself – Godfrey of Bouillon, stalwart of the Holy Roman Emperor.

Bohemond was the son of Robert Guiscard. Having been disinherited by a half-brother, he had honed his fighting skills in trying to carve out a territory for himself from the Balkan lands of the Byzantine empire. He was a late recruit to the enterprise as the crusader armies passed through Italy, almost certainly motivated by the prospect of personal gain as well as by religious zeal. Godfrey of Bouillon, meanwhile, led a separate group composed of his brothers, Eustace, Count of Boulogne, and Baldwin of Boulogne, and their followers, one of whom was Baldwin of Bourg. Yet another group, whose leadership was unspecified, consisted of Hugh, brother of the King of France, Robert Curthose, Duke of Normandy, and his relatives the Count of Flanders and Stephen, Count of Blois. Whether from Boulogne or southern Toulouse, from Normandy or the Norman kingdoms in Italy, they would all be referred to as 'Franks' by their Muslim opponents in the lands they sought to conquer.

While many of those who joined the crusade were younger sons or with limited prospects at home, it would be overly cynical to suggest they all came with an eye to advancement. There was undoubtedly a range of motives over the whole body of crusaders, but religious enthusiasm was clearly a major factor. Even Bohemond declared he had been inspired by the Holy Ghost to swear the oath taken by all participants and 'take the cross'. Many, including Robert Curthose, made great sacrifices to take part, and it should be remembered that with the hardships of the journey and the prospects of fierce fighting, a good number would not have expected to return home.

Setting off from mid-August 1096, the different groups, travelling by various different routes, straggled into Byzantium over a six-month period from November of that year until the following Easter. There the first culture clash became apparent as the Westerners were awed by the size of the place and the wealth and luxury on display. If they had expected to be supplemented by a vast army led by the emperor, however, they were to be disappointed. Though he showered them with gifts, Alexius had no intention of leaving his city. He had not anticipated such a response to his appeal for help and wanted only to be rid of these people he and his fellows regarded as barbarians as soon as possible. He was, too, highly suspicious of their motives, and demanded that the leaders should swear an oath of allegiance, promising to hand over to him whatever cities, fortresses and countries they should conquer. While most, including Bohemond, freely took this oath, it was perhaps indicative of things to come that Baldwin of Boulogne and Tancred quickly crossed the Bosphorus to avoid it.

Successes at Nicea and Dorylaeum in June 1097 bolstered the confidence of the crusaders and demoralised the already divided Turks, but the greatest challenge to the Westerners came from the summer heat and parched landscape they travelled through. Baldwin of Boulogne had brought his wife with him, and she was only one of many who now died of starvation, thirst or disease.

Baldwin and Tancred were sent to make contact with the Armenian Christians in Cilicia, successfully winning towns and support in that area. Friction between the two, however, led to Baldwin striking out on his own as 'liberator' of the Armenians from Turkish rule, and though his company was small it was brutally effective, taking a string of towns between Tarsus and the River Euphrates. It seems clear he was intending to carve out a territory for himself, but possibly Thoros, the Armenian ruler of Edessa, didn't realise this when he offered him an alliance against the Turks. One account describes a peculiar ritual whereby Thoros adopted Baldwin as his son, and the crusader was clearly welcomed to the city. A few months later, however, Thoros was murdered, some claim at the instigation of his new 'son'. Baldwin immediately styled himself Count of Edessa, married an Armenian woman, possibly called Arda, and settled down to rule the first Crusader State in the East.

Whether Baldwin of Bourg travelled with his namesake to Edessa or remained with Godfrey of Bouillon and the main army, we don't know. If the latter, he would have endured the hardships, divisions and long-drawn-out sieges of Antioch and Jerusalem, to see Godfrey at last acclaimed, not as 'King of Jerusalem', but 'Defender of the Holy Sepulchre'. By this time, however, the question of who would rule these conquered territories had already caused violent disagreements within the crusader ranks. Bohemond of Taranto had claimed Antioch as his own, on the basis that the Byzantines' failure to send support during the siege nullified his oath to the emperor. The papal legate Adhemar had died at Antioch, and with him any hope that Jerusalem might be claimed by the pope, and the last Greek Patriarch of that city had also recently died, to be replaced by the Frankish Arnulf of Chocques, who supported Godfrey.

If Godfrey refused to be called 'king', what he ruled was certainly not a Kingdom of the Holy Land. In the north, Bohemond held Antioch and Baldwin of Boulogne Edessa, while Tancred set about achieving his own lordship of Galilee, based on Tiberias. Between, though, and especially along the long coastline, Muslim towns such as Tripoli, Tyre, Acre, Caesarea and Ascalon remained unconquered, and to the east as well, all the land beyond the Jordan river was Muslim-held. To make matters worse, the majority of crusaders who had reached Jerusalem now returned home to Europe, having fulfilled the oath they had taken.

Godfrey himself did not have long to establish his rule, dying, probably of typhoid, during the hot summer of 1100. His dying wish was that Jerusalem should pass to his brother Baldwin of Boulogne, and though Baldwin took some time to reach the Holy City, when he arrived he had no hesitation in claiming the title of King of Jerusalem. He was duly crowned and anointed at Bethlehem on 25 December 1100.

It was, of course, crucial that Edessa should still be firmly held, preferably by some loyal person prepared to acknowledge the overlordship of this new king. As so often in these crusader states, family ties were paramount, and the man Baldwin turned to was Baldwin of Bourg, sometimes called his cousin, and sometimes merely a distant relative. He must have proved his worth over the preceding years, however, and now became Count of Edessa. In similar vein, Baldwin of Bourg would give his own cousin Joscelin de Courtenay a lordship based on the fortress of Tell Bashir, between Edessa and Antioch.

Like his predecessor in the role, the new Count Baldwin found a wife among the Armenian Christian population. Gabriel, the Armenian lord of Melitene, to the north of Edessa, nominally owed allegiance to Byzantium but was clearly on the lookout for alliances nearer home. He had married one daughter to Thoros of Edessa, and may have offered, or intended to offer, another, Morphia, to Bohemond, now calling himself Prince of Antioch. At this time, however, Bohemond was a prisoner of the Muslims. Baldwin of Edessa was nevertheless happy to receive Morphia, as *his* bride, together with a large and very welcome dowry. They married in 1103, and their first daughter, named Melisende after her paternal grandmother, was born early in 1105. Unfortunately, by then Count Baldwin's fortunes had taken a turn for the worse.

During Bohemond's captivity his nephew Tancred had had charge of Antioch, doing little towards raising his ransom. Baldwin, though, had been energetic in raising funds for his release, and thereafter they had campaigned together in the lands between them, threatening Muslim-held Aleppo. Then, in May 1104, they suffered a catastrophic defeat at the Battle of Harran, and while Bohemond and Tancred managed to return safely to Antioch, a rash charge following apparently retreating Syrian forces led to Baldwin and Joscelin being taken prisoner.

For the next four years Baldwin remained a prisoner, passed from one Muslim leader to another as their own internal politics dictated, and ending up in Mosul, held by its latest ruler, Chavli (Jawali). Throughout this time Edessa was subject to rule by Antioch. Bohemond, however, showed no inclination to raise a ransom, and, indeed, gave up entirely on the Middle East late in 1104. Leaving Tancred in his place, he returned to Europe ostensibly to raise another army, but he never returned, and it was no doubt a clue to his real intentions that, when he left, he stripped Antioch of all its wealth and manpower. Once in Europe he married Constance, daughter of Philip I of France, collected his army, but then led it against the Byzantine empire in the Balkans, rather than against the Muslims of the Middle East. Failing in this, he was forced in 1108 to sign the Treaty of Devol, accepting the Byzantine emperor as overlord of Antioch. Tancred, however, refused to acknowledge this treaty, having, by this time, expanded and solidified the borders of Antioch at the expense of the weakened Byzantines, drawing heavily on the resources of Edessa in order to do so.

In 1107 Joscelin de Courtenay had been ransomed by the people of Tell Bashir, and he in turn arranged the ransom of Count Baldwin, who was released the following year. Tancred, though had no intention of letting go of such a valuable asset as Edessa without a struggle. One of the conditions of Baldwin's release was an alliance with Chavli, who no doubt hoped for Frankish support against rival Muslim leaders. Now, though, the boot was on the other foot, and it was Baldwin who called on Chavli for help against Tancred. The matter came to blows before the Latin Patriarch of Antioch, religious authority for both territories, stepped in to force Tancred to hand over Edessa to its rightful count.

Tancred's aim of setting up Antioch as a rival to Jerusalem was to be further crushed in the next two years. At the siege of Tripoli in 1109, with all Frankish leaders present, Bertrand of Toulouse, son of Raymond and nominated by King Baldwin, was chosen as count of the newly conquered city, in preference to William Jordan, Tancred's candidate. Similarly, when the armies were re-united to defend Edessa against Mawdud, emir of Mosul, the following year, Baldwin of Bourg was definitively confirmed as count.

Through these troubled times we have no information as to the whereabouts of Morphia and her little daughter Melisende. It is probable they remained in Edessa, though Tell Bashir might have been an alternative sanctuary. Morphia's father Gabriel had been killed, and Melitene lost to the Muslims shortly after her marriage, so it is unlikely she moved very far from her new home. As a native of the East, albeit Armenian rather than Greek or Syrian, Morphia would have been better placed than a Frankish lady to ride out the turbulent times in relative safety. Certainly, the return of her husband would have been welcome, and the birth of a son would have made her position even more secure. The child born around 1109, however, was another daughter, christened Alice.

Although King Baldwin and Joscelin de Courtenay had also married Armenian wives, this trend for marrying local women was now over. When Bohemond married the French princess, he also arranged for Tancred to marry her young half-sister Cecile, daughter of Philip and his long-time bigamous 'wife' Bertrade.

Cecile was only nine years old at the time, and barely fifteen when Tancred died in December 1112. In the same year, Bertand of Tripoli died, and now his son Pons, the sixteen-year-old new Count of Tripoli, married Cecile. By one account this was at Tancred's direction, possibly to promote friendship between the two lands of Tripoli and Antioch where there had previously been animosity. A similar healing of a fractured relationship was a likely motive for the marriage of Tancred's nephew and successor, Roger of Antioch, to Cecilia, the sister of Count Baldwin of Edessa.

There was probably a different motive when King Baldwin of Jerusalem arranged to marry the widowed Countess Adelaide of Sicily at this time. She brought with her a large dowry and a force of fighting men, both urgently needed. She also stipulated that, if there were no children of the marriage – a likely result as he was in his fifties and she in her late thirties – her son Roger of Sicily from her previous marriage should be heir to Jerusalem. This marriage, though, was doomed from the start. Baldwin had earlier put aside his Armenian wife, committing her to a convent for vague and probably spurious reasons. The church, therefore, condemned this new marriage as bigamous and Baldwin was soon forced to agree to an annulment, sending Adelaide back to Sicily, and thus earning the long-term enmity of her son Roger. No aid from the powerful kingdom of Sicily could be expected for the crusader states for the foreseeable future.

Relations with neighbouring Muslims were variable at this time. Many were happy to buy peace by paying tribute, and power struggles within the Muslim world could lead to unlikely alliances. In 1115, for example, the entire Christian and Muslim leadership lined up against the Muslim commander Bursuq, when he was sent by the Sultan of Baghdad to take over Aleppo following the deaths of Ridwan of Aleppo and his son. Thus, Tughtegin of Damascus and his son-in-law Il-Ghazi of Mardin, the two Muslim leaders most closely affected by this move, called for and received the aid of Roger of Antioch, Baldwin of Edessa, Baldwin of Jerusalem and Pons of Tripoli. Such unity in war was rare, but it was not uncommon for truces, trading agreements and rights of pilgrims to be agreed between states and cities supposedly on 'different sides'.

By 1118 Baldwin of Edessa had added another daughter, Hodierna, to his family, but still had no son. With Edessa impoverished by frequent raids and skirmishes, he had taken back the lordship of Tell Bashir from Joscelin, who in turn had taken over Tancred's earlier lands as Prince of Galilee. Now, however, as Baldwin decided to travel to Jerusalem to celebrate Easter, his fortunes were about to get a major boost.

Early in that year Baldwin of Jerusalem had led a raid into Egypt with thoughts of expanding his kingdom in that direction. Camped by an easterly branch of the River Nile, however, he suddenly fell seriously ill. Variously blamed on the re-opening of an old wound or the eating of bad fish from the river, the illness proved fatal. He died on 2 April 1118, the return of his corpse to Jerusalem for burial coinciding with the arrival of Baldwin of Edessa.

Ignoring any possible claim Roger of Sicily might make, King Baldwin is said to have nominated his older brother Eustace of Boulogne as his successor, with the possible proviso that, if Eustace failed to come, Baldwin of Edessa should have the crown. There was, as yet, no settled method of succession, and on both previous occasions there had been a strong element of election in producing rulers for the Holy City. Now Joscelin de Courtenay – as Prince of Galilee a leading figure in the kingdom – began to campaign on Baldwin's behalf, backed up by the Patriarch of Jerusalem. Despite some opposition, Baldwin was duly anointed on Easter Sunday, 14 April 1118 – by some accounts as king, and by others as regent for Eustace. In return for his help Joscelin would shortly become Count of Edessa. As for Eustace, when approached by emissaries from Jerusalem he first refused the crown, then changed his mind and set out towards the Holy Land, only to hear Baldwin had been anointed, whereupon he renounced all claims and returned home.

Contemporary chronicles claim that the new King Baldwin II of Jerusalem truly loved his Armenian wife. Certainly, he seems to have delayed his coronation ceremony until December 1119 when she and their children had joined him in Jerusalem, though some suggest this was a second coronation, for his wife's benefit. The birth of another daughter, Yvette, around this time, was surely a disappointment, but though Baldwin was urged to divorce Morphia and take another wife who might give him a son, he refused to do so. In any case, he would have little time for family life in the coming years.

The first major challenge of his reign came even before his December coronation. In the summer of 1119 Il-Ghazi, now ruler of Mosul, assembled an army to march on Antioch and put an end to the constant threats from that direction. Instead of waiting for reinforcements, Roger of Antioch quickly assembled his own force and set out to oppose him. Once before by swift action on his own he had secured a victory and a notable amount of loot, but this time his intelligence gathering let him down. On 28 June 1119, outnumbered and surrounded, the army of Antioch was virtually wiped out, along with its prince, in what became known as the Battle of the Field of Blood. It was the worst defeat suffered by the Franks since first they came to Syria, and left Antioch itself wide open and almost defenceless, though Roger's wife Cecilia made shift to organise some sort of force within the city. In the event, Il-Ghazi failed to follow up his victory. Among both Muslim and Western chroniclers he had a reputation for drunkenness, and by one account he spent the weeks following the battle on a drinking spree. Others, more generously, suggest he concentrated instead on creating a buffer zone between Aleppo and Antioch.

By early August Baldwin had arrived with forces drawn from Jerusalem and Tripoli, and although Il-Ghazi had also been reinforced by men from Damascus, he was driven from the field at the Battle of Hab on 14 August and withdrew to Aleppo. While this ensured the survival of Antioch as a Christian state, that state was now leaderless, with not even a child of Roger's as heir. There was, however, a child of Bohemond's, now around twelve years old, living with his mother Constance in Apulia. It was thus agreed that this boy, also named Bohemond, was the rightful heir to the principality, but that until he came of age and arrived to claim his inheritance, King Baldwin would rule Antioch as regent. For good measure it was also agreed that this Bohemond would marry Baldwin's second daughter, Alice, then a child of about ten years.

Of the four crusader states, Jerusalem, Antioch, Edessa and Tripoli, which made up what was then known as Outremer, Baldwin now had a strong hand in three of them. This was not entirely to the liking of Pons of Tripoli, and when Baldwin called a general council at Nablus in January 1120, Pons stayed away, although they were later reconciled. The Field of Blood had been a severe shock, and the feeling at the council was that God had turned away from them due to their sins. One result was thus the establishment of a moral code, backed by law, to apply throughout the land. More pressing, though, was the recognition that outside help was needed to maintain the Christian states, particularly that of Antioch, in the face of increased pressure from the Muslim states surrounding them. Nor were hostile neighbours the only problem for the states of Outremer. In a letter to a friend, Warmund, the Patriarch of Jerusalem, also complained of plague, drought, and pests such as locusts that destroyed the crops. Famine was a regular threat at this time.

The nearest source of aid, of course, was the Byzantine empire, but given the continued claims of the emperor to be overlord of most, if not all, of the states, that was not to be considered by these Western Franks. Instead, they sent to the new pope, Calixtus II, requesting the calling of a new crusade. Calixtus in turn passed this request to the Doge of Venice, who in due course sent a well-equipped and well-manned fleet, though this would not arrive until 1123.

There were, of course, men, and indeed women too, constantly arriving in the Holy Land, but the majority of these were pilgrims and more of a headache than a help, as they were frequently attacked and robbed on their way from the coast to the safety of the Holy City. As early as 1113 the monastic order of the Hospital of St John of Jerusalem, founded by the Benedictine Gerard, had been formally recognised by the pope. Taking over the hospital already established on the site of the monastery of St John the Baptist in Jerusalem, they became known as the Hospitallers. Then, in 1119, an enterprising young French pilgrim, Hugh of Payns, established a similar monastic order, not to heal but to protect pilgrims travelling within the Holy Land. Originally with just a handful of fellows, they took vows of poverty, chastity and obedience to a master, and were approved at Nablus by King Baldwin and the Latin Patriarch of Jerusalem. Offered lodgings in a wing of the royal palace believed to be on the site of Solomon's Temple, they became known as the Order of the Temple of Solomon, or simply Templars. Soon afterwards the new master of the Hospitallers, Raymond of le Puy, established a military wing alongside its primary function. These Templars and Hospitallers would quickly grow in wealth and power, and they became ever more useful in preserving the peace within the crusader states.

An early supporter of the Templars was Fulk of Anjou, arriving in the Holy Land in April 1120. Around thirty years of age, he had recently been taking part in the wars between Henry I of England and his nephew William Clito over the duchy of Normandy, and in the words of Orderic Vitalis, had become 'anxious for the safety of his soul and very desirous of being reconciled to God'. Vitalis claims that in the sixteen months or so he spent in the Holy Land, he joined the Templars, though clearly only as a lay member, without taking any vows. When he returned home 'with their permission', he promised a yearly sum towards their upkeep and, we are told, his example was followed by other French lords.

With the promise of a Venetian fleet to support him, Baldwin's thoughts turned to the last two coastal cities held by the Muslims. Ascalon was firmly in the grip of the Egyptian Fatimids, but Tyre, further up the coast, had been weakened in earlier attacks and in 1122 was handed over to Tughtegin of Damascus. Before Baldwin could marshal his forces for an attack, however, his plans were thrown out completely. In September 1122, Joscelin of Edessa was captured by Il-Ghazi's nephew, Balak, who tried to force him to hand over Edessa. Il-Ghazi himself died shortly afterwards, but Balak held on to his prize, transporting him nearly two hundred miles north of Edessa to the fortress of Kharput, present-day Harput in Turkey. Worse still, the following April when Baldwin set out to rescue his cousin, he, too, was surprised and captured by Balak, joining Joscelin in his remote prison.

Orderic Vitalis, back in Europe, describes Kharput as 'a vast, stately and strongly fortified citadel, one of the first in the whole world of those fortresses which are the strength of tyrants.' He claims he collected his accounts of events in the east 'from those who were present at these transactions', but it is likely the tales grew in the telling, as he goes on to give a wildly romantic and detailed account of Baldwin's 'six years' in captivity, and Joscelin's escape and journey to fetch help. He claims Baldwin was 'tortured by fasting', only allowed food on Sundays and Fridays, while Joscelin's escape was aided by a Muslim peasant who recognised him, and whose little daughter he carried on the journey to safety.

In some respects, though, Vitalis is supported by other chroniclers such as Matthew of Edessa and William of Tyre, who were closer to the scene of the action. Thus, Vitalis claims, 'About this time, the queen of Jerusalem, who was an Armenian by birth, employed a hundred chosen men of her own race to disguise themselves as Turks in their dress and arms, and endeavour to give assistance to her husband in his captivity.' William says it was fifty men dressed as monks, and Matthew a mere fifteen, but the basic idea seems correct. While most of the men of Jerusalem were concerned with the siege now underway at Tyre, it was indeed Morphia who organised a rescue attempt for her husband. By trickery variously described by the different writers, they managed to get inside the fortress while Balak was absent, kill the guards and free the captives.

With the fortress in his hands there appeared to be nothing to prevent Baldwin from setting out for home. Instead, he remained at Kharput, sending Joscelin for assistance. It is possible he felt one man had a better chance of slipping through Turkish territory than two, and that his Armenian escort was too small to guarantee his safety. Both Vitalis and William of Tyre, however, suggest he felt Kharput was too valuable to abandon, and his intention was to take and hold the surrounding area. It seems an unlikely proposition, given how far it was from existing crusader states, and he no doubt regretted the decision when Balak stormed back and re-took his fortress shortly after, having in the meantime taken over Aleppo. The Armenians were tortured and killed, but Baldwin remained a prisoner with little hope of release until after Balak's death in May 1124.

Balak's son, Timurtash, was considerably less warlike and showed little interest in Aleppo, or in holding on to the Christian king of Jerusalem. Negotiations immediately began for Baldwin's release, and a huge ransom was agreed. To guarantee payment, numbers of Frankish children were to be handed over as hostages, with Baldwin's four-year-old daughter Yvette among the forty Vitalis says were required. Finally, at the end of August 1124 the King of Jerusalem was set free after some sixteen months of captivity (rather than Vitalis's 'six years').

He was no doubt delighted to find that in his absence the combined forces of Jerusalem and Tripoli, together with the Venetian fleet, had forced the surrender of Tyre the previous month. Buoyed by this, and realising the weakness of Aleppo, instead of returning to Jerusalem he immediately summoned Joscelin and his forces to besiege that city. From October 1124 to January 1125 the siege was maintained and was close to success when an unusual alliance between Bursuq of Mosul and Tughtegin of Damascus forced Baldwin to move off by threatening Antioch. Later that year, Baldwin had his revenge on Bursuq, soundly defeating him at the battle of Azaz and taking enough loot to pay his ransom and secure the release of the child hostages.

There had been no unseemly squabble to take over Baldwin's kingdom during his captivity, the Fleming Eustace Grenier having been chosen to act as viceroy in his place. The situation must, however, have thrown into sharp focus the fact that Baldwin, now around fifty years of age, had no obvious heir. It seems likely, though, that he was already clear in his own mind that his eldest daughter, Melisende, should be his chosen successor. Thus, when Bohemond II finally arrived in Antioch the following year – an 'amiable young prince,' says Vitalis – he was duly married to Baldwin's second daughter, Alice, and at about the same time the third daughter, Hodierna, aged around thirteen, was betrothed to Raymond of Tripoli, the son of Pons and Cecile. Melisende, however, now around twenty-one years old, remained unmarried. It would be a far more difficult task to find a suitable husband for the heiress to the kingdom.

All the girls had apparently been well educated, under the supervision of Morphia rather than Baldwin, who was rarely present. They also formed a bridge between the cultures of the Middle East and that of the crusaders, between Armenians, Syrians and Franks. Melisende would have learned Armenian from her mother, but also spoke Arabic and French, and could almost certainly read, if not speak, Latin. Certainly from 1125 onwards, it seems apparent that Baldwin was consciously preparing her for her role as heir to the kingdom.

Baldwin obviously trusted his daughter's intelligence and wisdom. What she lacked, though, was military training and the command required to lead an army into battle, something that would surely be needed in the years to come. Her husband must, therefore, be a man with military experience, a strong man, but not so strong that he would overpower his wife, whom Baldwin meant to rule in her own behalf. Marriage to a local lord would likely inspire factionalism and jealousy, and, indeed, the crusader families were already so interlinked that Melisende was related to most of them in one way or another. Connecting to the Byzantine empire was also out of the question considering the defiant independence of the crusader states.

A link with Western Europe was most desirable, something that might encourage more fighting men from France, Normandy, Germany or even England to bolster the manpower of Outremer, and it may possibly have been the Templar master, Hugh of Payns, who first suggested Fulk of Anjou as an ideal candidate. Not only was Fulk an experienced campaigner, but he also had an established reputation in Jerusalem itself. He knew the land and its people and was known by them. Indeed, he was probably already known to Melisende. Furthermore, he had connections, albeit unusual ones, with the throne of France, as it was his mother Bertrade who had become the bigamous 'wife' of Philip I. Cecile, wife of Pons of Antioch, was thus his half-sister, and some accounts suggest it was her other half-brother, King Louis of France, who originated the idea that Fulk should marry Melisende, possibly aiming to get rid of an over-powerful vassal.

It may not have been entirely a coincidence that the envoys sent by Baldwin to negotiate this marriage travelled with Hugh of Payns and his fellow Templar, Godfrey of St. Omer. They were on their way to seek formal approval from the pope for their new order but detoured to Anjou to assist in the negotiations. Fulk had lost his first wife in 1126 – the same year Melisende's mother Morphia had died – and was now busy settling the children of that marriage, negotiating, in particular, with Henry I of England who was urging the wedding of his daughter Matilda to Fulk's eldest son Geoffrey.

Fulk himself was by no means averse to returning to the Holy Land, especially with a crown in the offing, but drove a hard bargain. He was not prepared to be merely consort to a queen, he insisted on being king. After protracted discussions, and following a recommendation from Pope Honorius, a form of words was agreed that satisfied both parties. At home, however, Baldwin's intentions were made clear by the fact that, from March 1129, Melisende became associated with his rule in official documents, referred to as 'daughter of the king and heir to the kingdom of Jerusalem'.

Fulk of Anjou arrived in the Holy Land in May 1129 and was quickly married to Melisende. He was around forty years old and she twenty-four, but if he'd expected a meek and obedient little wife it is likely he was quickly disillusioned. Nonetheless, says William of Tyre, during Baldwin's lifetime he deferred to him and faithfully fulfilled the duties of a son. Baldwin, for his part, must have been considerably relieved. Now he not only had a solid support in Jerusalem, but his other son-in-law Bohemond appeared to be well settled and popular in Antioch, with a daughter already and the prospect of more children to come. It would have been a bonus when Melisende soon fell pregnant.

This happy state in the crusader lands contrasted with that in Damascus where the long-time governor Tughtegin had died in

1128. There, his son and heir Buri was having considerable trouble with the Nizari, a Shi'ite sect from Persia, also known as the Hashishin, due to their use of hashish. While not generally engaged in waging war, the Nizari held it to be a duty to kill individuals opposed to their creed – the word assassin derives from them – and Tughtegin had been suspected of using them in the past to dispose of rivals, hence their presence in Damascus.

The disturbances there, and the strength of his own hand, led Baldwin to set out in September 1129, along with his two sons-in-law, to try and conquer that ancient and most desirable city. It could have been a triumph, but instead turned to disaster. The chronicler Ibn al Qalanisi describes a surprise attack by Buri which wiped out a large foraging party, while William of Tyre says a mighty storm of thunder, lightning and torrential rain completed the job of forcing the would-be besiegers to abandon their camp and much of their baggage and straggle back to Jerusalem.

It was not an auspicious start, and the next year would prove to be worse. In February 1130 Bohemond of Antioch was killed in the course of a raid into Cilicia. His heiress was a two-year-old daughter, Constance, whose mother Alice immediately claimed the regency, though she herself was only around twenty. Bohemond, says Vitalis, had 'governed ... with distinction for four years, but like a bright flower he soon faded', and his fading threw the weight of Antioch back onto the shoulders of Baldwin.

Had it been closer he might have allowed Alice the role she craved, but it was too remote from Jerusalem and too close to hostile territory to be without a strong protector. When he arrived at Antioch, however, accompanied by the faithful Joscelin and by Fulk, he found the gates barred against him. Clearly, Alice had her supporters within the city. There were others, though, who were more inclined to Baldwin's view, and it was not long before Joscelin and Fulk were surreptitiously let in. First retreating to the citadel, Alice soon realised she had no cards to play and threw herself on her father's mercy. She was allowed to keep the towns of Latakia and Jabala and their lands, which had been her dowry, but was exiled from Antioch, where Baldwin was once again installed as regent, with Joscelin in immediate control. Whether Constance remained in Antioch or went with her mother is not recorded.

At some point in 1130 Melisende had her first child, a son, who was, of course, christened Baldwin. The king had little time to enjoy his grandson, however, as around the middle of 1131 he fell ill. We don't know what the illness was, but it clearly gave him time to prepare for the end. Exchanging his royal garments for a monk's habit, he had himself carried to lodgings near the Holy Sepulchre. Summoning his daughter and her husband and son to his bedside, he declared his will as to the succession. Whatever agreement he had made with Fulk – or which Fulk believed had been made – to bring him to the Holy Land, the dying king now committed his kingdom to the joint rule of all three of them, Melisende, Fulk and the baby Baldwin. Whether Fulk protested or not is not recorded, but if he did it had no effect. When the old king died shortly afterwards on 21 August, he had not changed his mind.

On 14 September 1131, the joint coronation of Melisende and Fulk was carried out by the Patriarch of Jerusalem, but whatever the appearances it seems Fulk had already made up his mind that he was the true king, and so it was recorded back in Europe. Thus, Orderic Vitalis declares that Fulk's marriage resulted in him 'obtaining easily by this union the kingdom of Jerusalem and the principality of Antioch'. He even claims that Baldwin offered him the crown immediately after the marriage, but Fulk refused to take it. Vitalis is more accurate, though, with what followed.

When he says that Fulk 'provided for the future with less caution than was politic', what he is describing is the attempted Angevin takeover of the kingdom. Fulk's first wife had been heiress to the county of Maine, and when it came to her he had immediately marched in and taken full control, replacing the existing officials with his own men and dealing with it as his own property. Now he tried to treat Jerusalem in the same way, 'too hastily appointing governors and changing other authorities without sufficient reason', and 'lending a too willing ear to strangers from Anjou and other newcomers who had no experience'. Those who had struggled through the early days to establish themselves and their families in the new kingdom were 'treated with coolness', the same coolness with which his wife was frozen out of the administration. All this was done solely in Fulk's name. Melisende does not even appear as a witness to his charters.

It may very well be for this reason that Alice abruptly returned to Antioch, with renewed claims to the regency she had been denied before. The faithful Joscelin had died a few weeks after Baldwin, and there seemed every prospect that Fulk would try to take over there as well. The fact that this time she was backed, not only by the citizens of Antioch, but also by Pons of Tripoli and Joscelin II, the new Count of Edessa, indicates that the northern states were all fearful of being absorbed into a greater Kingdom of Jerusalem. She may also have been backed by Melisende, but at this time Fulk was paying no attention to his wife's wishes.

Much to the astonishment of the Muslim chroniclers, a battle was fought before Pons and Joscelin were forced to back down. Then, rather than annexing Antioch, Fulk re-imposed a regency, with his nominated constable or chief military officer, Raynald Maseoir, in charge. Pressure from the Muslim warlord Zengi prompted a reconciliation between Fulk and Pons the following year, but it seems Alice tried repeatedly to return to Antioch, causing Fulk to seek a long-term solution to the problem.

By this time he would almost certainly have been aware of his increasing unpopularity among the nobility of the Kingdom of Jerusalem, so his part in the scheming to find a husband for the child Constance was more clandestine. The official version, as recorded by William of Tyre, was that the Patriarch and leaders of the people of Antioch begged him to find a suitable young man from Western Europe to come and marry their little princess. The 'young man' selected was Raymond of Poitiers, a son of Duke William IX of Aquitaine. Ideal for Fulk's purposes, he was a landless younger son of a good family, though his early life is obscure. Indeed, some have claimed he was illegitimate. He had been trying to make his way at the court of Henry I of England, and he would surely jump at the chance of such a marriage, even to a child. He would thus owe everything to Fulk and could be relied on for his future loyalty.

The only drawback – though not for Fulk – was that he was nearly thirty years older than his bride and would have made a better match with Alice. According to William of Tyre, indeed, that is how the new Patriarch, Ralph of Domfront, prevented Alice from protesting as the young man made his way across Europe. Becoming aware of his approach, possibly through spies in Antioch, she was persuaded to believe he was coming to marry her. As soon as he arrived, however, Constance was brought – without her mother's knowledge – to the Church of St Peter in Antioch and married by the Patriarch himself to Raymond of Poitiers. Even for that time she was far too young to be legally married, but once the event had taken place any support Alice might have had fell away. Most people, it seems, felt it was as good a solution as any to acquiring a protector for Antioch. As for Alice, she returned to her own court at Latakia and fades from the records. It may well be that she died shortly afterwards.

By the time of this marriage, which took place in 1136, Fulk's misdeeds had caught up with him. While he was in the north, Melisende had remained in Jerusalem, and she certainly inspired, if not orchestrated, the revolt that broke out on his return in around 1133. Vitalis declares that Fulk's high-handedness and exclusion of his wife 'occasioned deep resentment, and the pride of the nobles desperately revolted against the inexperienced prince'. He gives no details, though, not even the names of any rebels, merely claiming 'they long directed against their fellow Christians that warlike enterprise which they should have unanimously directed against the Heathen.' The piece was clearly written in 1137, for he says 'Fulk has been king for six years,' and it seems news was slow to reach him from far distant Jerusalem.

It is William of Tyre, writing decades later, who names the rebel leader as Hugh, Count of Jaffa, a second cousin of Melisende. Hugh was, he claims, the main protester against Fulk's rule, and still no details are given of what form that initial protest took. Vitalis's 'loss of many thousand men and of some strong places' seems to be linking together other events around that time, and attaching them all to Hugh's revolt, which may have amounted to no more than defiance and civil disobedience.

There is no record of an armed struggle at this point, and it may well be that Fulk found so many of the local nobility turned against him that this was not an option. Instead, his retaliation, again according to William of Tyre, was to have Hugh accused of conducting an affair with Melisende. Hugh, a young man in his mid-twenties, had only been in the Holy Land around ten years, having been born and brought up in Apulia. He had inherited the lordship of Jaffa from his father and had married the widow of Eustace Grenier. It was her son, Walter, from that earlier marriage, who in 1134 accused him of what at the time would have been regarded as incest and high treason.

Hugh was not some friendless outsider, however. A meeting was held of the Haut Cour – the council of the nobility, which also acted as a court – but it came to no firm conclusion. Instead, it was agreed the matter should be decided in the Frankish way by single combat between Hugh and Walter. A date was set for this, but Hugh didn't appear at the appointed time, and it has been suggested it was pressure from his wife that kept him away. She, of course, stood to lose either a son or a husband if the contest went ahead. Then, according to the rather hostile William of Tyre, the young man again seemed to lose his head entirely. Instead of appealing for backing from the already disaffected nobility of Jerusalem, he incited the Fatimids at Ascalon to rise up and attack the kingdom.

If anything was calculated to unite Jerusalem against him it was such an invitation to confirmed enemies, and with the Fatimid raiders defeated, Hugh found himself briefly besieged in Jaffa and then handed over to Fulk by his own people. Though the king might want to condemn him, however, the queen did not. The tale of an affair was almost certainly false, but Hugh had championed Melisende's rights as queen and she could not allow him to be put to death. Instead, with the intercession of the Patriarch, he was condemned to exile for a period of three years. That, however, was not the end of the story.

While in Jerusalem preparing for his departure, Hugh was attacked and seriously wounded by a knight from Brittany. Though he recovered sufficiently to travel to Apulia, he died there soon afterwards, and the immediate assumption was that the knight had been under orders from Fulk. He denied it, of course, and had the knight mutilated, though being careful not to have his tongue cut out, lest people should say he had silenced him. The knight suffered in vain.

The attack and subsequent death of Hugh proved to be a catalyst, not only for a major rift between Melisende and her husband, but also for the crystallisation of all the resentment felt against Fulk for his seizure of power and high-handed actions. The church and the nobility backed Melisende, while Fulk was cast as villain, particularly when he confiscated Hugh's lands at Jaffa. Thereafter he came 'under the queen's displeasure'. Anyone supporting him was barred from her court, and for a time it seemed they even feared for their safety. 'Even the king,' says William of Tyre, 'found that no place was entirely safe among the kindred and supporters of the queen.'

Surprisingly, it was Fulk that backed down. Perhaps he was canny enough to know this was an unnecessary fight, or simply recognised at last the value of an experienced and intelligent partner with local knowledge and strong local backing. Certainly, from that time on no policies were made or charters issued without the knowledge and consent of Queen Melisende.

Such recognition would have done much to heal the rift between them, but no doubt a few gifts would also have helped. In the British Museum is an exquisite little book known as the Melisende Psalter, reputed to have been a gift from Fulk to his wife, either as a peace offering, or possibly to celebrate the birth of their second son, Almaric, in 1136. Between intricately carved ivory covers, it contains psalms, prayers and a calendar of saints, executed by a number of different craftsmen clearly at the very top of their game. It also illustrates the cosmopolitan nature of Jerusalem society at the time, combining Greek, Islamic, Arabic, French, Latin and even English influences.

The new unity found in Jerusalem came not a moment too soon, with the crusader states, particularly those in the north, now threatened as never before. On the one side the Byzantine emperor, John Comnenus, found himself for the first time at liberty to turn his attention to those parts of the Middle East still, theoretically at least, subject to his overlordship. On the other, the Turkish warlord Zengi was a rising star in Mesopotamia, urging jihad against the Western unbelievers.

The Islamic concept of jihad embraces two different forms of struggle. The first, the greater jihad, is the struggle against one's own inclination to sin, while the second, the lesser jihad, is the struggle against the enemies of Islam. At the beginning of the twelfth century, the scholar 'Ali ibn Tahir al-Sulami emphasised that the first was much more important, and this had been the predominant view for a long time. 'Put the jihad against your souls ahead of the jihad against your enemies,' he declared, though he did add that this might lead to success in the lesser jihad as well.

It might be thought that Zengi was inspired to invoke the lesser jihad by the Christian insistence that the crusade was a holy war. On the other hand, the Seljuk Turks had also used religion as the basis of their struggle against the Shi'ite Fatimids. Indeed, religion had been as useful a veil for ambition as any other difference between humans for thousands of years.

In Zengi's case, ambition appears to have been at least the equal of religious zeal since his main target was clearly Damascus, rather than the crusader states, and he fought the Franks only when it was to his advantage, or when they interfered with his plans. Appointed governor of Mosul in 1127 following the death of Bursuq, he took over Aleppo as well in 1128, before focusing his attention on the towns to the south, between there and Damascus. Hama fell to him in 1130, and he was besieging Homs in July 1137 when he broke off to attack Tripoli. Earlier that year Count Pons had been killed, following a raid by the Mameluk commander Bazwij. Defeated and fleeing for safety to the hills, he was handed over by local Christians, presumably of a different sect, and executed. The response of his son, the new Count Raymond II, was to round up some local villagers, not necessarily the same ones, and have them tortured and killed. This weakness and disunity in Tripoli may well have prompted Zengi's attack, though he also had his eye on a very useful fortress at Baarin, which the Franks called Montferrand, part-way between Hama and Homs.

Raymond, in his mid-twenties and with an already weakened army, was in no condition to fight him off, and immediately appealed to Jerusalem for help. He was, of course, appealing to 'family'. Fulk was his uncle on his mother's side, while Melisende was the sister of Hodierna whom Raymond had married a few years before. According to Orderic Vitalis, Fulk 'summoned all who were able to bear arms', not only from Jerusalem but also sending to Edessa and Antioch. Those forces, however, were already engaged in fending off the Byzantine emperor. Nonetheless, Fulk, probably underestimating his opponent, clashed with Zengi at Baarin, where, says Vitalis, 'nearly the whole Christian army was annihilated.' While Raymond was taken prisoner, Fulk and some others escaped to the fortress where they were immediately besieged by Zengi. We don't know how long this siege lasted, though Vitalis declares the king and his fellows were reduced to eating 'horseflesh and other kinds of unclean and unheard of food', giving a bizarre picture of Fulk acting as steward and serving 'to each of his comrades morsels of the flesh of asses and dogs'.

The situation changed abruptly when Zengi got advance warning that a Christian army was approaching, led by Emperor John Comnenus, Raymond of Antioch and Joscelin of Edessa. Now he bargained to release Fulk and all the captives, in exchange for the fortress. Not knowing that rescue was at hand, Fulk quickly agreed. Montferrand was handed over and, having garrisoned it, Zengi departed in safety before the emperor arrived.

John was having a highly successful campaign. He had already subdued Armenian Cilicia and obtained from Antioch and Edessa an acknowledgement that he was their overlord. Now Raymond of Tripoli was reminded that his predecessor, Raymond of Toulouse, had sworn an oath to Emperor Alexius that he would hand over to the Byzantines anything he conquered in the Holy Land. As successor to that oath, Raymond, too, was now required to acknowledge John as overlord. When John then proposed to turn his armies against the Muslim-held fortresses at Aleppo and Shaizar, however, the response was lukewarm at best. Raymond of Antioch had been forced to agree he would hand over Antioch in exchange for these if they could be taken, and no-one wanted to see Antioch become a Byzantine stronghold. In the end problems elsewhere in his empire forced John to depart in 1138 with his ambitions unfulfilled.

Zengi would try again for Damascus in 1139, the government of that city being fatally weakened by internal division. Effective power lay with the military commander Unur, who had been a mameluk or slave soldier under Tughtegin. With the city under severe threat, Unur appealed to Jerusalem for help, offering money and the fortress at Banyas on the edge of the Golan Heights as an inducement. Even without that, Fulk may have felt that revenge for his earlier humiliation and a chance to dispose of Zengi was worth an expedition. In the face of this united opposition, however, the warlord withdrew to his lands in the north, and the following few years were blessed with relative peace.

It was a time of much building, both within Jerusalem and in the wider kingdom, with Melisende and Fulk overseeing the construction of a number of fortifications along their borders and in other strategic locations. Around Ascalon, a ring of fortresses at Gaza, Ibelin and Blanchegard aimed to restrict Fatimid action. To the south-east the mighty castle at Kerak beyond the Jordan was begun, while the impressive fortress at Beth Gibelin, between Hebron and Jerusalem, was handed to the Hospitallers, marking their development into a military order. Their most impressive fortification would be the Krak des Chevaliers, further north, on land given to them by Raymond of Tripoli, guarding the pass between Homs and Tripoli. The Templars, too, having achieved the backing of the pope in 1129, were supported in their castle building by Fulk and Melisende.

Nor was all the building military. In Jerusalem the Dome of the Rock had been thoroughly looted in 1099 by the first crusader army and was now to be extensively renovated as a Christian church. Similarly, the Church of the Holy Sepulchre was to be rebuilt on a far grander scale. Projects particularly associated with Melisende include the building of a convent at Bethany near the reputed tomb of Lazarus. Her youngest sister had become a nun, and it was the intention of the queen that she should be abbess of this new Convent of St. Lazarus. All in all, matters within the kingdom seemed to be progressing well after the royal couple's shaky start. Then in 1143 two freakish accidents occurred that shook the whole region.

In 1142 Emperor John Comnenus had returned to the east, once again putting pressure on Antioch and threatening a 'pilgrimage' to Jerusalem. Raymond of Antioch employed delaying tactics, and John was over-wintering in Cilicia when, early in April 1143, he cut his hand on an arrow while hunting wild boar. The wound became infected, and within days the emperor was dead, putting and end for the time being to plans for expanding Byzantine overlordship into Outremer.

Then in November of the same year, Fulk and Melisende were riding together outside the city of Acre. The king, who was fond of hunting, set off in pursuit of a hare that started out of a furrow. At full gallop his horse stumbled and fell, rolling on him and crushing his skull. He died on 13 November 1143, and at the age of thirty-eight Melisende was now sole ruler of the kingdom of Jerusalem.

There was no-one now to demand she must have a new husband. There was no-one, indeed, to command her at all. She was the queen, as she had been for the last dozen or so years. The question of who the strong male figure would be to lead the armies of Jerusalem never seems to have arisen. Melisende appointed her cousin Manasses of Hierges as her constable and carried on as before. The only advice recorded comes from Abbot Bernard of Clairvaux, one of the foremost religious leaders of the time and self-appointed advisor to all the royal families of Christendom. In a letter written soon after Fulk's death, he tells her how important her position is, then lapsing into the casual misogyny of the times:

> All eyes look to you, and on you the whole weight of the kingdom falls... Although a woman, you must appear like a man.

> Doing what is to be done in the spirit of wisdom and fortitude. You must dispose of all things so wisely and moderately that all who see them will suppose them the deeds of a king rather than a queen.

He continues in ever more patronising fashion by supposing Melisende might protest – '"But I am not," you say, "Capable of this. These great things are beyond my powers and my understanding."' He thus ignores the fact that she has been an equal partner in ruling the kingdom for a considerable time, with, in many ways, greater knowledge and understanding than her newcomer husband. That the letter is still extant suggests Melisende exercised Christian forgiveness in forbearing to tear it up.

There is even an implication in Bernard's letter that Melisende would be ruling on behalf of her eldest son, Baldwin, who, at thirteen years of age, was 'too young to bear the responsibilities of governing'. This was not the case at all. When Melisende was crowned again on Christmas Day 1143, although Baldwin was crowned jointly with her as Baldwin III, there was never a suggestion that hers was a regency role.

If the death of Fulk shook the kingdom, the events of the following year shook not only Outremer but the entire Western world. Zengi had made no further moves against Damascus but had concentrated his efforts on bringing the northern areas of Mesopotamia firmly under his rule. In the autumn of 1144, the ruler of one such area, Diyar Bakr, appealed to Joscelin II of Edessa for help, offering him land in exchange. Perhaps naively, Joscelin believed Edessa was safe while Zengi was busy elsewhere, and at once marched an army north. He was therefore not enjoying a life of luxury and pleasure at Tell Bashir, as the biased William of Tyre claims, but considerably further way when Zengi suddenly appeared outside the walls of Edessa late in November.

As usual, the warlord's spy network had informed him of the weakened state of the city, and he was quick to invest it, not only subjecting the walls to a constant bombardment, but also working to undermine them. When news reached Joscelin, he tried to assemble a relief force and sent to Antioch and Jerusalem for help. Melisende dispatched an army under Manasses, but Raymond of Antioch, who was considerably nearer, was busy trying to claim parts of Cilicia and failed to respond.

Before any relief appeared, on 24 December Zengi succeeded in collapsing one of Edessa's outer walls and his men flooded into the city. As the panic-stricken citizens strove desperately to reach the citadel, the Latin Archbishop Hugh, among many others, was trampled to death. Even in the citadel, however, there was no security, and that, too, fell on Christmas Day. The Muslim chronicler Ibn al-Athir, who was not there, claims that only the Franks were killed, the Armenians and Syrians being allowed to return to what was left of their homes after the soldiers had finished ransacking them. An Armenian native who was there, on the other hand, describes a bloody massacre, with no regard given to age or sex. Indeed, it is hard to picture the victorious army being quite so discriminating as to single out only the Franks in the immediate aftermath of their triumph. Later, no doubt, Zengi called them to heel, and then perhaps some return of non-Christians was permitted.

With the city firmly in the hands of Zengi there was no hope of immediate relief. Joscelin withdrew to Tell Bashir and Melisende's army returned home. As news of the fall of Edessa echoed around the Christian world, however, the fear now was that Zengi's momentum would be unstoppable. If he was indeed waging jihad against the crusaders, Antioch would be the next logical target. It was thus Raymond of Antioch who now sent for help, not, of course, to the new emperor in Constantinople with whom he was still at loggerheads, but to the pope in Rome and to the French king Louis. By the time his envoy Bishop Hugh of Jabala arrived in Rome, however, after a difficult winter journey, he found a situation almost as precarious as the one he had left behind.

For almost a decade following the death of Pope Honorius II in 1130, the church had been in a state of schism, with rival popes elected by cardinals supporting rival Roman families. Then, after the death of Pope Innocent II in September 1143, a rebellion led by the

Pierleoni family declared Rome a commune on the lines of ancient Rome, this republic being no longer answerable to any pope. Two more pontiffs rapidly came and went, the second of whom, Lucius II, was actually killed in a street battle with the 'republicans'. On the day of his death, 15 February 1145, a new pope was elected, a Cistercian monk who had studied under Bernard of Clairvaux, who took the name Eugenius III.

The popular suggestion at the time was that he was the only man brave enough, or foolish enough, to take on the role, and being blocked by the communards from reaching St Peter's for his own consecration, he lost no time in fleeing the city and establishing himself, first at Tusculum, some twenty miles away, and then at the more distant Viterbo. Nor was Bernard of Clairvaux exactly supportive. 'May God forgive you what you have done,' he wrote to the curia, referring to Eugenius as a 'mere rustic'. 'Is it ridiculous or miraculous?' he asked, 'Certainly one of these.'

Nonetheless, the new pope did what he could for his fellow Christians in Outremer. Having spent some time considering his response to Raymond's plea, on 1 December 1145 he issued a papal bull calling for a new crusade, the form of which drew heavily on Pope Urban's similar call to arms some fifty years before. Reminding the peoples of Western Europe of the valour of their fathers, and the blood willingly shed to take back the Holy Places from the unbelievers, Eugenius now called on them to display similar valour or have it said that their bravery and nobility had diminished in the interim. He spoke of the loss of Edessa, the first Christian city in Outremer, of the deaths and enslavement of its peoples and of the continuing threat to the other Christian states in the area, and called on them now to defend the eastern church and to rescue their captive brothers. Knights, he said, should direct their zeal towards acquiring suitable arms and horses, not the dogs and hawks and precious garments that marked their current licentious lives. The complete remission of punishment for sins – a prime selling point of the first crusade – is mentioned three times, particularly in a stirring conclusion, emphasising that this means complete absolution from all confessed sins for anyone undertaking the crusade and either completing it or dying in the attempt.

Like Urban before him, Eugenius may have hoped that this call to arms would unify Western Christianity behind his leadership. While Urban's oration had lit a fire across Europe, however, the letter of Eugenius was more of a damp squib. True, at his Christmas court that year Louis VII declared an intention to go to the aid of the crusader states, but it is not certain that the pope's letter had even reached him by that time. In the event it took the involvement of the influential and charismatic Bernard of Clairvaux before this second crusade really took off.

Bernard was already involved in the affairs of the Holy Land as patron of the Templars, and now, at the urging of the pope, he undertook a preaching tour in support of this new campaign, taking in cities in France, Flanders and Germany, while spreading the word additionally through the growing network of Cistercian monasteries. On 1 March 1146, the papal bull was re-issued, addressed specifically to Louis VII, 'illustrious king of the French', and to the princes of Gaul. Then at Vézelay at the end of that month Bernard preached a fiery sermon, following which both Louis and his wife Queen Eleanor committed themselves to the crusade, causing something of a sensation at the time.

Moving on to Germany Bernard continued his work, with miracles apparently following in his wake. Indeed, zeal for pursuing the enemies of Christendom ran so high, he had to angrily rebuke another Cistercian monk who advocated the massacre or forced baptism of the Jews in Europe as a precursor to dealing with the Muslims of the east. Sadly, Bernard was not in time to save those many Jews already murdered before he could speak against this distortion of his message.

Perhaps his greatest achievement was to persuade Conrad III, King of the Germans and Romans, to join the crusade. At fifty years old, Conrad had only recently made himself secure on the German throne following a civil war. Only when it was clear his greatest enemy, Welf VI of Bavaria, would also be going, did he consider participating, and some accounts claim he was extremely reluctant even then. Nevertheless, at Conrad's Christmas court at Speyer at the end of 1146, Bernard's persistence paid off and the German king committed himself to the crusade.

Of course it took time to raise the money, recruit the men and provide the equipment for so large an undertaking. No date had been set for the start, and, indeed, the specific object of the crusade had been left vague. By the spring of 1147 it had been expanded to include not only the conquest of the Moors in Spain, but also the Wends, a Slavic people of north-eastern Europe. By the time the Germans and French set off for the Holy Land, in May and June 1147 respectively, more than two years had passed since the fall of Edessa, and much had changed in that land.

In 1145, the mighty Zengi had strengthened his hold on much of the county of Edessa, giving him a great swathe of territory across northern Mesopotamia and Syria from Mosul to Aleppo. Those who called him 'Imad al-Din Zengi' –'Zengi the pillar of religion' – were probably still over-estimating his commitment to jihad, however. Certainly in 1146 he gathered a great army and no doubt Antioch feared the worst, but it was a Muslim fortress on the Euphrates he was besieging in September of that year, and many people suspected he still had his eye on conquering Damascus. Perhaps that is why, on 14 September 1146, he was murdered in his bed by an unknown assailant.

Zengi the Great was dead, and his lands were now divided between his sons. The eldest, Saif al-Din, took Mosul, and a younger son, Nur al-Din, took Aleppo, but if the leaders of the crusader states thought their troubles were over, or at least considerably diminished, they were mistaken. In October 1146, Joscelin II attempted to re-take Edessa, and with the help of some of the remaining Christians inside the city penetrated the outer defences. Taking the citadel, however, was a different matter. This mighty fortress topped a steep-sided natural hill some two hundred feet high, and in the six days that it took Nur al-Din to arrive with an army many thousand strong, Joscelin had barely had time to think how to begin. Now, caught between the force in the citadel and that outside the walls, Joscelin fled, and Nur al-Din proceeded to show he had learned well his father's lessons of brutality. No doubt his massacre of all the male Christians and enslavement of the women and children was intended as a demonstration to those in Aleppo and elsewhere that this young man in his late twenties was not to be trifled with. Then, before he departed, he razed the defences of Edessa, leaving the formerly vibrant Christian city, birthplace of Melisende, 'deserted of life, an appalling sight, enveloped in a black cloud'.

With one crusader state now totally lost, once again Antioch seemed to be the most vulnerable to imminent attack, particularly as Nur al-Din kept up a constant pressure on its eastern borders. If Melisende, far away to the south in Jerusalem, was tempted to feel more secure, however, this illusion must have been badly shaken by the friendly overtures made by Aleppo towards Damascus in 1147. Unur, the de facto ruler of Damascus, must have been wary, but his own position was not so well established he could overlook any such gesture. It had been his policy to be on good terms with all his neighbours as far as possible. Indeed, there was a longstanding truce with Jerusalem which allowed merchants and pilgrims to come and go between the two cities. The new alliance was cemented, however, with the marriage of his daughter Ismat ad-Din to Nur al-Din, and the immediate consequence was the breaking of this truce.

Who was the first to break it is a matter for debate. It might have been the alliance itself, or the support now offered by Jerusalem for the emir of Bosra who wanted to break away from Damascus and maintain his friendship with the crusader state. For the last few years, under the calm guidance of Melisende, Jerusalem had enjoyed relative peace. The troubles in the north had had little effect on the stream of pilgrims that brought prosperity with them, and among the many ongoing building works, the queen had commissioned a covered market area comprising three long rows of shops for the better comfort of the many merchants and their customers. Although Baldwin III had reached his fifteenth birthday two years after his father's death, and thus been regarded as 'of age', the joint rulership seemed to be working smoothly, and it seems clear Melisende was, at this stage, the senior partner. It has been suggested Baldwin showed little interest in the more mundane aspects of government, though he had participated in a number of skirmishes against the Muslims without any marked success.

It seems more likely to have been Baldwin that now urged armed support for the emir of Bosra, though the position of the town, across the Jordan and south of Damascus, made it attractive as a strategic ally. In the event, the army that set out rather cautiously under the seventeen-year-old king was harassed all the way by swift-moving mounted archers, and arrived at Bosra only to find it now occupied by the forces of Unur and Nur al-Din. There was no serious engagement as such at the time, but the return to Jerusalem was, to a large extent, a running battle, with the rearguard constantly forced to defend and cover the retreat. Though this, in absolute terms, was a minor conflict, nonetheless it was a harbinger of things to come.

On 10 September 1147, Conrad and his army arrived at Constantinople and passed on quickly across the Bosphorus, not without some unpleasantness on the way. In a matter of weeks, however, he had lost the majority of his best troops in battle with the Turks at Dorylaeum, and many others to hunger and hit-and-run attacks. In the forced retreat to Nicea Conrad himself was wounded, and the battered remnants of his army that reached that safe haven would not have impressed the French who were newly arrived there.

While Conrad returned to Constantinople to recover, Louis and his army tried a different route but fared no better, eventually giving up the idea of marching to Antioch and making for the coast at Adalia. After a two-month wait for ships to arrive, the king and part of his army finally reached Antioch in March 1148, the rest being left to make their own way as best they could.

Now came the first major disagreement. The primary reason for the crusade had originally been to win back the county of Edessa, but that cause was clearly already lost. To Raymond of Antioch the most urgent need now was to defeat Nur al-Din at Aleppo. Louis, however, would not consider such a campaign. His crusade was as much pilgrimage as military endeavour, and he was determined – as indeed the First Crusade had been – to press on to Jerusalem.

Further complications followed. Among the new crusaders, one, Alphonso-Jordan, had a possible claim to the county of Tripoli. When he died suddenly soon after arriving in the area, there were some who suggested he had been poisoned by its ruler, Count Raymond. Later accusations were even levelled at Queen Melisende, though it is hard to see how she could have benefitted by such an act. Most probably he was simply one of the many who succumbed to illness, probably dysentery, in the course of a long expedition. One result of this was that Raymond of Tripoli did not attend the council held at Palmarea near Acre on 24 June 1148, when the future progress of the crusade was determined.

Large numbers were present at this council. Louis and his chief supporters were there, and so, too, were the nobility and leading clergy of Jerusalem led by Melisende and Baldwin. Conrad was also there, having travelled by sea to Jerusalem in April of that year. It soon became clear, however, that, although Raymond of Antioch, supported by Melisende, argued strongly for an attack on Aleppo, neither Conrad nor Louis would agree to this. In the end it was agreed that Damascus would be the target. This was clearly a richer plum than Aleppo, and given the alliance between Unur, now confirmed as governor, and Nur al-Din, the conquest of Damascus would, it was argued, give greater security to the Holy Land and to Outremer as a whole.

In early July the combined armies mustered at Tiberias on the Sea of Galilee, and by the 23rd they were poised on the western outskirts of Damascus. There were no great fortifications to overcome. Instead, the way for the attackers lay through numbers of walled orchards. This approach had been chosen as the orchards could provide food for the army, but it also made the troops vulnerable to attack, split up as they were along the lanes between. According to William of Tyre, the men from Jerusalem led the way as they knew the lie of the land. They were to 'open up the way for the rest who were following them'. This proved easier said than done, with defenders laying ambushes from the orchards and side paths, so that 'on every side there was equal peril for the unwary, and danger of sudden and unforeseen death.' The advance was so slow that at one point Conrad, in charge of the forces at the rear, came pushing through to find out what was going on, and then brought up his own troops to prove he could do better.

By the end of the second day, they had fought their way through to the city walls, coming closer, says al-Qanisi, than any other army, either in ancient times or even more recently. Then came a sudden and fatal change of plan. The position for which they had fought so hard was abruptly abandoned and the whole army moved to the eastern side of the city, to an open plain. Then, finding that of no advantage, and furthermore lacking in food and water, the arguments and accusations began. Whether or not Unur, the governor of Damascus, had actually paid bribes to some of the Jerusalem barons to lift the siege, as William of Tyre claims, we cannot be sure. It seems clear, however, that he found some way to break up the precarious unity between the forces that attacked him. As claims and counterclaims of treachery and cowardice were heard within the camp, he further let it be known that he had sent to the mighty Nur al-Din for help, and that his armies were on their way. At this point the crusaders quickly abandoned their whole enterprise.

The retreat to Jerusalem was abject and humiliating. 'Thus,' says William of Tyre, 'a company of kings and princes such as we have not read of through all the ages, had gathered, and, for our sins, had been forced to return, covered with shame and disgrace, with their mission unfulfilled.' Not only had they failed, but they had failed in a way that destroyed for ever any notion that the crusaders were fearsome opponents that must be respected.

Back in Jerusalem the recriminations began, with the different leaders all blaming each other for the lack of success. A second expedition, this time against Ascalon, was mooted. Conrad made some preparations but then, finding no-one else backing him up, gave up the whole thing and sailed away to Constantinople to cement an alliance with Emperor Manuel Comnenus against Roger of Sicily. Louis stayed on in Jerusalem until the following spring, presumably so as to spend Easter in that Holy City, and then he and his followers also sailed back to Europe. As a military enterprise the Second Crusade was a complete fiasco. Edessa was still lost and nothing else achieved, and in Europe the one who bore the brunt of the recriminations was Bernard of Clairvaux, whose prestige never really recovered. He wrote a specific apology for the failure of the crusade addressed to Pope Eugenius, blaming the disaster on the sins of the crusaders. 'It was,' he says, 'as though the Lord, provoked by our sins, were almost judging the world before the time, with equity, indeed, but forgetful of his mercy... We all know that the judgements of the Lord are true.' Indeed, he claims to be happy for people to blame him rather than God for the fiasco, gladly welcoming 'the tongues that speak against me and the poisoned darts of blasphemers, if only they may not reach Him'.

In the east the alliance between Nur al-Din and Unur was bearing fruit. Despite the quiet renewal of the truce between Damascus and Jerusalem, in 1149 Unur joined his fellow Muslim in an attack on the territory of Antioch. The border between Antioch and Aleppo had gradually been pushed to the east of the Orontes River and the Belus Hills, and Nur al-Din now intended to push it back at least to the river. He targeted two Frankish outposts, at Harim, a bare dozen miles from Antioch itself, and Apamea, further south. The key to the latter was a bridge over the Orontes connecting it to Antioch, and in June 1149 he therefore began by besieging the fort at Inab, close to this bridge.

Raymond of Antioch responded quickly, many have said too quickly. Without waiting for reinforcements from Jerusalem or Tripoli, he set off with a relatively small force to relieve the fort. Initially, Nur al-Din withdrew, thinking this only the vanguard of a larger army, and Raymond believed he had driven him off. Camping on the plain by Inab, he discovered his mistake the following day, 29 June 1149, when he awoke to find his camp surrounded. In the ensuing battle – almost a re-run of the Field of Blood – Raymond was killed, his head being sent as a trophy to the Caliph of Baghdad.

His twenty-one-year-old widow Constance rallied the defence of the city of Antioch, but though it was briefly surrounded and Nur al-Din demonstrated his dominance by travelling to the coast and symbolically bathing in the Mediterranean, he made no serious attempt to attack it. Instead, Apamea and Harim were duly taken before the end of the summer, apparently setting the new frontier of Antioch at the River Orontes.

Raymond's son, Bohemond III, was a child of four, but the hereditary ruler of Antioch was still the Princess Constance. Therefore, although Baldwin of Jerusalem arrived soon after and relieved the pressure for a while by attempting to recover Harim, his standing was that of an ally rather than an overlord, that position having been conceded to Byzantium some years before. William of Tyre declares that Baldwin remained until the affairs of Antioch were restored to order, but it seems clear that Constance asserted her independence and right to rule as regent for her son. The confirmation of this would appear to be her summary refusal of a number of potential new husbands that Baldwin proposed for her in the ensuing year or so.

The precarious nature of life, at least for male rulers of the crusader states, was once again illustrated in 1150 when Joscelin of Edessa, under pressure in Tell Bashir, was captured by the Turks while on his way to try and enlist help. Handed over to Nur al-Din, one account declares that he was publicly blinded, and he certainly spent the remaining nine years of his life as a prisoner in Aleppo. His daughter Agnes had been married to Raynald of Marash, no doubt in the hope he could prove an able support for Count Joscelin. Raynald, however, had been killed at the battle of Inab. With little left of the county of Edessa, Joscelin's widow, Beatrice, saw no prospect of being able to secure the inheritance of her children, and the sale of Tell Bashir and its surrounds to the Byzantine empire was now negotiated. Baldwin, as overlord, met the representatives of the emperor at Tell Bashir to settle the deal, having travelled there accompanied by Raymond of Tripoli and Humphrey of Toron, a man he would soon appoint as his own constable. They, and all the forces they could raise, were then needed to accompany back to Antioch all those Franks and Armenians who had accepted the offer of refuge there, rather than remaining in the dismembered County of Edessa. Despite a determined attempt by Nur al-Din to destroy the column – the baggage wagons were reputedly so stuck with arrows they resembled porcupines – the refugees were safely delivered to their destination. Beatrice and her children then took up residence at Saône Castle near Latakia, an area that seemed to have become the sanctuary du jour for noble widows.

By this time, it was becoming clear that things were not running entirely smoothly between Baldwin and his mother Melisende in the Kingdom of Jerusalem. He was now twenty years old and had come of age, according to the custom of the kingdom, some five years before. According to William of Tyre, who was something of a champion of the king, he was well-grown, well-educated and intelligent, though there is a suggestion he may not have been that interested in the day-to-day running of the kingdom to this point. Certainly, from now on there seems to have been a tension between the joint rulers. Charters previously issued jointly were now, 'with the consent of ...' Separate scriptoria were established and factions opened up among the nobles. At times Melisende seemed to be excluding her son, though whether this was from doubts about his ability or in retaliation for him trying to wrest power from her is hard to say. Neither could challenge the legitimacy of the other's rule, however, without harming their own, since each derived from the will of Baldwin II. One result of this was the entrenchment of each in different areas of the country, Melisende in the south, and Baldwin establishing effectively a court of his own at Acre, and attracting his own supporters, independent of his mother.

It may well be that the differences between them involved policy as well as the eternal striving of the young to be free of the older generation. Melisende's rule aimed for peace, where possible, and support for the church and the ordinary people, the merchants, pilgrims and citizens of the kingdom. Baldwin, having witnessed the disaster of the crusade and the troubles in the northern lands, may have felt a more militaristic attitude was necessary. Troubles in the Fatimid caliphate of Egypt may also have encouraged his ambitions in that direction, for in around 1150 he set about strengthening the Frankish forts around the Fatimid stronghold of Ascalon. In addition, he is known to have clashed with Manasses of Hierges, Melisende's cousin and constable, a man with a reputation for haughtiness, who may have tried to treat him as an inexperienced boy. Baldwin increasingly claimed Manasses was driving a wedge between himself and his mother, and it may have made matters worse that Manasses, through his marriage in 1150, had his own lands of Ramlah and Mirabel to rule. Even Almaric, Baldwin's younger brother, was given his own lands as Count of Jaffa in 1151, while Baldwin, although titled king, had at least to consult with his mother in all actions relating to 'his' kingdom.

Matters came to a head in 1152. The sequence of events in that year is extremely hard to establish, though the following seems to be most likely in view of the few fixed points. At Easter, 30 March, Baldwin demanded that patriarch Fulcher of Jerusalem should crown him alone, without his mother's knowledge. When Fulcher refused, Baldwin appeared the following day self-crowned, some say with an actual crown and others with laurel leaves. At around the same time, however, trouble in Tripoli called attention away from this potential showdown.

Some time in February or March the Muslims had taken control of the town of Tortosa, between Tripoli and Latakia, possibly in response to Raymond raiding in the Beqaa valley the year before. With Nur al-Din involved, this implied a wedge was being driven between the southern crusader states and Antioch to the north. In fact, though, Tortosa was more or less a sideshow for the ruler of Aleppo, who since 1149 had also brought Mosul under his control, and still had his eye on Damascus. In that city Unur had recently died, leaving a very shaky regime in his place, and now it took little to persuade Nur al-Din to withdraw, though he destroyed the fortifications at Tortosa before he went. Raymond promptly gave the town to the Templars as part of a wider policy of engaging the military orders in the defence of his lands.

A council was now held at Tripoli involving Melisende and Baldwin, Raymond, Constance, the Haut Cour of Jerusalem and various church officials including the Patriarch of Antioch. Baldwin's ambitions toward Ascalon were discussed, along with the need for a military leader for Antioch, though Constance repeatedly refused to bow to pressure to take another husband. It is recorded that neither of her two aunts, Queen Melisende and Hodierna, Countess of Tripoli, could persuade her to accept one of those nominated for the role. It seems likely, however, that these two capable women did not try too hard, particularly as Hodierna's own marriage was breaking down at the time.

The reason for this seems to have been extreme jealousy on the part of Count Raymond, even casting doubts on the legitimacy of his eldest child, Melisende, which would later blight her marriage prospects. There was clearly concern at the time of the council about this marriage, and some form of negotiating took place to try and patch up the relationship. When the meeting ended, however, Hodierna and her children set off with Queen Melisende back to Jerusalem. Whether this was to be a permanent split or simply a short-term separation we will never know, for almost immediately Raymond was set upon and killed by a group of Assassins at the very gates of Tripoli. By one account he had ridden some way with his wife and her sister and was returning home, although it is possible he had been on an entirely different mission. All kinds of theories have been put forward, however, as to why he was murdered in this way.

The Assassins had never targeted a Christian before and had even been known to assist them against common enemies. To this point they had been at least tolerated in Tripoli, though now there was a certain amount of indiscriminate blood-letting, aimed at anyone who was not clearly a Frank. One suggestion is that Raymond's donation of Tortosa to the Templars, the sworn enemies of the Assassins, had caused his death, another that someone had simply paid them to kill him. Rather more far-fetched is the idea that they were not Assassins at all but simply people dressed up as Assassins, and either hired for the purpose, or perhaps exacting revenge for the death of another possible claimant to the County of Tripoli who had recently expired in suspicious circumstances. Probably the least likely theory is that Hodierna had hired this group to murder her husband, either with or without the connivance of her sister Melisende, though this has also been suggested, along with the idea that both sisters were unnaturally hungry for power.

Unlike Melisende, of course, Hodierna was not the ruler of Tripoli but merely the consort of one count and the mother of the next. Raymond III, however, was only twelve at the time of his father's death, and, with a regent urgently needed, Hodierna immediately turned back and claimed the role for herself. Count Raymond had apparently decreed that should his son be underage when he died, the county should be administered by the Templars. It may be that Baldwin was wary of the growing power of this group, or perhaps he simply accepted – or was persuaded – that Hodierna was a most experienced and capable woman. Either way, the decrees of Raymond were overridden and, with the approval of Baldwin and Melisende, the nobility of Tripoli now swore allegiance to Hodierna as regent, while young Raymond himself returned to Jerusalem with his aunt and cousin.

What this meant, of course, was that at this point all three remaining crusader states were effectively ruled by women, the daughters and granddaughter of Baldwin of Bourg and Morphia the Armenian. They were, by all accounts, a close and supportive family, and though later there were attempts to undermine their achievements and blacken their names, nothing at the time suggests they were anything but fully equal to the task they had undertaken. It may well be, however, that it was this unusual coincidence of female rulers that now spurred Baldwin to greater efforts to force his mother to give up her position in the kingdom of Jerusalem.

Each had supporters prepared to argue in favour of one or the other. For Melisende these included her younger son, Almaric, the constable Manasses and the powerful lord Philip of Nablus, along with many of the established nobility who had witnessed her rule over many years. Baldwin's backers included many from around Acre and Tyre where he had recently been based, although the marriage of Manasses to the heiress of Ramlah and the potential disinheritance of the Ibelin family this implied had inclined others of the landed nobility to his side. Initially at least, the clashes were verbal and carried out before a meeting of the Haut Cour, whose powers also included official responsibility for the election of kings. Perhaps unsurprisingly, a compromise was decided on. The kingdom should be divided, with Baldwin taking the northern part, including Galilee, Acre and Tyre, while Melisende ruled Judea and Samaria to the south, including Nablus and Jerusalem itself.

It must have been clear from the start that this could only be a short-term solution, and by all accounts it lasted a matter of weeks before Baldwin took matters into his own hands. Gathering the forces available to him – and these may have increased as it became apparent Melisende's power was diminishing – he attacked and defeated Manasses at Mirabel before moving south to confront his mother. She had moved for safety into the heavily fortified Tower of David in Jerusalem, along with her chief supporters, and when it appeared that Baldwin was preparing to attack the tower, Patriarch Fulcher, who had tried to remain neutral, attempted to reason with him.

William of Tyre, for whom this is clearly a painful episode, says Fulcher blamed Baldwin's friends for goading him to such an action, and called him ill-advised. The young king, though, was not to be moved. For several days he bombarded the tower using siege engines constructed for the purpose, and the fact that this had little effect on the massive structure may have made him more amenable to negotiation when Fulcher and other senior neutral figures again intervened.

It was a situation that could not be allowed to continue, and since Baldwin was adamant he would not back down, now Melisende was prevailed upon to do so. She conceded, says William of Tyre, in order to save the kingdom. The outcome was that that Kingdom of Jerusalem would be reunited under Baldwin, while Melisende, now in her late forties, would enjoy a comfortable 'retirement' at Nablus, with ample resources to sustain her as a king's mother should be sustained. Furthermore, Baldwin solemnly swore he would never disturb her thereafter, and, indeed, says, William, from then on he treated his mother with the utmost respect. Had the phrase been known to him, one can imagine him barely resisting the urge to add, 'and they all lived happily ever after.'

Although this looks like a complete victory for Baldwin, and a crushing of his mother's status as joint ruler, the agreement arrived at was clearly far more nuanced than that. Had the dispute been as bitter as some suggest, and had Melisende been completely overthrown and in her son's power, the most likely outcome would have been her banishment to a convent. Baldwin I had not scrupled to treat his first wife in such a way when she became 'inconvenient'. Instead Melisende retained sufficient support and recognition of her status as to be well provided for. Nor did her closest supporters lose by their association with her. Almaric and Philip of Nablus were both witnessing charters as part of Baldwin's inner court within a year, though his particular enemy Manasses found himself exiled.

It seemed to take little time, too, for Melisende and Baldwin themselves to be reconciled. By 1153 Melisende was again associated with Baldwin in charters, and once again she was undertaking public functions, particularly when her son was away from Jerusalem, which occurred frequently over the next half dozen years. It seems likely that, having firmly established his right to rule, as Melisende herself had done in her struggle with Fulk, Baldwin was happy to make use of the wisdom and wide-ranging experience of his mother. Her family links and influence in Tripoli and Antioch would also have been extremely useful, though these might have become a little less valuable when, in the next few years, Constance married the man of her choice, a French knight, Raynald of Châtillon, and Raymond III of Tripoli came of age.

It might be wondered why, during Jerusalem's time of trouble, nothing was heard of Nur al-Din, the Muslim leader supposedly devoted to jihad against the Christian states. In fact, at the time he was busy achieving his own chief objective, taking over Damascus in 1154, and then consolidating his rule there and in the north. This not only allowed Jerusalem to stabilise, but enabled Baldwin to concentrate on defeating the Fatimids at Ascalon, which, perhaps as a sign of complete reconciliation, he then handed over to his brother Almaric to add to his county of Jaffa.

Surprisingly, a two-year truce was signed between Baldwin and Nur al-Din in 1156, but when in the autumn of the following year the Muslim leader fell seriously ill, Baldwin could not resist attempting to recover land lost to the east of the River Orontes half a dozen years before. He gathered a substantial force from Jerusalem, Tripoli and Antioch and set about besieging the town and fortress of Shaizar. Raynald of Châtillon was one of the leaders of this force, and another was Thierry, Count of Flanders, who, having made several earlier visits to the Holy Land, had opportunely arrived again with his wife, Sibylla. The siege was on the point of success when a violent argument broke out between Raynald and Thierry as to who should have possession of Shaizar once it fell. Such was the bitterness involved that the siege was immediately abandoned, though, as partial consolation, Baldwin did succeed the following year in taking back the fortress of Harim, which would once again guard the borders of Antioch.

As before while the king was away, Melisende quietly dealt with affairs in Jerusalem, and on the death of Patriarch Fulcher in 1157 we have an unusual example of a committee of women appointing his successor. By this time Melisende's younger sister Yvette had been abbess of St Lazarus for more than ten years. Hodierna, the other sister, may have been residing there, too, or was perhaps with her older sister in Jerusalem, and Sibylla, Countess of Flanders had also decided to take vows as a nun there. Sibylla was a daughter of Fulk of Anjou by his first wife, and thus was a stepdaughter of Melisende, although only a few years younger. This family group now formally appointed Almaric of Nesle, prior of the Holy Sepulchre, as Patriarch of Jerusalem, and it shows the respect in which all these women were held that the appointment passed unquestioned.

In the same year, Melisende witnessed the marriage of one of her sons; not Baldwin, who was soon to seek a bride from the Byzantine Empire, but Almaric, who now married Agnes of Courtney. There is a suggestion they waited until this time because Patriarch Fulcher disapproved of the match. It was, indeed, later annulled on a rather contrived excuse of consanguinity, when it was felt Almaric should make a grander marriage. Their children remained legitimate, however, and each in turn would become ruler of the Kingdom of Jerusalem.

Baldwin himself married in 1158, his bride Theodora being the niece of Emperor Manuel. This marked a period when relations between the crusader states and the Byzantine Empire became warmer than they had previously been. Baldwin's attempts to persuade the emperor to marry his cousin Melisende, daughter of Hodierna, came to nothing, however, despite his raising an enormous dowry to go with her. The old shadow of illegitimacy raised by her father almost certainly counted against her, though it was claimed there were also concerns about her fragile health. Instead, Manuel married Maria, the daughter of Constance and Raymond of Poitiers, who thus became an empress.

After Baldwin's marriage, Melisende retired more and more to Nablus, and slips quietly into the shadows of history. She lived to see Almaric's daughter, Sibylla, born in 1160, but later that year suffered a stroke that left her paralysed. Taken to the Convent of St Lazarus that she herself had founded, she was cared for by her sisters Hodierna and Yvette, and by Sibylla of Flanders, until at the waning of the summer of 1161, she passed peacefully away on 11 September.

Writing of her later, albeit to please her son, William of Tyre declares, 'She ruled the kingdom with such ability that she was rightly considered the equal of her predecessors.' 'She was a very wise woman,' he says, but then – inevitably – adds that she had 'a manly heart' and 'completely triumphed over the handicap of her sex to take charge of important affairs'. Bernard of Clairvaux is also full of praise, describing Melisende as 'a strong woman, a humble widow, an exalted queen'. Writing to her at the time of the struggle with her son he declares that he has been told by those present in the kingdom that she held herself 'peacefully and calmly' and ruled herself and her affairs 'with wisdom and wise counsel'.

During her fifty-six years Melisende witnessed the turbulent birth of the crusader states, and in particular the rise of the Kingdom of Jerusalem. She herself embodied the fusion of east and west, tutored in eastern ways and traditions by her mother, and in the powers and expectations of a western ruler by her father. In her time that blend of eastern and western art and architecture that became 'crusader style' had blossomed, much of it commissioned by the queen herself. She also founded a school of book makers and a school of painters for the illumination of manuscripts. In Jerusalem, the Church of the Holy Sepulchre – although much altered and restored – stands as a lasting memorial, as does the legendary Street of Bad Cooking, part of the souk or covered market she commissioned.

Between them, Morphia the Armenian and her four daughters played a part in the development of each of the four crusader states. Among their children, grandchildren and great-grandchildren are found kings, queens, princes and at least one emperor and empress, something that must have seemed unimaginable at the time of Melisende's birth in 1105. By the time of her death in 1161, however, the glory of Outremer had already begun to fade. Baldwin outlived her by less than eighteen months, and although Almaric would reign for a further eleven years, already on the staff of Nur al-Din's general, Shirkuh, was a young man called Saladin who would prove to be the nemesis of the Kingdom of Jerusalem.

5

Eleanor of Aquitaine: Eagle of the Broken Treaty

'Give me a child until he is seven and I will show you the man.' Thus said Aristotle, but, with obvious amendments, he could have been speaking of Eleanor of Aquitaine. She spent most of her life in northern climes, among people who valued hard work, plain living and the decrees of the church, but her early years, those especially formative years, were spent far away, in sunnier regions and with a wholly different approach to life.

At the time of her birth the duchy of Aquitaine covered most of south-west France, including Poitou, Gascony and several lesser counties. Although nominally acknowledging the king of France as overlord, it was considerably larger than the area directly ruled by that sovereign, and had an independent spirit that, in the past, had led to frequent clashes. Fertile and well-watered, with abundant forests and a softer climate, it had little in common with the northern lands of the Ile de France. Even the language was different, a variation of French known as the 'langue d'oc,' as opposed to the 'langue d'oil' of the north. This reflected the different historical background of its people. Although conquered by the Franks centuries before, the southerners still retained more of their Roman heritage. Laws and customs were different, in particular in relation to the status and rights of women. In the south, women could own and manage property, leave it by will, and in general enjoyed a greater independence than those in the north who were subject to the heavier hand of misogynistic church leaders, still regarding all women as daughters of Eve the temptress.

The whole culture of the south was lighter, sunnier and, when not fighting among themselves, more given over to leisure and entertainment. Much of this was due to Eleanor's grandfather, William IX of Aquitaine, who would later become known as 'the Troubadour'. William of Malmesbury, who clearly disapproved of his lifestyle, describes him as a 'giddy unsettled kind of man', and certainly his major talents of womanising and song-making were not the kind of thing an English monk could be expected to endorse. Nonetheless, he filled his court with poets and troubadours, and did much to promote the idea of 'courtly love', that platonic worship of an idealised woman that would soon become fashionable. For William, though, the love was rarely platonic.

Through his wife Philippa he had a claim to the next-door county of Toulouse, which briefly became a reality when her uncle, Raymond of Toulouse, marched off to the crusade in 1096. It was thus in Toulouse that Eleanor's father, another William, was born in 1099. Philippa regarded herself as the rightful heiress to that county, which her father had ruled, and was probably furious when, a year or so later, William handed it back to Raymond's son Bertrand. Having refused the chance to participate in the First Crusade, he was anxious to join the force that departed in 1101, to win for himself some of the glory obviously awaiting anyone prepared to travel to the Holy Land. The money he needed to finance this expedition came from Bertrand, but William found the glory harder to achieve. After some preliminary skirmishes with the Turks of Anatolia, his entire army was wiped out on 5 September 1101 at Heraclea, William himself being one of very few to survive.

He did eventually reach Jerusalem before sailing safely home, but the only glory came from songs and poems he himself wrote in the following years. Nor did his trip to the Holy Land improve either his morals or his standing with the church. He was twice excommunicated, once over church taxes, and then, more importantly, when in 1115 he abducted the wife of a vassal to become his long-term mistress. She is known to history as

Dangereuse, Viscountess of Châtellerault, though 'Dangerous' was her description rather than her given name, and the lady was clearly very willing to be abducted.

In earlier years Philippa had turned a blind eye to William's constant infidelities, many of them celebrated in his coarser poems. She herself had given him five daughters after that first son, and then, most recently, another son, christened Raymond. When she found Dangereuse installed in her own apartments in the Maubergeonne Tower at the royal castle in Poitiers, however, it was the last straw. An appeal to the church for support brought no results. When William was rebuked by the Bishop of Angoulême, his response, as recorded by Malmesbury, was, 'You shall curl with a comb the hair that has forsaken your forehead, ere I repudiate this viscountess.' Adds Malmesbury, the bishop's 'scanty hair required no comb'.

Soon after, Philippa admitted defeat and took herself off to the abbey at Fontevrault, an abbey she herself had helped to found some fifteen years earlier. Fontevrault was the project of one man, Robert of Arbrissel, a celebrated preacher, with an attitude unusual for the times in that he declared women to be superior to men. Thus, when his 'honeyed diction' had won the funding for his abbey, and when Philippa had secured him land on which to build it, he established a community of both monks and nuns – soon separated into different buildings – to be ruled over by an abbess. Nor was Philippa the only noble lady on the premises. The abbey soon became famous not only for the nobility of its abbesses, but also for that of its novices and nuns. Philippa and her descendants would be associated with the abbey for more than a century, and when she died and was buried there in 1118, she would be the first of many to be entombed within its precincts.

The arrival of Dangereuse and the treatment of his mother may well have been resented by the younger William, now around sixteen years old. There is no contemporary record, however, of an alleged seven-year rebellion against his father. Rebellions among the independent-minded nobles of Aquitaine were fairly common, but none at this time has the name of young William attached.

Accounts agree, though, that the situation was eased when in 1121 William married a daughter of Dangereuse from her marriage to the viscount, the eighteen-year-old Aenor. Whether this was his own choice, or, as has been suggested, forced on him by his determined new mother-in-law, we will probably never know. Perhaps luckily for him, however, no-one would ever call his bride 'Dangerous'. Like many children of overbearing parents, Aenor seems to have been a quiet, gentle creature, who did what was expected of her, and whose personality has left no mark on history. Certainly, no complaint against her was ever recorded by her husband.

Their first child was probably born the following year, but since she was not the male heir they no doubt hoped for, the date and place of her birth was not noted. Only by counting back from references to her age at later dates can we arrive fairly securely at a birthdate some time in 1122. She was christened Eleanor, and, some have claimed, was the first to receive that name, it being derived from the phrase 'alia-Aenor' – 'another Aenor'. A sister, Aelith, arrived, probably in 1124, but though christened with that name she would be known from babyhood onwards as Petronilla. Finally, in 1126, the required heir, another William, was born. It was the year of the old duke's death, and, stepping into his shoes as William X of Aquitaine, Eleanor's father was surely glad to have the succession satisfactorily secured. A double tragedy in 1130, however, overturned all, when within a few months of each other both the four-year-old William and his mother died.

William X of Aquitaine was a greater man than his father only in terms of height. Standing over six feet tall, and with a reputedly gargantuan appetite to match, he seems always to have suffered from a comparison with the exuberant troubadour who preceded him. He inherited a court that was a centre for culture, music and the arts, and a land at peace when much of Europe was involved in wars of one sort or another. Yet he always seemed to come out just on the wrong side of the balance sheet. Thus, in 1130 when rival popes were elected, he chose to back Antipope Anacletus, despite the efforts of Bernard of Clairvaux to convert him to Pope Innocent. When Bernard departed, William promptly threw out all those bishops who backed Innocent, thereby earning for himself excommunication by that pope. Then in 1136, when he intended to marry Emma of Limoges, a group of nobles from Limoges, Angoulême and Lusignan decided her potential inheritance would make him too powerful, and she was swiftly abducted and married off to Count William of Angoulême instead. In that same year, William of Aquitaine joined Geoffrey of Anjou in invading Normandy, and in less than a fortnight was chased out again alongside Geoffrey himself.

Perhaps as a result of all these setbacks, William decided in 1137 that he would make a pilgrimage over the Pyrenees to the shrine of St James at Santiago de Compostela. Setting off on foot from Bordeaux in early spring, by 8 April, the day before Good Friday, he was some half a dozen miles from the end of his journey when overnight he fell seriously ill. Some have blamed contaminated water or tainted fish from a nearby river, but we can never be certain of the cause of his illness. The next day he insisted on struggling onward, but in the end he was carried the last part of the way, into the cathedral at Compostela. There, at the point of death, he made his last dispositions as to his duchy and his daughters.

Eleanor was named as his sole heir, to inherit the duchy in her own right. Knowing well, however, the inclination of his countrymen toward violence, and, indeed, the abduction of heiresses, he further named King Louis of France, his overlord, as protector of both his daughter and her lands until he had found her a suitable husband. Furthermore, William's death, now imminent, was to be kept completely secret until Louis had been informed, the sole exception being that the Archbishop of Bordeaux, who at present had custody of the girls, should be told, so as to be on his guard for any eventuality. His duty done, as far as it could be, William then received the Holy Sacrament and died, and Eleanor, at fifteen years old, became Duchess of Aquitaine.

What was she like, then, this girl who, at a stroke, had become the greatest heiress in France? Just as we have no details of her birth, so we can only infer her education from her later accomplishments. This seems to have gone well beyond the domestic arts usual for daughters of the nobility – needlework, spinning, weaving and household management. Eleanor could read and write, not only in her native Poitevin language, but in Latin, too. Arithmetic, history and even some astronomy were also included, and we might put this good educational grounding down to her quiet mother, who would have been her chief guide for the first eight or so years of her life. There is no evidence Eleanor was ever a 'bookish' child, but she seems to have been intelligent and keen to learn. As the daughter of a nobleman, riding, hunting and falconry would also have been part of her education, and in the glittering court of her father and grandfather, she would have been expected to appreciate music and literature, to play an instrument, dance, sing and engage in games such as chess and backgammon.

As far as looks go, Eleanor was acclaimed throughout her life as a radiant beauty and there is no reason to suppose that, at fifteen, she was any less attractive. Though we have no direct description of her, the twelfth-century model for beauty, as evidenced by the art of the time, generally involved blonde hair, blue eyes, regular features and white skin. The stamina and energy she retained into old age may well have derived from her father, while both nature and nurture would have contributed to her personality. William X was noted for his stubbornness and quick temper, both of which in Eleanor may have been leavened by her mother's quiet patience. She certainly had the liveliness of William the Troubadour, and, with Dangereuse as grandmother and role model, we don't have to look far for the streak of boldness and wilfulness we find in her character. Her position in her father's court would account for her self-confidence and independent spirit, as well as an ease in dealing with people and the problems of administration, while her travels with him around his duchy had given her a great love for the land of Aquitaine and its people that she would pass on to at least one of her sons.

William of Aquitaine was not the only significant figure to die in 1137. As his chief advisor and biographer, Abbot Sugar, records, King Louis of France 'was in the process of failing, not in mind but in body, as men habitually do, worn out by his corpulence and the continual strain of his tasks'. Late in May he was at his castle of Bethizy near Paris when the duke's messengers reached him. At once he recognised the opportunity being offered him, and not only gladly accepted the protectorship, but immediately had a husband lined up for Eleanor, his own son and heir, Prince Louis.

A 'noble cortège' was quickly assembled to accompany the prince to Bordeaux, and Louis, clearly alive to the potential dangers, added five hundred of the best knights to those noblemen who were meant to impress by their presence. In addition, says Suger, 'He added to the escort his close advisers, including myself,' the whole to be led by Theobald of Blois, currently in high favour with the king, and by Louis's own cousin Ralph, Count of Vermandois. They were provided with 'a sufficiency of treasure' and strictly forbidden to steal anything in Aquitaine, to damage the land or the poor, 'or to turn friends into enemies'. Louis wanted nothing to spoil this enormous expansion of the territory now to become directly subject to France.

They set off on 18 June and travelled through intense summer heat to reach Bordeaux on 11 July. With a purely political marriage such as this, no time was needed for courtship, and it is quite likely no-one bothered to ask the young couple what they thought of each other. Exactly two weeks later, on Sunday 25 July, they were married by Archbishop Geoffrey and formally recognised as Duke and Duchess of Aquitaine. Suger then seemed particularly anxious to return as quickly as possible to Paris. He may have been worried about the health of the king, but, by his own words, he was equally concerned about the troublesome nobles of Aquitaine. The royal party therefore set off immediately after the wedding and had reached Poitiers a week later. On that day, 1 August 1137, King Louis VI breathed his last in Paris. In less than four months Eleanor of Aquitaine had gone from heiress to duchess to Queen of France.

In theory, there was no reason why the marriage of Louis and Eleanor should not have been completely successful. Many political marriages of the time matched children with middle-aged or even elderly spouses – the eleven-year-old Matilda matched with Emperor Henry, some twenty years her senior, for example. Here, though, Louis, at seventeen, was only two years older than his new wife, and the expectation was that they would grow together and produce a string of healthy children for France. Unfortunately, just as Eleanor had been formed by her early background, so had Louis been formed by his, and they were diametrically opposed.

As the second son of the king, Louis had been destined from an early age for a career in the church. Thus, his education was among the cloistered monks of Saint-Denis, rather than in the rough and tumble of the royal court. By the time this destiny was overturned in October 1131, when his older brother Philip was killed in a fall from a horse, either nature or nurture had firmly established Louis's character as gentle, pious and devout. Even when taken from the cloisters and hastily anointed and crowned as heir to the throne, he had hurried back to Saint-Denis whenever possible, to pursue his studies among the, to him, more congenial company of the monks.

It would probably be unfair to say that Louis was afraid of women. They had simply never crossed his path, and his beautiful, vivacious bride must have seemed to him almost as a creature from another world. Eleanor, too, quickly recognised that her husband was not going to rank alongside the warrior figures of her childhood, or even the romantic knights that, no doubt, peopled her imagination from the songs of the troubadours. She might have been flattered, though, by his obvious infatuation, and appreciative of his courtesy and kindness when she was a stranger in a strange northern land, where even the language was difficult to understand. In the early days of their marriage he was happy to let her have her way in filling the halls with music and dancing such as had never been seen there before, and it took her only a matter of weeks to see off her disapproving mother-in-law, the Dowager Queen Adelaide. They were both prepared to do their duty, too, and it is likely that Eleanor was soon pregnant, though, sadly, this resulted in a miscarriage.

In Paris, though, Eleanor was like a fish out of water. Not only was it cold and, to her eyes, antiquated, but it was a city of intellectuals and scholars. Peter Abelard taught there, that shining star of medieval thought, though he was frequently in trouble for his advanced ideas. Students flocked to the place from across Europe, including a young Thomas Becket from England, and it was said that 'There is no knowledge under the sun, which brought to Paris does not acquire incomparable strength, of an excellence that may not be found elsewhere in all the world.' What they sought and debated, however, was the philosophy of Plato and Aristotle, and, in particular, the finer points of theology, subjects of only passing interest to the vibrant young queen from the south.

Nor did she play a large part in the public life of the young king, her husband. For advice in matters of state he turned to Abbot Suger, his father's counsellor whom he had known all his life. Soon after their marriage, a revolt broke out in Poitiers, and he did not turn to Eleanor for counsel, instead crushing the revolt and allowing Suger to placate the citizens. Queen Adelaide had regularly witnessed charters and participated in the policy-making of Louis VI, but Eleanor was given no such role. And when not involved in matters of state, the young king tended to retire again to the peace of Saint-Denis, to pursue his studies or take part in the religious offices.

In a word, Eleanor was bored, and like many bored people began to meddle and use the influence she undoubtedly had over her besotted husband to achieve her own ends. The year 1141 saw three events that would together prove calamitous, and in at least two of them we can see Eleanor's influence at play.

Several times since the 'selling' of Toulouse by William the Troubadour, Aquitaine had briefly succeeded in re-imposing its dominion over the county, but for the previous twenty years it had been ruled by Count Alphonse-Jordan, half-brother of Bertrand, who owed his name to the fact that he had been born in the Holy Land and baptised in the River Jordan. Now Louis, no doubt encouraged by his queen, attempted once more to add the county to Eleanor's lands, and thus to his own rule. In the summer of 1141 Eleanor accompanied him as far as Poitiers, with a household and retinue that included her beloved sister Petronilla, who had been by her side since they left Bordeaux in 1137.

The campaign for Toulouse was a complete failure, however, with Louis abandoning it as soon as Alphonse-Jordan showed he was prepared and determined to defend his lands. The rest of the summer was spent touring Poitou, and, by the time they returned to Paris in the autumn it was clear that Petronilla, now around seventeen years old, was at least in love, if not conducting an actual affair, with Ralph of Vermandois, some thirty years her senior. At the time, Ralph had been married for more than fifteen years to the sister of Theobald of Blois, and it may well have been rumours of this romance that kept Theobald from fulfilling his feudal obligation to provide forces for Louis in the Toulouse campaign.

Needless to say, her sister's happiness was paramount for Eleanor, and it was almost certainly at her urging that Louis now found three bishops willing to annul Ralph's marriage. His wife and their children were promptly dispatched to her brother, and Ralph and Petronilla were wed; but that was not the end of the matter. Theobald promptly complained to Pope Innocent, who, freed from the threat of Anacletus who had died in 1138, was no longer so concerned about upsetting the French monarch.

Innocent, indeed, already had his own quarrel with Louis. The Archbishop of Bourges had recently died, and the pious, monkish Louis, until now a faithful child of the church, had demanded his own chancellor be appointed in his place, disregarding the more correct appointment and consecration of Peter de la Châtre, who had been approved by the pope. Even here it is possible Eleanor had some input, since at the time there was a claim that the Archbishop of Bourges had authority over the Archbishop of Bordeaux. Uncharacteristically, Louis dug his heels in, refusing to admit the new archbishop, and, when Innocent declared he was acting like a petulant schoolboy, retaliated by swearing on holy relics that de la Châtre would not enter Bourges as long as he, Louis, was alive. Bernard of Clairvaux later described this oath as 'unlawful and accursed', and 'foolishly taken'.

It was Theobald who now offered shelter to the archbishop, and Theobald again who was blamed when, in 1142, Pope Innocent declared the first marriage of Ralph of Vermandois to be entirely valid and subsisting, and excommunicated both Ralph and Petronilla for ignoring this ruling. By that time Louis, too, had been excommunicated for his intransigence over the archbishop, and France put under an interdict. The result of all this was war between Louis and Theobald.

Louis himself led armies into Theobald's county of Champagne, ravaging and burning, but an incident at the town of Vitry-sur-Marne would have a profound effect on him. When the town was attacked and set on fire, the townspeople rushed to the sanctuary of the church where they should have been secure. To the horror of the watching king, however, by accident – a change in the wind, perhaps – or by design, the church itself was set ablaze. Upwards of a thousand people were burned alive, while some put the number as high as fifteen hundred.

Louis was devastated. At a subsequent meeting with Bernard of Clairvaux he openly wept, the abbot praising his repentance. 'These tears, if they do not quickly dry up,' Bernard told him, 'can extinguish all recollection of the burning of Vitry.' His consternation when Louis continued with the war, however, is documented in a series of angry letters to the king, accusing him of adding 'fires to fires and slaughter to slaughter ... under I know not what counsel of the devil.' Perhaps Bernard had some inkling of the 'devil' involved, for he also wrote to the king's supposed counsellors, Abbot Suger and Joscelyn, Bishop of Soissons, 'It is wonderful indeed if it is done against your advice; still more wonderful and mischievous if it is by your advice.' At this time, however, Suger was devoting most of his time and energy to the rebuilding of his church at Saint-Denis in an entirely new gothic style, which perhaps explains the absence of his usual restraint on the young king's actions.

A brief peace was achieved when Louis, having taken much of the county of Champagne, offered to withdraw if the excommunication of Ralph and Petronilla was lifted. It duly was, and he withdrew his troops. When Pope Innocent then asked Ralph to return to his first wife and was refused, however, they were excommunicated all over again and the war continued. Late in 1143, following the death of Innocent, the new Pope Celestine, in an attempt to break the deadlock, did lift all the excommunications, though a peace conference at Corbeil, arranged by Suger and Bernard, was a complete failure when Louis stormed out, feeling himself insulted. If he had only waited, Bernard wrote to him, all could have been explained, as 'Nothing was said by us that was an insult to yourself,' adding, 'We still stand and wait till your better nature return.'

It was in June 1144, at a splendid gathering to re-dedicate Suger's magnificent church at Saint-Denis, that Eleanor tried to take matters into her own hands. By this time she would have been well aware of the effect of the war, not only on France and Champagne, but on her own husband. Never really happy in his defiance of the church, Louis was suffering severe pangs of conscience. Withdrawn and morose, he may even have begun to blame his wife for his troubles. Worse, in the present circumstances, and after seven years of marriage, there seemed little immediate prospect of producing an heir for the throne of France.

We cannot be sure if it was Eleanor who arranged the private meeting with Bernard at Saint-Denis. Had she read his condemnation of court ladies, with their 'devilish vanity', their painted faces removed at night, their rich dresses made by 'the toil of worms' and their overload of gold, silver and jewels, she might have hesitated to seek an audience. Perhaps she thought her famous charm and native wit could win him over. Since they met alone, there is no direct evidence of what passed between them, but the chronicles claim Eleanor tried to bargain with the abbot – peace in Champagne, in return for the lifting of the excommunications on her beloved sister and her husband. Bernard, we are told, furiously rebuked her and told her to stop meddling in matters of state. Thereupon, apparently humbled and penitent, the queen confided her desperation to produce an heir. Having dealt with her father, who had shown no such penitence, Bernard then seemed to soften a little towards Eleanor. If you will promise to urge the king towards a better course of action, he told her, I will promise to ask God to send you a child. A short time later, Louis handed back to Theobald the lands he had taken and allowed Peter de la Châtre to take up his post as archbishop. In time, even the marriage of Ralph and Petronilla would be quietly recognised, though they would have to wait another four years for that. Long before then, just as Bernard had promised, Eleanor became a mother. It was not, however, the necessary son that she produced, to become heir to France. Instead, in 1145 she gave birth to a daughter who was christened Marie.

Great sins, so it is said, require great acts of penance, and it is likely that Louis's thoughts had turned towards a visit to the Holy Land even before Christmas 1145, when details were emerging of a possible response to the fall of Edessa the previous year. It was at this Christmas court, according to his secretary Odo of Deuil, that the king 'first revealed the secret in his heart'. Odo would go on to chronicle in some detail the zeal with which the king embraced the idea of a crusade, and would travel with him to the Holy Land, leaving a record of at least the first part of that enterprise.

Thus, he tells us of the gathering at Vézelay in Burgundy on 31 March 1146, in response to a papal bull and the preaching of Bernard of Clairvaux. The size of the crowd there on that Easter Sunday necessitated the building of a wooden platform in a field, so that Bernard, with Louis beside him, could address them. Then, he says, 'the heavenly instrument', that is to say Bernard, 'poured out the dew of the Divine Word', causing such a clamour for the cloth crusader crosses he had brought with him, that he had to resort to tearing up his own garments to make more. Needless to say, Louis was the first to take the cross, but Odo does not mention that Queen Eleanor and many other ladies also received a crusader cross that day.

Of course, Bernard knew something of the east through his contacts with the Templars and Queen Melisende, but it is a sign of the sheer ignorance of many as to what lay before them that, when Odo tells of Louis writing to the Byzantine Emperor, he admits he does not even know his name. Nonetheless, preparations went ahead with all speed for the coming expedition, and, while Louis contacted his fellow monarchs to establish possible routes to the Holy Land, Eleanor toured her lands to the south, drumming up support in terms of both manpower and funds. A special tax was imposed across France to finance the crusade, which, with numbers growing day by day, was anticipated to be many thousands strong. Nor were they all fighting men. Apart from Eleanor and her ladies – she later referred to them as Amazons – there were numbers of servants, cooks, armourers, men to handle the baggage animals and the flocks and herds brought along for food, falconers, and even minstrels and other entertainers. A significant number of simple pilgrims also attached themselves to the expedition, seeking protection on their dangerous journey.

On 11 June 1147, Pope Eugenius blessed the leaders at Saint-Denis, and they set off for Metz where the whole French part of the crusade was to assemble. Some attempt had been made to co-ordinate with the German section under Conrad, and the Germans had set off a few weeks earlier, probably to avoid too large an army passing along the same route at the same time and exhausting available food supplies. When the French finally got under way, Eleanor and her ladies travelled in a different part of the column from Louis, and probably with a very different mindset. For Louis it was, at least in part, a pilgrimage, for Eleanor more in the nature of a holiday. Probably neither of them at that point had given much serious consideration to the military undertaking on which they had embarked.

For the first part of the journey Odo gives us what is virtually a travelogue, listing the number of days journey between each town, and describing the scenery. The dense forests and rugged mountains of Germany impressed him, at least until he saw the mountains of Anatolia. The swollen rivers of Hungary were hard to cross, he says, and Bulgaria was well supplied with 'things that grow by themselves' and would have been good for other things, too, had there been farmers to grow them. Progress was slow but relatively easy and, at least at first, food was plentiful. Unlike on the First Crusade when the women travelled under the same conditions as the men, Eleanor had brought beds to sleep in and baths, and in her part of the camp, mainly among the contingent from Aquitaine, there was entertainment each night when the day's travelling was done. Apart from a few issues of looting – probably inescapable with such a large and varied crowd of people – the passage to the frontier of the Byzantine empire passed peacefully. 'Thus far,' says Odo, 'We had been at play.'

From the time they crossed that border, however, late in August, problems quickly began to multiply. The emperor, Manuel, had 'promised many things which he did not in fact carry out', says Odo, among them free access to markets and a fair exchange rate for their money. What they found were closed markets and exorbitant prices. In some places the Greeks refused to let them enter a town at all, letting down on ropes from the walls what they were prepared to sell. This was, of course, the second time a mass of crusaders had passed through this land, and this Second Crusade was not even a response to a request for help from the Byzantines. Nor had the passage of the German forces a few weeks earlier done anything to improve the Greeks' opinion of the barbarians from the west. Their looting and skirmishing was one reason for the reluctance to engage with the French, while another was the fact that a large part of the available food had already gone to feed that first army. Thus, with their own food supplies already exhausted, and with little other option, the French, too, says Odo, 'secured the necessary supplies by plundering and looting'.

Already there was bad feeling between the Germans and French, and Odo describes an encounter between French advance parties and German stragglers at a market where each was trying to buy food. The Germans, he claims, would not allow the French to buy anything until they had all they wanted. A major brawl followed between the supposedly allied crusaders, until, says Odo, 'God put an end to this wickedness, for night soon fell.'

It was in a more sombre mood, therefore, that Louis and his followers reached Constantinople at the beginning of October. If they had had any doubts that they were unwelcome in this land, they would have been dispelled by now by the sight of dead Germans, apparently ambushed along the road and left unburied. Nor was their stay of almost a fortnight in this fabled city entirely untroubled. While Louis and Eleanor were comfortably housed in a palace that was, at other times, Manuel's hunting lodge, the army was left to fend for itself outside the city walls. As a result, says Odo, they burnt the houses of the Greeks and their olive trees, 'either because of a lack of wood, or else because of the violence and drunkenness of fools'. Louis tried to maintain order, cutting off the ears, hands or feet of offenders, but with little effect.

It was here, too, that they would have begun to realise exactly what faced them on the rest of their journey. Although a large part of Anatolia was nominally part of the Byzantine empire, in practice only a relatively narrow coastal strip had any kind of security. Even here there was constant pressure from Mesud, the Turkish Sultan of Rûm, whom Manuel had been battling for some time. Threatened now by Roger of Sicily, Manuel had just concluded a twelve-year truce with Mesud, though this truce clearly did not cover the crusaders. Knowing little of the intricacies of local politics, there were cries of betrayal when this was discovered, and even demands that Constantinople should be attacked. With a distinct lack of trust on both sides, the emperor was more than happy to provide food and advice, and to ship his unwanted visitors across the Bosphorus as quickly as possible.

Perhaps as a result of this advice Louis decided to follow the coastal route to Antioch, rather than striking straight across country as Conrad and the bulk of his army had done a few weeks before. Nothing had been heard of them since, though as the French left Constantinople there were rumours of a battle and a victory.

There had indeed been a battle, but the victory was not to the Germans. Instead, Mesud had followed the example of his father Kilij Arslan in the First Crusade, attacking the crusaders at Dorylaeum and leaving Conrad's mighty army in ruins, with the king himself bearing a serious head wound. Only a few days into their journey the French began to meet the survivors struggling back, mere hundreds where thousands had set out. The scale of the defeat was shocking, not only men lost, but all their baggage, animals, arms and supplies. No doubt it awoke in Eleanor memories of her grandfather's stories of death and devastation on the plains of Anatolia.

There was nothing to be done but to continue, and the remnants of the German army – Conrad, too, when they came up with him – joined them on their march towards Ephesus. By now winter had set in, and cold, rain and swollen rivers added to their difficulties. The food supplied by Manuel, supposedly enough to last them to Antioch, had almost gone, and when they made camp near Ephesus on Christmas Eve, they had their first encounter with Turkish raiders. The fact that they saw them off with some ease put heart into them, and it was decided that, instead of continuing around the coast, they would strike inland to Laodicea where they hoped to pick up fresh supplies of food. Conrad left them at this point to return to Constantinople by ship to recover from his wounds.

The French reached Laodicea on 6 January 1148, and it was immediately apparent there would be no food supplies there. The place was almost deserted, and all around were signs that they were not the first Westerners to pass that way, and that their predecessors had fared badly. It was, in fact, the place where another, largely non-combatant, part of Conrad's army had come to grief. Led by Conrad's half-brother Otto, Bishop of Freising, they had run out of food there and succumbed to the Turks. Many were killed, others captured and led away to slavery, and just a few, Otto among them, had managed to escape and would make their way back to Constantinople.

Once again, plans were changed. All ideas of marching on to Antioch were abandoned. Instead, they would go to the coast and take ship to their destination. There was no thought of going back to Constantinople, though, or even to Ephesus. No, decided Louis, they would go forward, over the mountains to the port of Adalia. It would have been a difficult journey in summer with fit, well-supplied men. In the depth of winter, frozen, half-starved and continually attacked by Turkish raiders, it was a disaster waiting to happen.

The disaster duly arrived on the day in mid-January when the army was to cross a high pass on Mount Cadmus, a ridge so lofty, declares Odo of Deuil, that it seemed to touch heaven, while from there the plain below seemed like the depths of hell. Leading the vanguard was Geoffrey de Rancon, the lord of Taillebourg in Poitou, with probably the bulk of the forces from Aquitaine around him, and close behind, Queen Eleanor. Far away at the rear of the column, Louis had elected to ride with the rearguard, a vulnerable position usually given to a seasoned warrior. Between them, climbing the steep and rocky path up the mountain, stretched the mounted knights, the foot soldiers, the baggage train and the pilgrims.

Geoffrey's orders were to cross the ridge and then make camp while the rest of the army closed up with him. It says much about the king's lack of control over his forces, however, that when Geoffrey reached the designated stopping place about noon, he decided to go on further. Had Louis been closer, of course, he could have consulted him, but there was no possibility of reaching him, far below on the narrow way. Instead, he consulted the king's uncle, the Count of Maurienne, who agreed they should move on.

A variety of reasons have been suggested for this decision. Geoffrey might have assumed the king had overestimated the time it would take to cross the mountain. He might have thought the proposed camp was too exposed in winter weather, or scouts might have informed him there was a much better place further on. One theory that gained credence in later years, however, was that it was Eleanor and the other women who urged him to find a more congenial camping place. Likewise, Eleanor's baggage was blamed for slowing up the rear of the column, which could not hope to travel as swiftly as the mounted men at the front.

For whatever reason, Geoffrey and the vanguard moved on, together with Eleanor and the other women. The column crossing the ridge became stretched thin and then broken, and the ever-watchful Turks moved down to occupy the summit. Then, around mid-afternoon, they fell on those still climbing up from below, mainly the foot soldiers, the pilgrims and the baggage, overwhelming them like a great wave on the sea. There was little chance of escape. The choice was to perish by the sword or by the fall into the abyss, and only a very few escaped both.

Odo was one who did, and Louis another. Had the king been dressed in regal splendour he would, no doubt, have been a major target, but his plain clothes and crusader tunic made him one of a crowd. While his noble bodyguard was slain, he managed to scramble onto a rock above the mayhem and defend himself until finally the Turks withdrew as night fell. Odo recorded that that was the only help they received from heaven that day.

No doubt several miles away across the mountain, nothing was heard of this in Geoffrey's camp, and it was only late in the day that men were sent to discover why the rest of the column had not arrived. They found the remains of the slaughter scattered over the mountainside, and eventually, around midnight, the king himself, struggling on towards safety with a few of the survivors.

No longer in a fit state to command, Louis put what was left of his army in the hands of a group of Templar knights who had been travelling with them, and thus they finally reached Adalia towards the end of January. Even now, the king was wholly impractical, thinking like a pilgrim rather than a commander. Antioch was still forty days march away across hostile territory, while it could be reached in three days by sea. Louis proposed they should undertake the march and give their lives like martyrs, and, says Odo, had to be forced by his barons to consider and adopt the latter alternative.

We are not told Eleanor's opinion, but by now she seems to have become totally disillusioned in her husband. He had failed in Toulouse, he had failed her sister, and now he had failed uncounted numbers of men and women who had blithely followed him into this wilderness. It took two months to assemble a fleet of ships, and during that time they seem to have had little to do with each other. In the event there were far too few ships, and the prices demanded for their passage were out of the reach of many. Thus, when eventually Louis, Eleanor and the elite of their forces embarked for Antioch, many thousands were simply abandoned to their fate at Adalia – another failure for Louis.

It was at Antioch that Eleanor's marriage really began to disintegrate. Raymond of Antioch was her father's younger brother, an uncle only eight years older than herself, and whom she may well have remembered from her early years at Poitiers. His welcome was effusive, and after her recent privations, that and the luxury of the court at Antioch must have done much to restore her spirits. Once again, she was among her fellow countrymen – for many Poitevins had followed Raymond to Antioch – speaking the language of her youth and enjoying the relaxed court life with its love of music and verse, so reminiscent of her far-off days of childhood. While Eleanor enjoyed herself, however, those who had disapproved of her conduct in Paris found even more to deplore in this foreign land. Rumours spread that she was conducting an affair with Raymond, a most unlikely, incestuous relationship, but one still touted by William of Tyre some thirty years later. In fairness, he also states that Raymond showed equal honour to the king and was a generous host to all the French.

In truth, what Raymond most wanted was for the French army to back him in action against Zengi's son, Nur al-Din, the Turkish lord who now held Edessa, and whose growing power threatened Antioch itself. He no doubt reasoned that obtaining Eleanor's support would bring him one step closer to achieving this. In fact, the opposite was true. The more Eleanor urged backing for Raymond, the more Louis resisted the idea. At a meeting of the leading crusaders when Raymond outlined his plans, the king immediately rejected them, saying his pilgrim vow meant he must travel on to Jerusalem before undertaking any other enterprise.

We have no record of what passed between Louis and Eleanor at this time, Odo of Deuil having tactfully ended his chronicle at Adalia. It is impossible that the king would not have heard the rumours about his wife, and very likely there were serious arguments. He would have been aware, too, that he cut a poor figure alongside the dashing Prince of Antioch, and may quite simply have been jealous. He would have been stunned, though, when Eleanor suddenly announced that she was going no further and wanted a divorce. Some five years earlier Bernard of Clairvaux had suggested the marriage was illegal as they were too closely related, and this is the idea Eleanor now resurrected, though almost certainly for her own ends, rather than from any real conviction as to the illegality.

Panic-stricken, Louis fired off a letter to Abbot Suger, at the time acting as regent of France. Suger's advice, when it came, was that all matters relating to the marriage should be postponed until they returned from the Holy Land. More immediately practical advice, however, was given by advisers close at hand. Whatever she said, Louis must not permit Eleanor to remain at Antioch. Thus, in the dead of night on 28 March 1148, the king mobilised his army and departed the city, with Eleanor, according to John of Salisbury who may have heard it from Louis himself, 'torn away and forced to leave for Jerusalem'.

They travelled south via Tripoli, but whether Eleanor went under a form of 'house arrest' or with a show of willingness and courtesy to her husband in order to save face, we cannot know. Once at Jerusalem, and kindly welcomed by Queen Melisende and her son King Baldwin, the French queen fades into the background, as Louis once more took up the idea of military action. Something was certainly needed to make all the vast expense and loss of life on this expedition seem worthwhile.

By now Conrad had arrived in the Holy City, having travelled by sea with another German army, in ships provided by his new friend the emperor Manuel. At a meeting held at Acre on 24 June, the Western kings readily fell in with a proposal put forward by the leaders of the kingdom of Jerusalem. This was for a full-scale attack, not on Edessa, far to the north, but on the ancient and wealthy city of Damascus. None of the northern rulers were present at this meeting, and Edessa, now seen as a lost cause by those who were there, was not even mentioned.

If the earlier part of the crusade had been a shambles, that was as nothing in comparison with the attempt on Damascus that got under way late in July 1148. With an army made up of forces from Jerusalem, France, Aquitaine, Germany and elsewhere, and multiple leaders, none of whom entirely trusted the others, the potential for division and recrimination was ever present. It was presumably King Baldwin and his advisers who decided they would attack on the western side of the city, through five miles of narrow paths and walled orchards. Says the Muslim chronicler Ibn al-Qanisi, who was probably there, they deluded themselves that that would be an easy way to approach, as town and country districts merged together in that region.

In the event they remained there only four days, under attack by defenders the whole time. The decision was then made to move the whole of the forces around to the east of the city where there was an open plain. Here, though, there was no food, and they were still under constant attack. During all this time, apparently, Unur, the governor of Damascus, was doing his best to negotiate, and possibly spinning different stories to different leaders. Later, even Raymond of Antioch was accused of bribing men to abandon their enterprise, to thwart any chance of glory for Louis.

Unur had also, however, made a very reluctant plea for help to his ally, Nur al-Din, and it soon became generally known that that warlord was on his way with an army. The situation was too much for Louis. If they remained where they were, they would be in a trap between two Muslim forces. Their previous position to the west had already been re-occupied by forces from within the city. Retreat was the only option, and retreat they did, all the way back to the Kingdom of Jerusalem, harassed the whole way by Muslim archers and leaving a trail of dead and dying behind them.

The crusade was effectively over. Conrad left almost at once, but Louis showed no signs of wanting to go home. Though Suger wrote repeatedly to urge him to hurry back, he lingered through autumn and winter, touring the holy places, and behaving more like a pilgrim monk than a king. It may well be that he didn't want to return. There were likely to be all manner of recriminations over the money wasted and lives lost on a crusade that had been his own dearest project. As Robert of Torigny would later write, 'nothing worthy of being remembered occurred in this expedition.'

At home, too, he would have to face up to the reality of his shattered marriage. There is nothing to show that Eleanor had changed her mind about the divorce. She may even have become more insistent. Certainly, the actions of her husband at

Antioch and at Damascus would have done nothing to repair her opinion of him. It is easy, given the pious demeanour and general ineffectiveness of Louis, to fall into the trap of picturing him as an old man. In fact, at this time he was only twenty-seven years of age, and Eleanor a year or two younger. They had their whole lives before them, and it was a life Eleanor had no wish to share with her husband. It is no doubt indicative of the situation between them that when they finally sailed for home after Easter 1149, they went in separate ships.

The ships were provided by Roger of Sicily, now at war with the Byzantine empire. They were supposed to sail in convoy, but when suddenly confronted by Manuel's navy they scattered. A storm made matters worse, and while Louis, briefly captured by the Byzantines, was driven in one direction, Eleanor disappeared in another. For more than two months nothing was known of either of them and there were even stories that both had perished. Then, in mid-July, Eleanor finally came ashore at Palermo in Sicily.

Described as more dead than alive, she had apparently spent some time on the northern shores of Africa, though what adventures she might have gone through there remain a mystery. It took several weeks for her to recover enough to travel, and what her thoughts were during that time when she may have believed Louis was dead, we can only guess. During that period, however, she would have heard that he, too, had reached Italy safely, landing near Brindisi two weeks after her own arrival. About then she would also have learned that her uncle Raymond of Antioch had been slain in battle against the Turks. It would have been in no very happy state of mind that she eventually rejoined her husband.

We don't know whose decision it was to visit Pope Eugenius on the way back to France. He was, of course, the ultimate arbiter on legal and illegal marriages, and one or both could have been eager to have the matter settled once and for all, though from very different viewpoints. The meeting with the pope – at Tusculum, since he was at the time barred from Rome – is described in detail by John of Salisbury, who was then a secretary at the papal court. Eugenius heard each party separately, Eleanor claiming the failure to produce an heir was because the marriage was unlawful, and Louis, doing all he could to retain his beautiful wife (and her beautiful duchy), protesting that he loved her passionately.

Eugenius came down firmly on the side of Louis. Not only did he declare in writing that the marriage was lawful, but he forbade anyone to question it again. Furthermore, if it was the lack of an heir that worried them, he had a remedy for that, too, insisting that they sleep in the same bed, a bed he had blessed and decked with hangings from his own chamber. He did everything but tuck them in and kiss them goodnight.

Whether it was the pope's blessing or otherwise, soon after they returned to Paris Eleanor was pregnant again. Had she produced a son her fate would have been sealed, and she would have spent her life as a very reluctant queen of France. But early in the summer of 1150 another daughter was born and christened Alix. And now the queen found she had some allies in her quest for a divorce, as the French nobility began to urge Louis to set her aside and marry again in the hope of producing an heir.

By that time, however, Louis was already being dragged into someone else's war. The struggle for the crown of England had been going on for nearly fifteen years, after Stephen of Boulogne, brother of Theobald of Blois, had seized it from Matilda, the designated heir of Henry I. Fortune had favoured first one side and then the other, and the rise in Matilda's prospects, together with Louis's own conflict with Theobald of Blois, had enabled her husband Geoffrey Plantagenet, Count of Anjou, to seize Normandy, a fact Louis had been forced to recognise in 1144. In 1148 Matilda had retired to Normandy, but there was no question of her giving up the fight for her birthright. Instead, the focus now shifted to her son Henry. Early in 1150 Geoffrey handed over Normandy to this seventeen-year-old, entirely without consulting his overlord Louis, and, with Stephen's star apparently on the wane, people on both sides of the Channel began to view Henry as a likely successor to the English crown. For the past ten years the French king's sister Constance had been married to Stephen's own son, Eustace, and when Stephen and Eustace now proposed to take their war to Henry in Normandy, Louis felt obliged to join them.

Abbot Suger was strongly against the war, and equally strongly against a divorce from Eleanor. This was not time, he argued, to be giving up the extensive lands of Aquitaine, which might then fall into the hands of another enemy. Suger, though, was an old man and in January 1151 he died. A few months later, in the summer of that year, the war duly took place. While Eustace energetically attacked the north-east of Normandy, however, Louis fell ill of a fever before even facing his foes in battle. A truce was arranged, brokered by Abbot Bernard of Clairvaux, which grew into a peace agreement. In August 1151 Geoffrey and Henry came to Paris in order to sign it.

If we are to believe the accounts of Robert of Torigny and Abbot Bernard, their behaviour was insolent in the extreme, the abbot even being stung into prophesying that for his blasphemies Geoffrey would be dead within a month. Whether it was this singular lack of reverence for her husband that first drew Eleanor's attention, we cannot be sure, but drawn it certainly was, in particular to the younger of the two.

We have a very detailed description of Henry from Gerald of Wales, who knew him well some thirty years later. Subtracting from that the features that would be due to late middle age, we can say he was of average height, of sturdy and muscular build, red-haired, with a round head and ruddy complexion, and grey-blue eyes that could flash with anger. At eighteen he was some ten years younger than Eleanor, in the full flush of youth, and with an active, energetic presence that contrasted strongly with Louis's pale and pious demeanour. He was no more like the romantic image of a courtly lover than Louis but was otherwise as opposite to her husband as a man could reasonably be.

There is no record of their meeting in Paris at that time, but given what followed they surely must have done, and there must have been other messages passed between them later as well. It is generally assumed that the immediate attraction was physical – at twenty-nine Eleanor retained her beauty – but it could equally well have been political. Nothing had yet been said openly about a divorce from Louis, but it seems clear Eleanor was now confident of regaining her freedom, and with it her duchy of Aquitaine, though it might still take a little time. She was shrewd enough to know the duchy would immediately become a target for fortune-hunters, and, no doubt, preferred to pick her own protector. For Henry, of course, the duchy had the same attractions as it had for Louis. Whether or not the young man boasted of his plans for an invasion of England – and offered her an English crown in place of a French one – we will never know. Those plans had to be put on hold for a time, however, when Bernard's prediction came true, and Geoffrey of Anjou died suddenly of a chill on his way home from Paris.

That Eleanor's plans were progressing nicely is confirmed by the tour of Aquitaine she made with Louis that autumn. While he was accompanied by a considerable number of barons and bishops, she had a separate retinue of clergy and nobles from the duchy, and as they went, royal garrisons were quietly withdrawn from castles and towns. Clearly the divorce was now imminent, and the careful separation of France and Aquitaine had begun. They celebrated Christmas together at Limoges, then, early in the New Year, Louis returned to Paris and Eleanor to Poitiers. The scene was set for the final act in their marriage.

It is probable that Louis was still in love with his wife, but the urgent need now was for a male heir and clearly Eleanor was not going to provide one. Instead of divorcing her for adultery, using evidence from those who had accused her in Antioch, he fell back on the old excuse of consanguinity. Ignoring the prohibition of Pope Eugenius, the matter was examined by a church council, with the backing of Bernard of Clairvaux, and on 21 March 1152 Eleanor was summoned to Beaugency and told that her marriage had been annulled and her duchy restored to her. Her two daughters, though, were declared legitimate and they would remain with their father. They were, after all, the only heirs he had at present. Whether Eleanor suffered a pang at parting from them, the younger less than two years old, we cannot know, though she had apparently felt no qualms at abandoning Marie at a similar age to go off on crusade.

Eleanor had been around fourteen years old when her father's intended bride had been abducted and married off, and she would have been well aware that she was once again a most valuable prize for any man brave enough to do the same to her. We are told, indeed, that two such men existed. Ambushes were laid for her by both Theobald of Blois, second son of the recently deceased Count Theobald, and Geoffrey of Anjou, second son of the newly deceased Count Geoffrey. She avoided them both. Eleanor had no intention of becoming the wife of a second son.

Once again, we have no record of any communication between her and young Henry, now Duke of Normandy, but communication there must have been, for she had been in Poitiers only a matter of weeks before Henry arrived with just a few companions. They were married on 18 May 1152, 'not very splendidly in proportion to their rank', says William of Newburgh, 'but with guarded prudence'. Robert of Torigny, close in time and place, uses the peculiar phrase that they married 'either suddenly or deliberately', the wedding clearly being a complete surprise to contemporaries. Newburgh, though, with the benefit of hindsight, explains the need for secrecy, 'lest any pompous preparation for their nuptials should allow any obstacle to arise'. The obstacle in question, of course, would be Louis, who, as overlord of both, should have been consulted, and who would certainly have forbidden it. Discovering now how he had been duped, the king, says Torigny, 'became incensed against the duke'.

A new alliance was formed against Henry with Louis calling on his major vassals to defeat this upstart. Thus we find allied together Robert of Dreux, together with Theobald, newly Count of Blois, and Henry, newly Count of Champagne, these being the sons of old Count Theobald of Blois, and, surprisingly, Henry's own brother Geoffrey who felt himself badly treated under their father's will. With Eustace of England joining the alliance, Henry found himself ringed with enemies intent on 'stripping him of all his possessions'. His response was characteristically swift and decisive. Between June and the end of August the alliance was shattered, as first the Blois brothers and then Geoffrey were driven to seek peace. Nowhere did he directly challenge Louis, but the French king, too, was quickly forced to abandon his campaign, leaving the new husband free to return to his wife in Poitiers.

Eleanor, no doubt delighted by this display of prowess, was already happily signing herself, 'Eleanor, by the grace of God, duchess of Aquitaine and Normandy'. It was time now for Aquitaine to meet its new duke. Despite repeated pleas for Henry's presence in England, for the next few months the couple toured the duchy, not only consolidating the new regime, but also allowing Henry to obtain men and resources for his forthcoming campaigns. By the time he left her at Poitiers in December, Eleanor was pregnant.

Throughout the whole of 1153 while Henry was pursuing his destiny in England, his formidable mother Matilda was put in charge of Normandy, but Eleanor was given custody, not only of her own duchy of Aquitaine, but also Anjou. It argues considerable confidence in a new wife that she should be trusted with such a responsibility, but she proved herself an able administrator and revelled in this opportunity to use her considerable intelligence and experience. In August, around the time Henry was, perhaps reluctantly, accepting the proposal of a negotiated settlement with Stephen, she gave birth to her first son, who was christened William. Whether this was a tribute to her own father, following the tradition in Aquitaine, or a nod towards Henry's all-conquering great-grandfather, we don't know.

It was the following Easter before young William could be introduced to his father, Henry returning then with his succession to England assured but not expected to take place for some years. Now Eleanor travelled to Rouen for the first time to meet her mother-in-law, the Empress Matilda. She would already have discovered that she had not the influence over Henry she had had over the infatuated Louis. Henry had ideas of his own. He was young, though, and open to advice, and it may have been resented by Eleanor, now relieved of duties in Aquitaine, that when he wanted such advice he turned to his mother rather than to her. Nor did Matilda approve of the flightier elements of Eleanor's court, the troubadours being quickly sent packing back to Aquitaine. Nonetheless, the two women would probably have developed at least a respect for each other during the time they spent at Rouen, while Henry typically rushed around his domain imposing order. The news that Louis had married again, this time to Constance, the quiet young daughter of Alphonso of Castile, would have been of some interest, but by then Eleanor was pregnant again and hoping to give her husband another son.

Then, early in November, came much more startling news. Stephen, king of England, had died suddenly on 25 October, and Henry's presence was urgently requested to take over the kingdom. There was a delay while Henry was summoned from distant parts, and a further delay due to storms in the Channel. On 8 December, however, the new king arrived in England, accompanied by his wife, now six months pregnant, and one-year-old son. Eleven days later, on Sunday 19 December 1154, with 'becoming pomp and splendour (and) amidst universal rejoicings', Henry was crowned as King of England in Westminster Abbey. Eleanor, too, received a crown, becoming in the process the only person to have been indisputably crowned both as Queen of France and as Queen of England. Just over two months later, on 28 February 1155, she gave birth to her second son, who would of course be christened Henry.

If Eleanor had hoped that, away from his mother, the king would now turn to her for advice and involve her in the administration of his extensive realm, she was to be disappointed. Instead, he appointed a number of senior officials, among them Richard de Luci and Earl Robert of Leicester as joint chief justiciars, the latter being the first of the senior nobility in England to support his cause against Stephen in 1153. Nigel, Bishop of Ely, nephew of the great Roger of Salisbury, became Treasurer, while Theobald, Archbishop of Canterbury, recommended one of his own household – a man recently appointed archdeacon of Canterbury in recognition of his usefulness – to be the king's chancellor. The man's name was Thomas Becket.

Some thirteen years older than Henry, Becket had been born in London, schooled at Merton Priory, and well, though not brilliantly, educated later, including a year studying in Paris. At the time the post of chancellor was not the mighty office of state it would later become, involving mainly supervision of the royal chancery or writing office, keeping the Great Seal and acting as chaplain to the king. Much of its enhanced function about this time, however, derived from the ambition and abilities of Thomas Becket, together with the extraordinary friendship that grew up between himself and the king.

His initial task, though, was humbler, being the complete refurbishment of the royal residence, variously described as the palace at Westminster or the Tower of London. This he accomplished so quickly that, from substantial dilapidation at Easter, it had become fit for the royal family to move into by Whitsun. So many carpenters and other workmen were employed together, says William fitzStephen, Becket's biographer, that they could not hear each other speak. No doubt it was this energy in accomplishing the tasks given to him that endeared him to Henry, and soon more and more was devolved to the most useful chancellor, who, says fitzStephen, 'discharged his duties with energy and authority'.

If Eleanor had been jealous of Matilda's influence over her son, she had at least as much cause to feel jealous of Thomas Becket as his star inexorably rose. In particular, one burden he took from Henry's shoulders was that of lavish entertaining. Henry, ever mindful of his tendency to put on weight, disliked the feasting and the pomp involved in holding court for the nobility, or providing important visitors with suitably impressive entertainment. Thomas, though, relished the role. His house, provided by Henry, and his lavish table were open to all, and among the earls, bishops and foreign dignitaries dining there on a daily basis, the king himself could be found there when the mood took him. Thus, the splendid and lively gatherings over which Eleanor would have been delighted to preside were increasingly to be found, not in her hall, but in that of the chancellor. Furthermore, as time went on, in the little leisure time he allowed himself, Henry was more frequently found in the company of his chancellor rather than his wife. Says fitzStephen, 'When the daily round of business was completed, the king and Thomas would sport together like boys of the same age.' One thing Eleanor would have known, however, was that an openly jealous wife now in her mid-thirties, would have held very little attraction for a much younger husband.

In September 1155, she moved to secure a measure of independence. A council was held at Winchester important enough to draw the Empress Matilda from Normandy. The major debate concerned whether or not to invade Ireland with a view to conquest, the pope having issued a bull approving this move in order to bring the Irish church into line with Rome. This was firmly vetoed by Matilda and the idea shelved. Now, however, a proposal was put forward to award Eleanor 'the Queen's Gold'. For every 100 silver marks due to the king, one gold mark would be paid to the queen, thus ensuring she had an income of her own not dependent on ownership of estates. The proposal was approved, and from then on Eleanor ensured that the Queen's Gold came to her on a regular basis.

Before Henry left to deal with continental troubles at the start of 1156, Eleanor was pregnant again, this time delivering a daughter in June of that year, who would be christened Matilda in deference to the empress. At some point in this year, however, her first-born son William died, a not unusual occurrence for a child under five at the time, but a blow nonetheless. He would be buried at Reading Abbey at the foot of the tomb of his great-grandfather, Henry I.

Later that year Eleanor and the remaining children joined Henry in Aquitaine, but it would not be as joyful a homecoming as she might have wished. In England people rejoiced that Henry had reimposed order after the chaos of the Anarchy, reviving and developing the laws and courts of his grandfather, and establishing strong centralised government. It annoyed him that the people of Aquitaine took the opposite view. Lukewarm to him at best, they resisted efforts to make them pay homage and conform to a system of government they regarded as alien. Now, determined to bring them to heel, he set about destroying castles, taking hostages for oaths of allegiance, and appointing Normans and Norman garrisons in place of what he regarded as ineffective southerners. For Eleanor, this was the wrong policy for 'her' people, and they may well have argued about it, but Henry was unmoved, and, in any case, soon the queen was once more back in England, and once more pregnant.

The latest child, another boy, was born on 8 September 1157 and christened Richard. From the first he seems to have been Eleanor's favourite, but even so he was soon handed over to a wet nurse as the queen joined her husband on a progress round England that would last the best part of eleven months and cover well over three thousand miles. If this progress was in any way similar to one described later by Peter of Blois, Eleanor may well have felt grateful for her experiences of rough travel while on crusade. Henry, apparently, travelled on a whim, frequently changing itinerary and living in spartan fashion. Even if plans had been made and lodgings arranged in advance, he rarely arrived when and where he was expected, by such means keeping local officials uncertain as to when their activities might be inspected. With a train of servants, clerks, courtiers, chaplains and others, often more than two hundred strong, food seemed the least of Henry's concerns, and though the lodgings for himself and his queen would certainly be the best available, his sudden appearance and equal restlessness meant that supplies might be short and food undercooked, while those lower down the scale simply had to fend for themselves. Many a time Eleanor must have wished she was on one of her father's leisurely tours, or even the meticulously planned progresses of Henry I.

After taking in the extreme north, most of the Midlands, the Welsh Marches and the West Country, the grand tour finally ended at Winchester at the end of July 1158, by which time Eleanor must have been in some discomfort as she was again seven months pregnant. Almost at once she was left as co-regent with Richard de Luci, while Henry rushed off to the continent to further ambitions in two important areas.

The lesser of these was the securing of Brittany following the death of his brother Geoffrey, who had been inserted as duke some years before. Far more important was a scheme that might result in the French throne becoming joined to the English. Earlier in the year, Louis's second wife Constance had presented him with another daughter, christened Margaret. Immediately, Henry had dispatched Thomas Becket to negotiate a marriage between the child and his own son Henry. Surprisingly Louis had seemed amenable to the suggestion – possibly overawed by the extreme ostentation of Becket's entourage, so that 'the person of his liege lord might be honoured in his envoy,' as fitzStephen records. The details were now thrashed out by the two kings, meeting in person at Gisors, with the Vexin agreed as Margaret's dowry. Then, almost as if to spite Louis, as Henry neatly disposed of one son, on 23 September 1158 Eleanor bore him another, who would be christened Geoffrey.

Having ended 1158 on the most amicable terms with Louis, it seems perverse of Henry to immediately plan to deprive him of a southern county. Toulouse had been a sore point in Eleanor's family ever since it had been lost generations before. Whether it was at her urging that the king now assembled forces to attack it, or whether it was simply his ambition to add a rich prize to his 'empire', we cannot be sure. He had reassembled all the parts that Stephen had lost, and even Wales and Brittany now acknowledged him as overlord. Perhaps he accepted Eleanor's claim that Toulouse was a legitimate part of her territory. Indeed, the fact that Louis himself had attacked it on her behalf some eighteen years earlier may have persuaded him there would be no protest on the part of the French king. Things had changed since then, however. Louis's sister Constance, widowed on the death of Eustace of England, had married Count Raymond of Toulouse, and when, in the summer of 1159, Henry put the city under siege, Louis neatly checkmated him by arriving with a small escort and quietly requesting permission to enter and visit his sister. Now, says fitzStephen, 'from foolish scruples and respect for the king of France', Henry immediately called off the siege and withdrew.

This was the occasion of the first recorded disagreement between Henry and his chancellor, Becket arguing that Toulouse should be taken and Louis made a prisoner, while the king declared it would set a bad example to his own vassals if he took such action against a man to whom he had paid homage. Henry thereupon returned to his wife in Poitiers, while the disgruntled chancellor, who had provided 700 knights for the army from his own household, satisfied his ambitions by storming and taking three castles in the area.

The failure to take Toulouse was the first real setback to the grand Plantagenet plan, and Eleanor may have been personally annoyed at Henry meekly giving way to Louis. She may, though, have been quietly pleased at the first sign of a rift between the king and Becket, who had far greater influence over her husband, and, indeed, saw far more of him, than she did herself. It was in many ways a strange marriage, even for the times, for while Henry continued his relentless travelling around his vast territories, Eleanor was for much of the time not even in the same country. It is clear Henry trusted her implicitly, frequently requiring her to supervise England while he was away and calling on her for specific tasks when needed. In the winter of 1159/60, for example, she arranged the collection of coin from the treasuries at Westminster and Winchester, and then escorted it personally to Barfleur for Henry's use, before returning at once to England. In like manner, later that year, she brought the five-year-old Prince Henry to Rouen so he could be married to the two-year-old French princess Margaret, thus enabling Henry to claim her dowry of the Vexin.

Wherever they had been during the year, they usually met for the holding of a royal court at Christmas, and the romantics might claim the flame of love still burned bright on those occasions, as witness the number of their children born in September or October. By the time her second daughter, Eleanor, was born on 13 October 1162, however, the queen herself was forty years old and had borne six children in nine years, one a year for the first five years of her marriage. She would have two more, a daughter, Joan, in 1165, and finally John, born on 24 December 1166, by which time she was in her forty-fifth year. It argues strongly for the queen's inherent stamina and fortitude that all these pregnancies had in no way diminished her good health and keenness to participate fully in royal life.

Thus far, she had done her duty as a mother rather than as the partner she had hoped to be, but she was already making plans to alter that situation. Possibly the fall from grace of Thomas Becket a few years earlier had convinced her that Henry was never going to turn to her for advice, as he still did to his mother. When in 1162 the king had proposed making Becket archbishop of Canterbury, the Empress Matilda is recorded as trying to dissuade him, but there is no suggestion Eleanor was even consulted. Throughout the clash of wills that followed, when the new Archbishop Thomas showed a surprising willingness to defend the church from what he viewed as Henry's attempts to undermine its independence, the queen seems to have remained merely an onlooker. Perhaps she, like many at the time, viewed Thomas as a hypocrite given his earlier relish for worldly wealth, though most likely it was simply his nature to intend to be the best archbishop, as before he had intended to be the best chancellor. Certainly, when he was in exile later and his supporters appealed to her for backing, they were informed they could expect none, and she was no doubt glad that her son Henry, who had been placed in Becket's household for his education, was now returned to her.

It is probably true to say that Eleanor had never been very interested in small children. She had left two daughters with Louis of France, and her travelling, pregnancies and supervisory roles in England and elsewhere would have given her little time for nursery games with her later brood. Now, though, as her sons were getting older, and their futures and those of her daughters were coming under discussion, Eleanor's thinking seemed to embrace a change to a different kind of family life. Young Henry, at eleven years, was already married, his young wife now being brought up in Eleanor's household. Matilda, too, now nine years old, was promised to the thirty-six-year-old Henry the Lion of Saxony, and would leave for Germany soon. Richard had once been promised to the daughter of Count Raymond of Barcelona, though that had come to nothing. Now, though, there was talk of his marriage to Alys of France, the younger daughter of Louis and Constance, while in June 1166 Geoffrey, aged eight, was betrothed to the five-year-old Constance, heiress to the duchy of Brittany. It must have come home to Eleanor that, if she wanted to have any influence over her children, it must happen soon, and could not happen under her existing peripatetic lifestyle.

She wanted, too, more of a political role than she was at present being given. In England where Henry was solidly established this was unlikely, but she was, after all, Duchess of Aquitaine in her own right. It is thus clear that, from around 1166, Eleanor was contemplating a long-term separation from her husband, and equally clear that Henry had no particular objection to this. The motives on both sides, however, have been muddied by wild stories that later grew up around a young beauty known to history as 'Fair Rosamund'.

Rosamund Clifford was the daughter of a minor Marcher lord, Walter Clifford, of Clifford Castle near Hereford. We have very few facts about her life except that she was born some time before 1150, possibly as early as 1140, and may have been educated at Godstow Abbey in Oxfordshire. At some point she came to the attention of King Henry, and in 1174 was publicly acknowledged as his mistress. She later fell ill, returned to Godstow and died in 1176. On these bare bones, however, the popular story grew up that Henry met Rosamund at her father's castle after his failed expedition to Wales in 1165, fell head-over-heels in love with her and installed her at Woodstock Palace, near Oxford, as his mistress almost at once. At the time Eleanor was at Angers, acting as regent while Henry was in England. Late in 1166, though, she returned, heavily pregnant, to England, possibly having heard rumours of Rosamund, and found her occupying her own quarters at Woodstock. As a result, Prince John was born at another royal residence in Oxford instead of at that more favoured palace. Incensed at her husband's behaviour she then demanded a separation, to which Henry readily agreed, having tired of his wife. Eleanor subsequently spent years plotting revenge and turning her children against their father.

There is much in this that could be circumstantially true, if unproven, but the tale comes suspiciously close to that of her grandfather installing Dangereuse in the apartments of his wife at Poitiers. Nor is it likely Eleanor would be surprised or shocked by Henry's infidelity. He had, no doubt, had women aplenty in the course of his travels, and had at least one illegitimate child who was being brought up alongside her own children. If Henry himself had made declarations of love to Rosamund and had shown he intended her to replace Eleanor in his affections, that might have made a difference, but it would have been uncharacteristic. In the event, she was not even acknowledged publicly for another eight years, and there is no evidence she ever bore him a child. If this *was* a royal love affair, indeed, it could well have assisted Eleanor in her plans for a separation, thus mitigating any jealousy she might have felt towards the younger woman.

On the other hand, the story of the cheating husband, the wronged wife and the fair mistress was far too good to let go easily, and future generations heaped more and more lurid detail upon it, until Rosamund became the innocent victim and Eleanor something akin to the wicked witch. Thus, in one version Henry had built a tower for Rosamund, known as Rosamund's Bower, near his palace, and set it within a labyrinth so intricate that only he could find the way. Eleanor is then said to have followed a silken thread that had fallen from Rosamund's embroidery chest, confronted her rival and murdered her. Woodstock Palace itself was totally destroyed in the building of Blenheim Palace. Near to the site there is a pool known as Rosamund's Well, supposed to have been a bathing pool in the garden Henry made for his mistress. Archaeological exploration has, however, failed to find any trace of Rosamund's Bower.

The supposed murder was also elaborated over the years. In a fourteenth-century French chronicle Rosamund was roasted between two fires, stabbed and thrown into a bath of scalding water, surely an unnecessarily involved and lengthy way of disposing of a mistress, even by way of revenge. Later tales claim she was given a choice between poison and stabbing with a dagger, and chose the poison. This far neater version was the one much favoured by the Pre-Raphaelite artists of nineteenth-century England in their depictions of Rosamund and Eleanor. The simple truth, however, is that at the time of Rosamund's death Eleanor was in no position to murder anyone, being herself under lock and key at Old Sarum. It is unlikely the two women ever laid eyes on each other. Henry did, though, pay for a lavish tomb for his mistress at Godstow, where she lay before the main altar until, after his death, the Bishop of Lincoln insisted she be moved to the cemetery outside the church. Godstow Abbey itself was ruined at the time of the Dissolution of the Monasteries, but some have suggested the site is haunted by the ghost of a 'Grey Lady', identified with the unfortunate Rosamund Clifford.

Whatever the motives of the king and queen, late in 1167, after the departure of young Matilda for Germany, Eleanor collected her belongings and left England. Then, early in the New Year, Henry escorted her to Poitiers, and they parted apparently amicably, Earl Patrick of Salisbury remaining with the queen to supervise and protect her. Most nobles in Aquitaine were delighted to have their duchess back but there were exceptions, and before he left, Henry took action against the lords of Angoulême and Lusignan, sending several hurrying to the protection of Louis in Paris. He had barely departed, however, before Geoffrey and Guy de Lusignan set an ambush for Eleanor. Earl Patrick was killed – some said stabbed in the back – but the furious defence set up by a young man of Patrick's household, caught Eleanor's attention even as she escaped. William Marshal, the earl's twenty-two-year-old nephew, was wounded and captured, but the queen quickly ransomed him, and for the next two years he would serve her in Aquitaine before, almost certainly on her recommendation, becoming companion and tutor-in-arms to her son Henry.

After the death of Earl Patrick, no replacement was sent, and, to a large extent Eleanor now had the role she had wished for, effectively in command in Aquitaine, at least in day-to-day matters. She established her own court, complete with poets and troubadours, and encouraged a revival of the atmosphere of culture and civilisation that had been in abeyance during the more heavy-handed Angevin rule. Rather than crushing dissent by force, she endeavoured to defeat it by charm and a lighter touch, travelling around the duchy and encouraging a renewal of traditional fairs and festivals. For a time, at least, it seemed to be a successful policy, and Aquitaine enjoyed a period of relative peace.

One of the more fanciful images from this time is the idea that Eleanor established a 'Court of Love', where women were regarded as the dominant civilising sex to whom men must apply for guidance. A partner in this enterprise was said to be her eldest daughter Marie of France, now married to Henry, Count of Champagne, who came from her own court at Troyes for a visit. Between them, it is claimed, they persuaded Andreas Capellanus – Andrew the Chaplain – to write a book called 'De Amore', 'About Love'. The first part of this promises instruction to a young man called Walter on the art of love. The second consists of a number of dialogues offering guidance to men on how to win fair lady, followed by questions apparently posed to a 'Court of Love' presided over by Queen Eleanor, Marie and others, with answers provided by that court. The book finishes with a set of rules of love, including that it is not proper to love someone that one would be ashamed to marry, that every lover turns pale in the presence of his beloved, and that one entertaining thoughts of love eats little and sleeps less. One question apparently posed to the court is whether love is possible within marriage. Possibly drawing on their own experiences, the ladies answer that it is not impossible, merely unlikely.

Sadly, there is no evidence that Marie visited her mother at this time, or indeed that she ever saw her after her divorce from Louis. Though both Eleanor and Marie are specifically mentioned, it seems most likely that the book, or at least part of it, was written some time later, and may have been intended as a satire on the idea of 'courtly love' that was then fashionable throughout the courts of Europe. Certainly, a final part of it may have been added later, for it seems to refute the earlier sections. Called The Rejection of Love, it advises that love should be avoided for a variety of reasons, but especially because women are untrustworthy, avaricious, weak-minded, loud-mouthed gossips, unfaithful and vain. It is hard to picture Eleanor of Aquitaine willingly lending her name to such views.

At least at first the queen had most of her children with her in Aquitaine, her sons Henry, Richard and Geoffrey, and daughters Eleanor and Joan. Missing, though was baby John, never given overmuch of his mother's affection. Instead of travelling to Poitiers, he was left at Fontevrault Abbey, with the possible intention that he should be brought up for a career in the church, though any such idea seems to have been quickly abandoned. The futures of the other children would, however, be decided in the near future.

It may be that Eleanor was given a free hand in Aquitaine because in the late 1160s Henry had more pressing matters on his mind. One of his schemes, at least, had come to nothing when, on 22 August 1165, Adela of Champagne, the third wife of Louis of France, at last gave him the son and heir he craved. Christened Philip and known at first as Philip 'Dieu Donné' – God Given – his arrival seemed to put new life into the French king. Giving shelter and support to Thomas Becket was just one challenge to Henry, while skirmishes over the Vexin and encouragement of rebels in Brittany and Aquitaine came close to provoking open warfare. Pope Alexander had also given support to Becket, but troubled by yet another antipope supported by the Holy Roman Emperor, he now did all he could to try and reconcile the French and English kings, both of whom supported his papacy, and to bring an end to the Becket affair. Papal legates negotiated with all parties and in January 1169 a meeting was held at Montmirail, near Chartres, with a prospect of resolving all issues.

In the event little progress was made with Becket, but a large part of the tension between Henry and Louis was removed by the English king declaring an intention to divide his vast territory between his three sons, who had accompanied him to the meeting. The young Henry, now nearly fourteen years old, was to have Normandy, Anjou, Maine and the overlordship of Brittany. Richard, aged eleven, was to have Eleanor's duchy of Aquitaine, a decision of which she whole-heartedly approved. Ten-year-old Geoffrey, already betrothed to Constance of Brittany, was to have Brittany and do homage for it to his elder brother, while Henry and Richard now performed homage to Louis for their lands. This highly satisfactory arrangement was sealed by the betrothal of Richard to Louis's daughter Alys, his second pair of daughters thus allied to the Plantagenet brothers, as his first pair had been to the brothers from Blois. To complete Henry's dynastic arrangements, soon afterwards his daughters Eleanor and Joan were betrothed to two southern kings, Alfonso of Castile and William of Sicily respectively. As a further sign of his good intent, Henry had his elder son crowned King of England in 1170, while Richard was acclaimed Duke of Aquitaine in 1172.

Between these two events, however, the king suffered his most traumatic reverse. The proposal to crown his son caused another rift between Henry and the church. Thomas Becket claimed only the Archbishop of Canterbury was entitled to crown an English king, and he was backed up by the pope who also rightly declared that this crowning in the lifetime of an existing king was not an English custom. When it appeared Henry would go ahead with his plan, the pope issued a bull addressed to the Archbishop of York and all the English bishops commanding 'on Apostolic authority' that 'none of you shall presume to confer the crown upon the prince.' Henry later claimed this did not arrive in time, and on 14 June 1170, says fitzStephen, 'contrived to have his son, Henry crowned king in London, by the hand of Roger, Archbishop of York, against the desire and opinion of almost everyone in the kingdom'.

Apparently, Eleanor approved of this coronation but the pope did not, immediately threatening Henry with excommunication. Nor did Louis of France, furious that his daughter Margaret, the young Henry's wife, was not crowned with her husband. In the face of this, and possibly aware he had blundered, Henry finally agreed to a reconciliation with Becket. Early in December of that year the archbishop returned to England and immediately began excommunicating those involved in the coronation – which both the pope and the king had authorised him to do – sending bishops scurrying across the Channel to protest to the king. Then, says William of Newburgh, in his rage Henry 'poured forth the language of indiscretion'. The exact words are variously reported, but whatever he said it was interpreted by four knights as a desire to have Becket killed. They therefore crossed to England and on 29 December 1170 murdered the archbishop in his own cathedral.

The outrage that followed this deed wholly undermined the position of the king. While he protested his innocence of any intent to harm the archbishop, it took him over a year to convince Pope Alexander. Even Eleanor stood aloof, holding her own Christmas court in Aquitaine in 1171, instead of joining her husband has she had done before. Henry, too, absented himself from his domains, and by the time he returned to Avranches in May 1172 to swear his innocence on the gospels in public and be formally reconciled with the church, he had gone a long way towards conquering Ireland.

If Henry now anticipated living in peace with the active support of his sons, however, he was to be disappointed. The contemporary Gerald of Wales, who would later serve the king and knew all the family, offers an outsider's view. Henry, he says, 'was the kindest of fathers to his legitimate children during their childhood and youth, but as they advanced in years, looked on them with an evil eye, treating them worse than a step-father.' Furthermore, he says, 'he could never bear to think of them as his successors.' The major point of contention was the division of his lands, which he had announced in 1169. At that time the king was thirty-six years of age, and, whatever anyone else might have expected, clearly had no thought of retirement. On the other hand, after his coronation, and certainly as he grew to manhood, the junior Henry – known to history as Henry the Young King – began to demand the sharing of power that his new status seemed to suggest.

It is possible the English king had no great opinion of his son's fitness or readiness to rule. Gerald of Wales describes the Young King as courteous, affable and generous, saying 'he considered he had lost a day when he had not secured the attachment of many by various acts of liberality, and bound them to him, body and soul, by multiplied favours conferred.' Unfortunately, with no estates or resources of his own, there were few favours he was able to confer, and his generosity, and his practice of living in the manner of a king, had already landed him deeply in debt. Moreover, he preferred to spend his time at jousting and tournaments, which Henry had banned in England, rather than learning the business of statecraft. There is a strong resemblance here with the situation of William the Conqueror and his eldest son Robert Curthose, and the outcome was exactly the same.

Matters came to a head early in 1173 when, in arranging a marriage for his forgotten son John – already referred to as 'Lackland' – Henry carelessly promised as dower four castles that, in theory at least, formed part of the Young King's manorial holdings. Says the chronicler Roger of Hoveden, in service with the king at the time, the Young King immediately protested that he 'would in nowise agree thereto, nor allow it to be done', particularly since Henry had not even given to him any part of his lands where he and his wife could live. In turn he demanded that Normandy or England or Anjou should be made over to him, and when Henry refused, 'could not even converse with him on any subject in a peaceable manner'.

He took himself off to his father-in-law, Louis of France, who was more than happy to support him in any attempt to undermine the power of the English king. Roger of Hoveden, indeed, declares that it was Louis who suggested he demand a territory of his own. Others, however, give a large share of the blame for what Gerald calls the 'grievous dissensions' between Henry and his sons to Eleanor, particularly in light of the fact that Richard and Geoffrey, fifteen and fourteen respectively, now left her court at Poitiers to join their elder brother.

William of Newburgh declares the princes left 'with her connivance, as it is said', and other chroniclers also imply her involvement as a matter of hearsay. Only Gervase of Canterbury, a contemporary chronicler and monk at Canterbury, names Eleanor as the leading force behind the rebellion that now took place. None speculates as to her motives, and it seems to be stretching the evidence to suggest, as some have, that she deliberately plotted with her first husband to bring down her second out of jealousy over the Fair Rosamund. It would appear more plausible that the whole rebellion was simply a revolt against the heavy controlling hand of Henry. She may well have argued before that, having taken the step of crowning his son, it was foolish to continue treating him as a child, and may have reminded him that his own father had stepped aside as soon as he made him Duke of Normandy. She would, too, have had her own complaints, among them that the revenues of Aquitaine continued to be paid to Henry rather than to herself, and that, on Raymond of Toulouse at last submitting to the English king, his homage had been paid to Henry, rather than to the Duchess of Aquitaine, as was her right.

The fact that so many joined in this rebellion lends weight to the claim it was a carefully developed plot, but then again, Henry's power and ambitions had made him many enemies. If they thought, though, that the king would be crushed by the concerted forces of France, Flanders, Brittany, Scotland and some leading English magnates, they were quickly disillusioned. Most of Normandy and England stood beside Henry, and with substantial mercenary forces and the aid of Richard de Luci, his justiciar in England, by the autumn of 1173 the rebels had been defeated and put to flight.

At this point it seems Eleanor might have suffered a loss of nerve. She had been at Poitiers supporting Richard, the last of the sons still fighting, but now she abruptly fled for Paris, disguised as a knight, so we are told, and riding astride. She never reached that city. Captured and handed over to Henry, for a period of months she disappears completely. It is the following July before we hear of her again, travelling with the king as he crosses the Channel to England. She is clearly a prisoner and on arrival is dispatched to her prison, probably the castle at Old Sarum in Wiltshire, where she would remain under fairly spartan conditions for the next ten years.

A few months later, victorious over all his enemies, Henry gathered his sons around him at Montlouis, near Tours, and forgave them all. Apparently penitent, they were given castles and allowances and promised to serve him faithfully in future. For

Eleanor, though, there was no forgiveness. It is claimed Henry considered divorcing her if she would go quietly to Fontevrault, but she refused. She was now fifty-two years old, a good age for that time, and possibly Henry expected her to fade away and die in her prison. Eleanor, though, was not the fading type.

How much she knew of events in the outside world we cannot tell. Possibly she heard in 1177 that the Young King's wife had had a baby son in Paris, who died within a few days, and maybe that, in the same year, her youngest son John had been crowned King of Ireland. In 1179 she may have known of King Louis's visit to Canterbury to pray at the tomb of Thomas Becket – now Saint Thomas Becket – for the health of his seriously ill son, and how, on his return, the French king suffered a stroke that left him paralysed and unable to attend the coronation he had planned for the fourteen-year-old Philip. The death of her former husband the following year would surely have been reported to her. It seems impossible, too, that she would not have known of the renewed hostilities between her husband and sons that flared up in 1183, when Richard, having spent the previous ten years subduing the rebellious lords in Aquitaine, repeatedly refused homage to his brother the Young King, who then tried to take the duchy by force. With Henry this time aligning with Richard against the Young King and his brother Geoffrey, the comment of Gerald of Wales seems particularly apt: 'There was never any good agreement, either of the father with his sons, or of the sons with their parent, or between themselves.'

In June 1183 the death of the Young King mid-campaign – from dysentery rather than in battle – must have come as a shock, but it may have prompted the first change in Eleanor's situation. Having begged in vain for his father to visit him on his deathbed, the young Henry's dying wish was a plea for mercy for his mother. It was another year, though, before Eleanor suddenly appeared in public again. We don't know whether it was the Young King's plea, or possibly the visit of her daughter Matilda with her husband, Henry the Lion of Saxony, that prompted the release of the queen. It was clearly parole, rather than freedom, however, and most likely because in 1184 Henry wished to make use of her. The new King Philip of France was demanding the return of his widowed sister's dowry, the Vexin, while Henry insisted it had been given to his own queen and could not be returned. More importantly, when she appeared at the Christmas court at the end of the year he wanted her to back his re-distribution of lands between his remaining sons.

The Young King's death had left Richard as heir presumptive to England, Normandy and Anjou, though Henry refused to confirm that presumption, possibly having learned a lesson from his crowning of his elder son. What was bad for one son may, however, have been good for the other, with Richard now left in no-man's-land and constantly expecting to be passed over for John who, at eighteen, was clearly emerging as the king's favourite. In 1184, indeed, Henry had tried to force Richard to hand over Aquitaine to John and had been flatly refused. Eleanor's presence helped defuse the situation, and in the end John was sent to Ireland – where he conspicuously, and probably deliberately, failed to impress – while Richard was ordered to hand Aquitaine back to his mother, which he was more than willing to do.

If Eleanor had thought this would lead to a triumphant homecoming, she was soon disillusioned. Though she remained for some time with Henry she was clearly still in custody, and when he had no more use for her, she was returned to her 'prison' at Old Sarum. It was there she would have heard of the death of Geoffrey in August 1186, at a tournament in Paris where he had been plotting mischief with his friend Philip of France. There, too, the final breakdown between Henry and Richard in 1188 would have been reported to her. With only two sons left as potential heirs, still the king had refused to confirm Richard as his choice, spurring the man already referred to as Lionheart to offer homage to Philip, and take up arms once more against his father. By the time they met for the last time Henry was a very sick man. Forced to concede all that was demanded of him, even a kiss of peace for his renegade son, he died a few days later on 6 July 1189. At last, and indisputably, Eleanor's favourite child would now be king.

Here Roger of Wendover, writing with the benefit of hindsight and clearly a fan of the writings of Geoffrey of Monmouth, fashionable at the time, refers to one of the obscure 'prophecies of Merlin' contained in Monmouth's 'History of the Kings of Britain'. The specific prophecy he quotes reads, 'The Eagle of the broken treaty shall rejoice in her third nestling,' and he goes on to explain that Eleanor is the 'eagle', stretching her wings over the kingdoms of France and England. The 'broken treaty' refers to her two broken marriage contracts, the one with Louis ended by divorce, and with Henry, effectively ended by her imprisonment. Richard, of course, is her 'third nestling' if we count only the sons and remember the short-lived William, and, says Wendover, he was certainly a 'source of joy to his mother', thus triumphantly fulfilling the prophecy.

It was, indeed, Richard's first act to order the release of Eleanor from her confinement. She was now sixty-seven years old, and a lesser woman might have looked forward to a quiet retirement. There was no such thought for Eleanor of Aquitaine, however. The new king was practically unknown in a country where she had been queen for more than thirty years, and it was perhaps for this reason that his order was accompanied by an instruction that she was to have a free hand in England until he arrived there himself. So while Richard was being invested as Duke of Normandy, Roger of Hoveden reports that Eleanor 'moved her royal court from town to town and castle to castle, just as she thought proper', demanding oaths of fealty to Richard, and winning popularity for him by such measures as liberating prisoners, in particular those who had fallen foul of the hated forest laws, provided they promised to uphold the peace and support the new king. When Richard finally arrived, therefore, on 13 August 1189, it was on a wave of goodwill, further enhanced by his mother escorting him on a brief tour of southern England and culminating in a magnificent coronation in Westminster Abbey on 3 September.

The new king had no intention of remaining long in England, however. Like many – including Henry and Philip of France – he had answered the call for a new crusade to the Holy Land, following the fall of Jerusalem to the sultan Saladin in 1187.

Before he could leave, though, he needed money, and thus, says Hoveden, 'the king put up for sale everything he had, castles, vills and estates.' Even the Bishop of Durham had to buy back his see, becoming an earl in the process, while William Longchamp bought the office of chancellor for three thousand pounds. So much was sold that a tale grew up that Richard was selling his kingdom as he had no intention of returning from the east.

One who was not required to pay was the ever-unreliable Prince John, who now had honours, lands and revenues in England and Normandy heaped on him, along with a rich wife, Isabelle of Gloucester, in order to discourage mischief. Of course, if the king was to die while fighting in the east, John would be his heir, a prospect which Eleanor clearly did not relish. For more than twenty years Richard had been betrothed to Alys of France but had made no move towards marrying her. Indeed, it was widely believed that in that time she had become his father's mistress. The king surely had no intention of marrying her now, although her half-brother Philip was to be his companion on crusade.

Before he departed he was pushed by Eleanor into naming an alternative bride, Berengaria of Navarre, whom he had met briefly some years before. As Richard left for Sicily, therefore, where he was to overwinter before taking ship for the Holy Land, Eleanor set out southwards to collect his chosen wife. It would have been an arduous journey on horseback even for a young woman – down through Aquitaine, and over the Pyrenees to Pamplona, the capital of Navarre, then across the Alps in mid-winter and down the length of Italy – but Eleanor was sixty-eight years old when she set out. Nonetheless, Berengaria was duly delivered to Richard at Messina in Sicily in March 1191. Since it was by then the season of Lent when weddings were not allowed, they were married later at Cyprus on 12 May, by which time Eleanor was well on her way home.

Arriving back in England in June 1191, Eleanor then played a considerable role in stabilising the government of the country. This had been much disturbed since Richard's departure by conflicts between the chancellor and the nobility and senior clergy.

Chancellor William Longchamp is described by the admittedly biased Newburgh as 'an intolerable tyrant,' having 'most consummate arrogance' and 'for audacity and artifice ... almost without an equal'. The situation was not helped by the interference of Prince John, who had returned to England though he had promised to remain abroad for three years. Longchamp attempted to secure his position by bribing the prince for his support. When this was discovered, says Newburgh, John was 'reproached for it by his mother' and when the chancellor was eventually expelled from the kingdom, it was by the whole of the nobility, including John, 'together with the queen'.

Nor was Richard's crusade the most successful. Not only did he fail to re-take Jerusalem, but he managed to fall out with all his allies. Philip, outraged at his final rejection of Alys, returned home at the end of 1191 to make mischief with John, while a gratuitous insult to Duke Leopold of Austria would have serious repercussions when, late in 1192, Richard sailed for home. Blown well off course by gales, he was shipwrecked on the Gulf of Trieste near Venice. Trying to make it overland to his brother-in-law in Saxony, he was recognised in Austria and handed over to Duke Leopold.

For some time he disappeared completely, and when news reached England of his capture by an enemy, John immediately declared he was dead and did homage to Philip for the Angevin territories in France. Soon, however, it appeared that the king was in the hands of Holy Roman Emperor Henry VI, who demanded 100,000 silver marks for his release. William of Newburgh does not specify who organised the vast collection that now took place in England, saying merely that 'The royal officers now accelerated the business ... without sparing anyone; nor was there any distinction made between clergy and layman, ... but all indifferently were compelled to pay the stipulated sum for the king's ransom.' Gervase of Canterbury, however, states that Eleanor was in charge, John being too busy intriguing with Philip of France. Indeed, the 'unnatural John' as he is referred to, together with his partner in crime, tried to bid more for the emperor to hold on to his prisoner, and it was only with difficulty that Henry was dissuaded from accepting this offer. According to Newburgh, the first collection of money was found to be insufficient, which was 'supposed to have happened through the fraud of the officers'. A second, and then a third collection was made, even taking the sacred chalices from the churches, for, as he eloquently phrases it, 'the locust might eat the leavings of the caterpillar, the palmer-worm the leavings of the locust, and the mildew the leavings of the palmer-worm.' England was stripped bare, but finally, early in January 1194, Eleanor personally delivered the ransom to the emperor, and, says Roger of Hoveden, Richard was 'released into the hands of his mother'.

Twice now England had been stripped of money and would pay again for the wars Richard waged against Philip, retaking the lands John had let slip during his captivity. As for John, he was quickly forgiven by his brother, his plotting being put down to his youth and bad advice. Even Gerald of Wales is moved to be lenient, saying of him, 'As … he has obeyed the laws of green youth, so he will conform to those of subsequent age.' He would live to know better.

Eleanor's greatest concern at this time would have been Richard's continued failure to produce a legitimate heir. He and his wife had spent little time together either before or after his exploits in the Holy Land, and he no doubt thought there would be plenty of time when all was peaceful. It was not to be. Reconnoitring a castle he wished to attack in the early months of 1199, the king was shot in the shoulder by a crossbow bolt. A physician he summoned – Hoveden calls him a 'butcher' – 'carelessly mangled the king's arm in every part' in trying to remove the arrow head and gangrene quickly set in. It took him twelve days to die, by which time Eleanor had rushed to his side. On the evening of 6 April 1199, he passed away in her arms.

Less than a week later she buried her favourite child at Fontevrault, at the feet of his father as he had requested. She did not have long to mourn, however, for although John had been named by Richard on his deathbed as heir to all his lands, he had muddied the water by, some years earlier, giving that nomination to his nephew, Geoffrey's son Arthur, now twelve years old. Some debate followed as to whether a younger brother ranked ahead of the son of an older brother. England immediately accepted John, but Philip of France, still determined to break up the Angevin empire, had no compunction about abandoning his erstwhile friend and backing Arthur. Even as John moved north, to be invested as Duke of Normandy on 25 April and crowned King of England on 27 May, Philip was attacking Normandy, Maine and Anjou on behalf of Arthur.

In Maine and in the south of Anjou, however, he met unexpected resistance. Commanded by Eleanor and led in the field by Mercadier, Richard's mercenary chief, says Roger of Hoveden, 'they entered Anjou and ravaged it, because its people had received Arthur.' Then, leaving Mercadier to continue the struggle, Eleanor travelled south to Aquitaine, reclaiming her role as hereditary duchess, and buying goodwill with favours as she toured her old homeland. Finally, in July, she met with Philip of France at Tours, doing homage for her duchy and thus effectively preventing him from claiming it for Arthur. It was probably the first time the two had met, though no doubt Philip had heard tales about his father's first wife throughout his life. What he thought of this indomitable old woman – now seventy-seven years old – who knelt before him to swear fealty, we can only speculate.

Clearly the new King John did not regard his mother as an old woman. As part of a peace treaty agreed in January the following year, Philip's son Louis was to be married to John's niece, the daughter of his sister Eleanor, Queen of Castile. Then, says Roger of Hoveden, John 'sent his mother Eleanor to Alphonso, King of Castile, to obtain his daughter in marriage for Louis'. Once more the long journey south was undertaken, over the Pyrenees, through Navarre and on to Castile, to meet the daughter who was her namesake and whom she had not seen for more than thirty years. In that time the Queen of Castile had given birth to nine children and was probably pregnant with her tenth (who in due course would be named Eleanor). John had apparently left it to his mother to choose which of her grand-daughters would be the wife of the French prince, and in the event she chose the younger of the two who were of appropriate age, the twelve-year-old Blanche.

After a stay of some two months in Castile, grandmother and grand-daughter set out on the return journey. By early April they had reached Bordeaux but now, finally, Eleanor began to feel her age. The murder of her mercenary captain Mercadier in that city by rivals in the service of King John may have contributed to her uncharacteristic surrender to weakness. Mercadier was to have escorted the party on the final leg of their journey to Paris. Instead Blanche was handed over to the Archbishop of Bordeaux to be escorted the rest of the way. 'After this,' says Hoveden, 'Queen Eleanor, being fatigued with old age and the labour of the length of the journey, betook herself to the abbey of Fontevrault and there remained.'

At seventy-eight years of age, no doubt even Eleanor now looked forward to a peaceful retirement, but John had one more move to make that would again spur her to action. In 1200 he had put aside his wife Isabelle on the grounds of consanguinity and ten childless years of marriage. The following summer he married the twelve-year-old Isabella of Angoulême, ignoring the fact that she was already promised to Hugh de Lusignan, one of the more rebellious lords of Aquitaine. Hugh complained to Philip of France, theoretically John's overlord for his French possessions, and when, in April 1202, John refused to appear before Philip's court, the French king declared all his lands in France forfeit and bestowed them on Arthur.

Aquitaine was included in this declaration, despite Philip having accepted Eleanor's homage for the duchy, and this threat to her land was enough to stir her again. She had been ill at Fontevrault, some suggest she was even bedridden, but now she set out, albeit slowly, for Poitiers, on the way recruiting powerful lords for John, who was at Le Mans guarding Maine and Anjou. At the end of July, however, it came to the notice of Arthur and his Lusignan friends that she was at Mirabeau castle, vulnerable to attack, and would make a most useful hostage.

The town was quickly stormed and taken, with Eleanor retreating to the stone keep, but they hadn't reckoned on John's reaction. Furious at the attack on his mother, he blazed down the country, covering some eighty miles in under 48 hours. At dawn on 1 August

Arthur and his friends were taken completely by surprise, soundly defeated and made captive.

With these trump cards in his hand John should have been triumphant over his enemies. Possibly Eleanor believed he would be, but even before she returned to Fontevrault he had begun to let things slip away, breaking promises, acting capriciously and losing allies, holding those he should release and freeing those he should hold. In the following year rumours began to spread that he had murdered Arthur and more allies fell away. By this time, though, Eleanor was eighty years old and increasingly frail. John would have to fight his own battles now.

Throughout that year, Philip kept up the pressure on Normandy, and though Roger of Wendover accuses him of extreme idleness and inaction, John did resist, albeit with decreasing success. We can only speculate how much of this was reported to Eleanor and what her reaction might have been to the shortcomings of her least favourite son. Then, some time early in 1204 she slipped into a coma. She would thus have been unaware of the loss, on 6 March, of the mighty Chateau Gaillard, her beloved Richard's 'Saucy Castle' and the key to eastern Normandy. A few weeks later, on 1 April 1204, Eleanor of Aquitaine, indomitable wife and mother of kings, quietly passed away.

She was buried at Fontevrault Abbey, as, no doubt, she had wished, alongside the two men she had most passionately loved, her second husband Henry and her son Richard. During the French Revolution the tombs were opened and the bones scattered and lost, but the effigies remain, restored now to peace and dignity. Indeed Eleanor, depicted as quietly reading a book, may well have viewed the chaos and desecration with the same calm disdain she had shown in many earlier times of crisis.

From teenaged Queen of France to octogenarian Dowager Queen of England, she made her own choices in life and stuck to them, whether they led to triumph or disaster. In 1193, during the captivity of Richard, she wrote to Pope Celestine describing herself as 'pitiful but unpitied'. With two sons already dead, one now in chains and one trying to usurp his kingdom, she was, she claims, 'defiled with grief ... my flesh ... wasted away'. 'I long for death,' she writes,' I am weary of life.' Yet she would live a further eleven years, mourning another son, but making unprecedented efforts to secure the throne and duchy for the one that remained.

She outlived two husbands and all but two of her ten children, and among her children and grandchildren were numbered kings and queens of England, France, Castile and Leon, together with one highly controversial Holy Roman Emperor. She would not have wanted to be remembered only for her offspring, however. Although she rebelled against her husband, the first Plantagenet King of England, she did more than anyone else to ensure the dynasty remained in power in that kingdom. Not only did she support her sons' rights to rule in turn, but it was Eleanor's original promotion of William Marshal that led to him taking the role of king-maker, when John's death in 1215 left her nine-year-old grandson to become King Henry III.

Eleanor is almost certainly the most famous of the medieval women of power, and rightly so, since her choices and actions secured the throne of England for her direct descendants for the next three hundred years. And even today, while it is more usual to look at the male line of descent, Queen Elizabeth II and her children and grandchildren can trace their ancestry back through more than twenty generations to the indomitable woman who was Eleanor of Aquitaine.

A Note on Sources

Queen Emma

Queen Emma would, no doubt, prefer that the *Encomium Emmae Reginae* was accepted as the last word on her life, at least up to the point when her son Harthacnut became King of England, which is when it ends. Completely contemporary, and written specifically for her by an anonymous monk of St. Bertin's Abbey in Flanders, its major drawback, however, is that its acknowledged aim is to praise Emma and present her own view of the times she lived in. Equally contemporary, and generally far more objective, is the *Anglo-Saxon Chronicle*. This, in fact a collection of chronicles, is based on an original of the ninth century which was then copied and distributed to monasteries around England. These copies were added to, using available information on national and local events until late in the eleventh century and in one case up to the death of King Stephen in 1154. Often written immediately after the events in question, the Chronicle is not blighted by hindsight, and gives a useful corrective to some of the wilder flights of fancy of the Encomium. Many later chronicles, including those of John of Worcester (d. c1140) and William of Malmesbury (d. c1143) drew on the *Anglo-Saxon Chronicle*, including on some additional manuscripts which have since been completely lost. Norman perspectives for this era are given in chronicles compiled by two Norman clerics, Dudo of Saint Quentin and William of Jumièges.

Matilda of Canossa

Like Emma, Matilda of Canossa had her story written during her lifetime. The work now usually known as *Vita Mathildis (Life of Matilda)* was begun as a general history of the counts of Canossa, but the emphasis shifts in the second part to focus on Countess Matilda herself. It was written by Donizo, a monk of the monastery of St. Apollonio at Canossa, and completed very soon after Matilda's death in 1115. Thus, not only was the author contemporary, but also very well placed to learn about the events he described, at least from the point of view of one side in the ongoing conflict between papacy and Holy Roman Empire. A similar bias is apparent in the *Liber ad Amicum (Book to a Friend)* another contemporary work justifying Matilda's actions, written by Bonizo, Bishop of Sutri, who at the time was sheltering from his enemies with the countess. Her role in sheltering bishops from the wrath of the empire meant that she also figured in contemporary works extolling their lives and virtues, such as those by Ranger of Lucca and Pseudo-Bardo. A slightly different viewpoint is found in contemporary chronicles of the deeds of the Normans of Southern Italy by Geoffrey Malaterra and William of Apulia, while the *Chronicle of Montecassino* also covers events involving Matilda and the papacy. For the other side of the coin we have *Ad Heinricum IV, Imperatorem, libri VII (Seven Books to Emperor Henry IV)* by Bishop Benzo of Alba, supporting the imperial view of the struggle, and the equally contemporary but anonymous *Vita Heinrici IV Imperatoris (Life of Emperor Henry IV)*.

Matilda the Queen and Matilda the Empress

This was, in many ways, a golden age of history writing. In England, William of Malmesbury took as his model for his *Chronicle of the Kings of England* the careful work of the Venerable Bede some four centuries earlier, and while Orderic Vitalis in Normandy is a little looser in his approach to the past in his *Ecclesiastical History of England & Normandy,* he gives a detailed picture of events in his own time. Both were monks, born of Anglo-Norman parentage at the end of the eleventh century, and both were well placed to hear details of current affairs. Vitalis in particular is scathing about the early attempts of Geoffrey of Anjou to claim Normandy for his wife. Both Malmesbury and Vitalis died, however, in the early 1140s, leaving the story of the struggle for the crown to be continued by others. Henry of Huntingdon was close to events, but being commissioned to write by Bishop Alexander of Lincoln, showed a rapid disillusionment with King Stephen. By contrast, the anonymous *Gesta Stephani* sets out to champion the king and justify his taking the crown, only later, and possibly with a different author and the benefit of hindsight, referring to Henry II as the 'rightful heir'. Writing just a little later, William of Newburgh, a Yorkshireman and canon of Newburgh Priory, aimed for a precise and accurate description of events, to counter the 'ridiculous fictions' of Geoffrey of Monmouth, whose 'History of the Kings of Britain', with its tales of Arthur and Merlin, had become fashionable at the time.

Melisende of Jerusalem and her Family

As the most spectacular events of the age, the crusades, and then the struggles of the crusader kingdoms of 'Outremer', were well documented on both sides. For the Europeans, the *Gesta Francorum (The Deeds of the Franks and the Other Pilgrims to Jerusalem)* written by an anonymous soldier attached to Bohemond's army, gives eyewitness accounts of the First Crusade from his own point of view, while the *Chronicle* of Fulcher of Chartres, later chaplain to Baldwin of Boulogne, gives a more clerical approach. For the Eastern view, we have Matthew of Edessa, representing the native Armenian Christians, and *The Damascus Chronicle* of Ibn al-Qalanisi, native of that city giving the Muslim side of the story throughout the first half-century of the crusading period, including the disastrous Second Crusade. Back in Europe, Albert of Aachen wrote his *History of the Journey to Jerusalem* based on information gleaned from those returning, while Orderic Vitalis, though usually well informed, shows a male bias typical of the times in dealing with Fulk of Anjou as King of Jerusalem. Some of the tales reported to him concerning events in the crusader kingdoms also seem to have grown in the telling. Again, the copious writings of Bernard of Clairvaux, patron of the Templars, give much useful information concerning events in the east. Closer to the action, William of Tyre was born in Jerusalem around 1130 and grew up there before completing his education in Europe. He would later become Archbishop of Tyre. Though he only began writing his *History of Deeds Done Beyond the Sea* around 1170, being strongly associated with Melisende's son Almaric, he would have been well placed to give an insider's view of the recent history of the area.

Eleanor of Aquitaine

Once again, the life of Eleanor of Aquitaine was well documented, though with significant gaps. Abbot Suger of Saint-Denis, advisor to Louis VI and chronicler of his life, was one of the party sent with Prince Louis to Aquitaine to oversee his marriage to Eleanor. Afterwards, Suger would continue to advise the new Louis VII, and the abbot remained close to Louis's court until his death in 1151. Much concerning Eleanor's court in France can be gleaned from the letters of Bernard (later Saint Bernard) of Clairvaux, in his dealings with most of the royalty and senior clergy of Europe. Odo of Deuil's *Crusade of Louis VII, King of France* gives a full account of the earlier part of the Second Crusade, in which he participated, though he tactfully ends his story before the disintegration of Eleanor's marriage and the disaster at Damascus. Details of that debacle are provided by Ibn al Qalanisi among others, while John of Salisbury, at that time a clerk at the papal court, gives an account of the attempts of Pope Eugenius to mend the royal marriage. A number of writers express varying degrees of surprise at the divorce and re-marriage of Eleanor, including William of Newburgh in England, and Robert of Torigny, Abbot of Mont St. Michel in France. Gerald of Wales, later clerk and chaplain to Henry II, in his *Concerning the Instruction of Princes*, gives a detailed description of that king and his sons, and the breakdown of relations within the family, while William fitzStephen was an eyewitness to much of the story of Thomas Becket, having served in his household for many years and been present at his death.

Another royal servant, Roger of Hoveden, witnessed the later reign of Henry II, and afterwards that of Richard I, accompanying the latter on the Third Crusade, while keeping a detailed journal of events which became the *Annals of Roger of Hoveden*. The latter part of Eleanor's life is then covered by Roger of Wendover, a monk of St. Albans, writing early in the thirteenth century, and carefully selecting from earlier writings as well as contemporary knowledge for his *Flowers of History*.

Select Bibliography

Primary printed sources

Acts of King Stephen & the Battle of the Standard, Richard of Hexham, trans. Rev. Joseph Stevenson (London: Seeleys, 1856)

Ad Heinricum IV, Imperatorem libri VII, Benzo of Alba, ed. Hans Seyffert, MGH SS rer. Germ [65] (Hanover: 1996)

A History of Deeds Done Beyond the Sea, William of Tyre, trans. Emily A Babcock & A.C. Krey (New York: Columbia University Press, 1943)

Anglo-Saxon Chronicle, ed. & trans. J.A. Giles (London: G. Bell & Sons, 1914)

Annals of Roger of Hoveden, trans. Henry T. Riley (London: Henry G. Bohn, 1853)

Arab Historians of the Crusades, sel. & trans. F. Gabrieli (Berkeley: University of California Press, 1969)

Cantica canticorum et de sancta Maria ad comittissam Matildam, John of Mantua, eds. Berhard Bischoff and Burkhard Taegar (Freiburg: Universitätsverlag, 1973)

Chronica Boemorum, Cosmas of Prague, ed. Bertold Bretholz, MGH SS rer. Germ. N.S.2 (Berlin 1923)

Chronica monasterii Casiensis, H. Hoffman MGH SS 34 (1980)

Chronicle of Henry of Huntingdon, ed. & trans. Thomas Forester (London: Henry G. Bohn, 1853)

Chronicle of Ibn al-Qalanisi, in *The Damascus Chronicle of the Crusade,* Ibn al-Qalanisi, trans. H.A.R. Gibb (London: 1932)

Chronicle of John of Worcester, trans. Thomas Forester (London: Henry G. Bohn, 1854)

Chronicle of the Kings of England, William of Malmesbury, ed. & trans. J.A. Giles (London: Henry G. Bohn, 1847)

Chronicles of Robert de Monte, trans. Rev. Joseph Stevenson (London: Seeleys, 1856)

Chronicles of the First Crusade, ed. Christopher Tyerman (London: Penguin Classics, 2012)

Concerning the Instruction of Princes, Gerald of Wales, in *Church Historians of England, Vol. V,* trans. Joseph Stevenson (London: Seeleys, 1853)

Ecclesiastical History of England & Normandy, Vols. 1-4, Orderic Vitalis, ed. & trans. Thomas Forester (London: Henry G. Bohn, 1853)

Encomium Emmae Reginae, ed. Alistair Campbell (Cambridge: Cambridge University Press, 1998)

Flowers of History, Roger of Wendover, trans. J.A. Giles (London: Henry G. Bohn, 1849)

Gesta Normanorum, Dudo of Saint Quentin, trans. Felice Lipshitz (New York: Internet Medieval Sourcebook, 1998)

Gesta Normanorum Ducum, William of Jumièges, ed. J. Marx (Rouen: SHN 1914)

Gesta Stephani, The Acts of King Stephen, ed. & trans. Thomas Forester (London: Henry G. Bohn, 1853)

Heimskringla, Snorri Sturlusson, ed. E. Monsen & A.H. Smith (Cambridge: 1932)

History of Recent Events in England, Eadmer, trans. Geoffrey Bosanquet (London: Cresset Press, 1964)

History of the Journey to Jerusalem Vol I, Albert of Aachen, ed. & trans. Susan B. Edgington (Oxford: Clarendon 2007)

History of William of Newburgh, trans. Rev. Joseph Stevenson (London: Seeleys, 1856)

Letters of Royal & Illustrious Ladies of Great Britain, Vol I, Mary Anne Everett Green (London: H. Colburn, 1846)

Liber ad Amicum, Bonizo of Sutri, ed. E. Dümmler, MGH Ldl I (Hanover 1891)

Liber Eliensis, trans. Janet Fairweather (Woodbridge: Boydell & Brewer, 2005)

Life & Works of St. Bernard, Abbot of Clairvaux, Vol II, ed. Dom John Mabillon, trans. & ed. Samuel J. Eales (London: Burns, 1889)

Life of King Louis the Fat, Suger, trans. Jean Dunbabin (Internet Medieval Sourcebook)

The Crusade of Louis VII, King of France, Odo of Deuil, in *The Crusades: A Documentary History,* trans. James Brundage (Milwaukee, W.I.: Marquette University Press, 1962)

The Deeds of Count Roger of Calabria & Sicily and of Duke Robert Guiscard his brother, Geoffrey Malaterra, trans. Graham A. Loud (2005 Internet Archive)

The Deeds of Robert Guiscard, William of Apulia, trans. Graham A. Loud (1995 Internet Archive)

The Deeds of the Franks and the Other Pilgrims to Jerusalem, ed. Rosalind Hill (London: Thomas Nelson, 1962)

The First Crusade, The Chronicle of Fulcher of Chartres & Other Source Materials, ed. Edward Peters (Philadelphia: Penn Press, 1998)

The First Crusade: The Accounts of Eyewitnesses and Participants, August C. Krey (Princeton: 1921)

The Historia Pontificalis, John of Salisbury, ed. & trans. Marjorie Chibnall (London: Thomas Nelson, 1956)

The Historical Works of Geraldus Cambrensis, ed. Thomas Wright (London: George Bell, 1905)

The History of the Archbishops of Canterbury, Gervase of Canterbury, in *Church Historians of England, Vol. V,* trans. Joseph Stevenson (London: Seeleys, 1853)

The Life and Death of Thomas Becket, William fitzStephen, ed. & trans. George Greenaway (London: Folio Society, 1961)

Vita Heinrici IV, imperatoris, ed. W. Wattenbach, MGH SS 12 (1852)

Vita Mathildis, Donizo, trans Alison Creber (Academia.edu.)

Vita metrica sancti Anselmi Lucensis episcopi, Ranger of Lucca, eds. E. Sackur, G. Schwartz and B. Schmeidler, MGH SS 30/2 (1926)

Vita Sancti Anselmi episcopus Lucensis, Pseudo-Bardo, ed. R. Wilmans, MGH SS12 (Hanover 1856)

Secondary sources

Ashbridge, Thomas, *The Crusades, The War for the Holy Land* (London: Simon & Schuster, 2012)

Barlow, F., *The Godwins* (London: Pearson Education Ltd., 2002)

Barlow, F., *Feudal Kingdom of England 1042-1216* (London: Longman, 1972)

Bradbury, Jim, *Stephen and Matilda, The Civil War of 1139-53* (Stroud: Sutton Publishing, 2005)

Brook, C., *From Alfred to Henry III 871-1272* (London: Sphere Books, 1969)

Carpenter, David, *The Struggle for Mastery* (London: Penguin, 2004)

Cassagnes-Brouquet, Sophie, *In the Service of the Just War: Matilda of Tuscany (eleventh-twelfth centuries)* trans. Michèle Greer, (Clio [Online] 39/2014

Castor, Helen, *She-Wolves, The Women Who Ruled England Before Elizabeth* (London: Faber & Faber, 2010)

Chibnall, Marjorie, *The Empress Matilda, Queen Consort, Queen Mother & Lady of the English* (Oxford: Blackwell, 1992)

Cronne, Henry Alfred, *The Reign of King Stephen 1135-54: Anarchy in England* (London: Weidenfeld & Nicholson, 1970

Crouch, David, *The Reign of King Stephen 1135-1154* (Harlow: Pearson Educational, 2000)

Davis, H. W. C., *England Under the Normans & Angevins 1066-1272* (London: Methuen, 1921)

Davis, R.H.C., *History of Medieval Europe, From Constantine to Saint Louis*, ed. R.I. Moore (Harlow: Pearson Education, 2006)

Duff, Nora, *Matilda of Tuscany, La Gran Donna D'Italia* (London: Methuen, 1909)

Hay, David J., *The Military Leadership of Matilda of Canossa 1046-1115* (Manchester: Manchester University Press, 2008)

Hollister, C. Warren, *Henry I* (New Haven & London: Yale University Press, 2003)

Huddy, Mary E., *Matilda, Countess of Tuscany* (London: John Long, 1905)

Jones, Dan, *Crusaders, An Epic History of the Wars for the Holy Lands* (London: Head of Zeus, 2019)

Keen, Maurice, *The Pelican History of Medieval Europe* (Harmondsworth: Penguin Books, 1969)

Kneale, Matthew, *Rome, A History in Seven Sackings* (London: Atlantic Books, 2017)

Mayer, Hans E., *Studies in the History of Queen Melisende of Jerusalem – Dumbarton Oaks Papers Vol. 26* (Dumbarton Oaks: Trustees for Harvard University, 1972)

Meade, Marion, *Eleanor of Aquitaine* (London: Phoenix Press, 2001)

Newman, Sharan, *Defending the City of God, A Medieval Queen, The First Crusades & the Quest for Peace in Jerusalem* (New York: Palgrave Macmillan, 2014)

Norwich, John Julius, *The Popes, A History* (London: Vintage Books, 2012)

O'Brien, Harriet, *Queen Emma & the Vikings* (London: Bloomsbury, 2005)

Poole, A.L., *Domesday Book to Magna Carta, 1087-1216* (Oxford: Oxford University Press, 1955)

Stafford, Pauline, *Emma, The Powers of the Queen in the 11th Century* in *Queens & Queenship in Medieval Europe*, ed. Anne J. Duggan (Woodbridge: The Boydell Press, 1997)

Stenton, Sir Frank, *Anglo-Saxon England* (Oxford: OUP, 1997)

Trow, M.J., *Cnut, Emperor of the North* (Stroud: Sutton Publishing, 2005)

Tyerman, Christopher, *The World of the Crusades, An Illustrated History* (Newhaven & London: Yale University Press, 2019)

Weir, Alison, *Queens of the Conquest, England's Medieval Queens 1066-1167* (London: Jonathan Cape, 2017)

Index